BRITISH STEAM
PACIFIC POWER

BRITISH STEAM
PACIFIC POWER

Keith Langston

WHARNCLIFFE
TRANSPORT

First published in Great Britain in 2013 by
Wharncliffe Transport
An imprint of
Pen & Sword Books Ltd
47 Church Street
Barnsley
South Yorkshire
S70 2AS

ISBN 978 1 84563 156 7

A CIP catalogue record for this book is
available from the British Library.

Typeset in 11pt Minion by Mac Style, Driffield, East Yorkshire
Printed and bound in India by Replika Press Pvt. Ltd.

Pen & Sword Books Ltd incorporates the Imprints of Pen & Sword Aviation,
Pen & Sword Family History, Pen & Sword Maritime, Pen & Sword Military,
Pen & Sword Discovery, Wharncliffe Local History, Wharncliffe True Crime,
Wharncliffe Transport, Pen & Sword Select, Pen & Sword Military Classics,
Leo Cooper, The Praetorian Press, Remember When, Seaforth Publishing
and Frontline Publishing.

For a complete list of Pen & Sword titles please contact
PEN & SWORD BOOKS LIMITED
47 Church Street, Barnsley, South Yorkshire, S70 2AS, England
E-mail: enquiries@pen-and-sword.co.uk
Website: www.pen-and-sword.co.uk

CONTENTS

Chapter 1

A CENTURY OF STANDARD GAUGE BRITISH PACIFIC STEAM LOCOMOTIVES

The century marker for British Pacific locomotive building was passed in August 2008 when Loco No 60163 TORNADO (a project supported by public subscription and built under the guidance of the 'A1 Steam Locomotive Trust') moved in steam for the first time. One hundred years earlier a 4-6-2 locomotive design by Great Western Railway (GWR) engineer G.J. Churchward rolled out of Swindon Works, and that loco No 111 THE GREAT BEAR was the first ever British-built Pacific steam locomotive. No 60163 is pictured in the company of 'A4' class loco No 60007 SIR NIGEL GRESLEY during a 2009 visit to the Barrow Hill Roundhouse Railway Centre. *David Gibson*

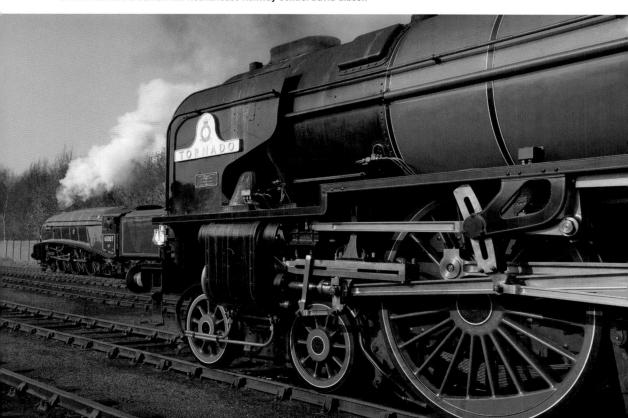

The term 'Pacific' when used in relation to steam locomotives is a direct reference to the 4-6-2 wheel arrangement, as listed in the 'Whyte Notation' listings devised in America by Frederick Methvan Whyte and reportedly first published in 1900. In those listings a locomotive with two leading axles (and therefore four wheels) in front, then three driving axles (six wheels) and then one trailing axle (two wheels) is classified as a 4-6-2.

The reason for use of the name Pacific in relation to that wheel arrangement attracts differing opinions. The naming of wheel arrangements almost certainly has its origin in the United States of America, many of which refer to the company who used them on their locomotives; for example 4-6-2 was used by the Missouri Pacific Railroad during the 1920s. However, some railway historians prefer the explanation that the American locomotive manufacturer Baldwin Locomotive Works supplied the New Zealand Railways Department with 13 'Q' class 4-6-2 configured engines in 1901, that wheel arrangement was then appropriately named Pacific in relation to New Zealand's position in the ocean of the same name.

The advantages of the Pacific (4-6-2) configuration are aptly illustrated by noting the design request given to the Baldwin Locomotive Works by the New Zealand railway. They requested a locomotive 'capable of burning efficiently poor quality lignite coal from mines on the South Island' of that country. In order to comply with that request the engineers came up with an engine possessing a large grate area; to accommodate the associated larger type of firebox a trailing axle was added to what was an otherwise 4-6-0 configuration. The Pacific design became popular with British railway companies, and indeed throughout the world. During the most 'steam active' period of the post-1948 British Railways era that company operated 147 ex-Southern Railway Pacifics, 58 ex-LMS Pacifics and 318 ex-LNER Pacifics; in addition BR built a further 67 Pacific locomotives between 1951 and 1954.

Use of the term Pacific quite rightly evokes in railway enthusiasts thoughts of powerful express passenger tender-type engines hauling trains the length of Britain, during the greater part of the steam era. However, not all Pacific types were tender locomotives; in fact ten

The first Pacific locomotive ever built in Britain; GWR 4-6-2 No 111 THE GREAT BEAR is seen in this rare image. The 1908 Churchward engine was rebuilt by Collett in 1924 as a 'Castle' class 4-6-0 loco retaining the same number but being renamed VISCOUNT CHURCHILL. *Laurence Waters/Great Western Society*

British Standard Gauge Pacifics – Timeline

Year	Designer	Company Original class	BR Class	Build total	BR 1948 Number series
1908	Churchward 4-6-2	GWR '111' The Great Bear	Converted to 'Castle' 4-6-0	1	111 as 'Castle' class
1910	Marsh 4-6-2T	LBSCR 'J1'	'J1'	1	32325
1910–1911	Worsdell/Raven 4-6-2T	NER 'Y' class	'A7'	20	69770–89
1911–1916	Bowen-Cooke 4-6-2T	LNWR 'Superheater Tanks'	N/A	47	N/A
1912	Marsh 4-6-2T	LBSCR 'J2'	'J2'	1	32326
1914–1916	Robinson 4-6-2T	GCR '9N'	'A5/1'	30	69800–29
1914–1916	Worsdell 4-6-0T Converted to 4-6-2T	NER 'W' class 'Whitby Tanks'	'A6'	10	69791, 69793-98
1917	Pickersgill 4-6-2T	CR '944' 'Wemyss Bay Tanks'	'944'	12	55350, 55352–54, 55356–61
1921–1922	Urie 4-6-2T	SR 'H16'	'H16'	5	30517–20
1922	Gresley 4-6-2 Rebuilt Thompson 1945 LNER	GNR 'A1' LNER 'A1' and 'A1/1'	'A1/1'	1	60113
1922–1948	Gresley 4-6-2	GNR 'A1' LNER 'A10'/'A3'	'A3'	78	60035–112 51 ex 'A1' + 27 new build
1922–1924	Raven 4-6-2	NER/LNER 'A2'	N/A	5 (NER numbers 2400-04)	N/A
1925–1926	Gresley 4-6-2T	LNER 'A5/2'	'A5/2'	13	69830–42
1931–1936	Gresley 4-6-2T Rebuilds from Raven NER 'D' class 4-4-4T	NER 'D' LNER 'H1'/'A8'	'A8'	45	69850–94
1933–1952	Stanier 4-6-2	LMS/BR 'Princess Royal'	'Princess Royal' 'Turbomotive'	12 1	46200-01, 46203–12 46202
1935–1938	Gresley 4-6-2	LNER 'A4'	'A4'	34	60001–34
1937–1948	Stanier 4-6-2	LMS/BR 'Princess Coronation/Duchess'	'Princess Coronation/ Duchess'	36 2 (Ivatt)	46220–55 46256–57
1941–1949	Bulleid 4-6-2	SR 'Merchant Navy'	'Merchant Navy'	30	35001–30
1943–1944	Thompson 4-6-2 Rebuilds from 'P2' 2-8-2 built (1934-36)	LNER 'P2/A2/2'	'A2/2'	6	60501–06
1944–1945	Thompson 4-6-2	LNER 'A2'	'A2/1'	4	60507–10
1945–1951	Bulleid 4-6-2	SR/BR 'Battle of Britain & West Country'	'Battle of Britain & West Country'	110	34001–110
1946–1947	Thompson 4-6-2	LNER 'A2'	'A2/3'	15	60511–24
1947–1948	Peppercorn 4-6-2	LNER/BR 'A2'	'A2'	15	60525–39
1948–1949	Peppercorn 4-6-2	BR 'A1'	'A1' see also 'A1/1'	49	60114–162
1951–1954	Riddles 4-6-2	BR 'Britannia'	'Britannia'	55	70000–54
1951–1952	Riddles 4-6-2	BR 'Clan'	'Clan'	10	72000–09
1954	Riddles 4-6-2	BR 'Duke of Gloucester'	'Duke of Gloucester'	1	71000
2008	Peppercorn 4-6-2	A1 Trust 'A1'	'A1'	1	60163 (BR number series)

classes of 4-6-2 (4-6-2T) tank engines are included in the overall total list of classes. In all, 648 standard gauge Pacific locomotives were constructed in the UK, work which involved the completion of exacting tasks coupled with the use of groundbreaking construction methods. Famous locomotive engineers and designers worked in unison with vast numbers of skilled workers in order to make Britain a world leader in 'Pacific' steam locomotive technology in particular and steam locomotive building in general.

The railway company who first gave Britain a 4-6-2 type was the Great Western Railway (GWR), that locomotive designed by G.J. Churchward and built at the famous Swindon Works being introduced in 1908. By 1924 that pioneering design was no more! Thereafter GWR completely abandoned their use of the 4-6-2 configuration. The London & North Eastern Railway (LNER), the London Midland & Scottish Railway (LMSR) and the Southern Railway (SR) all utilised 4-6-2 types on their premier express passenger services and from 1951 onwards British Railways produced three types of Standard Pacific engines to complement the then existing designs.

As the last British-built Pacific type No 71000 DUKE OF GLOUCESTER left the works to enter service, the almost universal opinion was that the BR Crewe-built Riddles-designed '8P' would mark the end of 4-6-2 steam locomotive production in Great Britain. If the past decade has proved anything it has proved that age old adage 'never say never', as in August 2008 railway enthusiasts looked on in delight as a further member of the Peppercorn 'A1' 4-6-2 class was completed, and No 60163 TORNADO 'steamed' into 21st century revenue earning service. To use a cricketing analogy it is fair to say that the Pacific type then passed the '100 Not Out' mark!

The last British Railways-built Pacific type No 71000 DUKE OF GLOUCESTER returned to Crewe Works during the September 2005 'Great Gathering' event, where the loco is seen whilst being serviced after a mainline charter. *Keith Langston*

Brighton built Bulleid light Pacific No 34028 EDDYSTONE is one of 20 of the type which have been preserved. The loco is pictured during March 2004 at Corfe Common on the Swanage Railway. *Paul Pettitt*

Stanier 'Princess Coronation/Duchess' class Pacific loco No 46251 CITY OF NOTTINGHAM makes a magnificent sight at Charwelton in the early morning sunshine, whilst heading *The East Midlander* an R.C.T.S. railtour from Nottingham Victoria to Eastleigh and Swindon on 9 May 1964. This Crewe-built Pacific was withdrawn by British Railways (BR) in October 1964 and cut up two months later. *Dave Cobbe/Rail Photoprints Collection*

Preserved Un-Rebuilt Bulleid Battle of Britain light pacific No 34081 92 SQUADRON is based at the Nene Valley Railway but often visits other heritage railway centres. The loco is seen in the yard at Sheffield Park on the Bluebell Railway during a 2007 visit. *Paul Pettitt*

Gresley Pacific 'A3' class No 60079 BAYARDO was for many photographers an elusive member of the class; the loco is seen being serviced at Edinburgh Haymarket shed (64B) in July 1958. Those familiar with the location will instantly recognise the huge concrete coaling plant which in this image dominates the skyline. *David Anderson*

Raven-designed Gresley-rebuilt 'A8' class 4-6-2T BR No 69855 is pictured between turns at Eaglescliffe during September 1955; note that this loco has been fitted with an enlarged coal bunker (hopper). This loco was withdrawn in January 1960 and cut up a month later. *Mike Stokes Collection*

Gresley 'A3' class Pacific No 60066 MERRY HAMPTON is pictured at London Kings Cross station in August 1959; the engine was at that time allocated to Kings Cross depot (34A). This North British Locomotive Co-built loco was withdrawn in September 1963 and cut up in the following month. *A.E. Durrant/Rail Photoprints Collection*

Chapter 2

DESIGNERS OF THE PACIFICS

Before examining in detail all the locomotive classes which combine to make up the definitive list of British Pacific standard gauge steam locomotives it is appropriate to learn a little about the engineers who designed and oversaw the construction of those engines. The biographic details of those 'loco builders' are listed approximately in the chronological order in which their Pacific class/classes first came into service.

The reader will notice regular reference to apprentice or apprenticeship, as in those long past times Britain really did have a vibrant and diverse manufacturing industry, to 'get on' in which an apprenticeship (in the appropriate trade) was all important. It should be remembered with pride that the skills required to build a steam locomotive were many and varied and that following, in many cases, only a rudimentary formal education, the young 'would be artisans' were taught all they needed to know by the 'company', or perhaps more to the point directly by the seasoned tradesman they were directed to work with.

Building, operating and maintaining large fleets of steam locomotives, their associated rolling stock and ancillary equipment required a huge amount of engineering know-how, and importantly for those times the industry was a major source of employment. In modern times we have rightly marvelled at space travel, air travel and electronic wizardry of all kinds but way back in the days before computers etc. the combining of all the various skills to create a living breathing steam locomotive, from a drawing on a piece of paper, should be considered at least as impressive in its own right. Accordingly, the achievements of past steam locomotive designers and their combined workforces should not be forgotten.

The building in the 21st century of a steam locomotive from a mid 20th century design (No 60163 TORNADO) is in itself a fitting complement to the locomotive builders of Britain. There were of course many other great locomotive designs and configurations but in this instance let us salute the achievements of the designers and workers who built the Pacifics!

George Jackson Churchward, CBE – Great Western Railway

George Jackson Churchward was born on 31 January 1857 at Stoke Gabriel; he was the son of a farmer.

He was educated at Totnes Grammar School.

From 1873 until 1876 Churchward was employed by the South Devon Railway (SDR) at their Newton Abbot Works and was a pupil under John Wright. He moved to the Swindon Works of the Great Western Railway (GWR) in 1876, where he first served an apprenticeship as a pupil of William Dean, thereafter becoming employed by the GWR in 1877.

He held several senior positions which included serving as the Manager of Swindon

Churchward's GWR pioneer Pacific No 111 THE GREAT BEAR seen awaiting to depart from London Paddington station in this historically significant 1910 image, note that this is before the loco's boiler was converted to include a 'top feed'. The gentleman wearing the straw boater appears to be studying the then unique 4 cylinder Pacific express passenger locomotive. Note that the other loco is a 'County Tank' 4-4-2T, No 2225 an Oxford-allocated engine which was built September 1906 and scrapped in December 1934. *Robert Brookman Collection*

Carriage Works (1889) and then as the Manager of the Locomotive Works (1895) before being appointed as the principal assistant to Dean in 1897. In 1902 Churchward succeeded Dean as Locomotive Superintendent of the GWR, and that job title changed to Chief Mechanical Engineer (CME) in 1916. Churchward retired on 31 December 1921.

During his tenure he was responsible for the design of 23 locomotive classes which included only one Pacific class, which comprised a single locomotive, No 111 THE GREAT BEAR.

He was awarded the CBE in 1918.

George Jackson Churchward died on 19 December 1933, in Swindon.

Douglas Earle Marsh – London Brighton & South Coast Railway

Douglas Earle Marsh was born at Aylsham in Norfolk on 4 January 1862.

He was educated at Brighton College and thereafter at University College London.

His introduction to railway locomotive engineering began at the Great Western Railway (GWR), where he worked under William Dean. He was appointed Assistant Works Manager, Swindon, in 1888, a position he held until leaving the GWR in 1896. He left in order to take up the post of Chief Assistant Mechanical Engineer at the Great Northern Railway (GNR). At

Marsh-designed 'J1' class 4-6-2T No 325 ABERGAVENNY seen in London Brighton & South Coast Railway lined Grey livery, which the loco only carried for a short period. This wonderful period image was taken on the LBSCR mainline in 1912 and shows the 'J1' 4-6-2T with a down train to Brighton comprised of 'Pullman' stock at Preston Park. The service is a running of the daily all-Pullman train (Victoria–Brighton) introduced in 1908 and later named the 'Southern Belle'; it was common practice on the LBSCR not to carry headboards. This loco passed into British Railways (BR) ownership in 1948 and was withdrawn June 1951, being cut up a month later (BR No 32325). *Mike Morant Collection*

Doncaster Works, Marsh served under H.A. Ivatt and participated in the design of the 'Ivatt Atlantics'.

Marsh moved to the London Brighton & South Coast Railway (LBSCR) on 23 November 1904, where he succeeded R.J. Billinton as the Locomotive, Carriage and Wagon Superintendent. At Brighton Works, Marsh was associated with the design of 10 locomotive classes, one of which included a pair of Pacific Tank engines, the first specifically 'Express Passenger' 4-6-2T types to be built in Britain. Marsh retired on the grounds of ill health in July 1911, but later went on to work for the Rio Tinto Company.

Douglas Earle Marsh died in May 1933, at Bath.

Raven 4-6-2T North Eastern Railway 'Y' class (BR 'A7' class) is seen in LNER days as No 9772, at Hull Dairycoates depot. This loco passed into BR ownership in 1948 and was withdrawn in December 1957 and cut up in February 1958 (BR No 69772). *Ben Brookshaw*

Sir Vincent Litchfield Raven KBE – North Eastern Railway

Vincent Litchfield Raven was the son of a clergyman and he was born in the Rectory at Great Fransham, Norfolk, on 3 December 1859.

He was educated at a Brighton boarding school and thereafter at Aldenham School, Hertfordshire.

He joined the staff of the North Eastern Railway in 1876 and was initially based at the railway's Gateshead Works. On being appointed Chief Assistant Locomotive Superintendent in 1893, Raven transferred to Darlington Works. He became Chief Mechanical Engineer for the NER in 1910 and began his first phase of locomotive building. In 1915, Raven became Superintendent of the Royal Arsenal in Woolwich, and two years later was conferred the honour of a KBE. He then transferred to the Admiralty, returning to the NER in 1919 to start a second phase of locomotive building. He was responsible for a single class of Pacific Tank locomotives and one class of 4-6-2 tender engines. Raven was a leading figure in early NER electrification schemes. When the London & North Eastern Railway (LNER) superseded the NER in 1922 Raven became Technical Advisor for that railway under Gresley. Raven resigned from the LNER in 1924. LNER locomotive designer Edward Thompson was Raven's son-in-law.

Sir Vincent Litchfield Raven KBE died on 14 February 1924 whilst on holiday in Felixstowe.

Bowen-Cooke London & North Western Railway (LNWR) 4-6-2T 'Superheater Tank' No 2669 has steam to spare when seen at Crewe station; note the advertisements for 'Swan Pens'. In this image the loco has an LNWR number but LMS tank side lettering, presumably because the engine was repainted at Crewe Works a little while before the LMS livery had been chosen, therefore dating the picture to circa 1923. *Colour Rail*

Charles John Bowen-Cooke – London & North Western Railway

Charles Bowen-Cooke, the son of a church minister, was born on 11 January 1859 at Orton Longueville, Huntingdonshire.

Bowen-Cooke was educated at Cheltenham College and thereafter at King's College London.

He began his apprenticeship at Crewe Works in 1875 as a pupil of the highly regarded locomotive engineer Francis William Webb (a man often referred to as 'The King of Crewe'). In 1893 Bowen-Cooke wrote and caused to be published a book entitled *British locomotives: their history, construction; and modern development*, following that up with a revised second edition of the same title in 1894; a second book entitled *Developments in Locomotive Practice* was published in 1902. Bowen-Cooke served the LNWR as CME for a little over 11 years, taking over the post from George Whale in 1909. He was the first engineer to introduce superheated locomotive boilers to the railway and amongst his highly successful designs were the LNWR George the Fifth 4-4-0 class and the Claughton 4-6-0 locomotives. In modern times Bowen-Cooke is remembered for his involvement with the LNWR G1 0-8-0 freight locomotives. He was responsible for the design of the LNWR 'Superheater' class of Pacific Tank locomotives.

Charles John Bowen-Cooke died 'in service' on 18 October 1920.

Robinson-designed Great Central Railway (GCR) '9N' class engine is seen as LNER 'A5/1' class No 5165; the exact date on which this image was taken is not known. However, the loco carried that number/livery combination during the LNER 1st Grouping Period, the engine later became LNER No 9800 and subsequently BR No 69800. The location is not known. This loco was withdrawn in August 1959 and cut up a month later. *Colour Rail*

John George Robinson, CBE – Great Central Railway

John George Robinson was born on 30 July 1856. He was educated at Chester Grammar School, Cheshire.

In 1872 he embarked upon an engineering apprenticeship with the Great Western Railway (GWR) at Swindon, where he was a pupil under the engineer Joseph Armstrong. Upon the completion of his indentures he joined the GWR's Bristol depot as assistant to his father, Matthew Robinson.

John George Robinson left the GWR in 1884 in order to take up the post of Locomotive, Carriage and Wagon Assistant Superintendent with the Waterford & Limerick Railway (became the Waterford Limerick & Western Railway in 1896). After only one year he was promoted to Superintendent with that company.

In 1900 Robinson returned to Britain and joined the Great Central Railway (GCR) as Locomotive & Marine Superintendent; two years later he took over the post of Chief Mechanical Engineer (CME), a position he held until 1922. He was awarded the CBE in 1920.

Prior to the GCR's grouping into the London & North Eastern Railway (LNER), Robinson turned down the opportunity of becoming CME with that company, instead stepping aside to allow the younger Nigel Gresley to take up that post. Amongst his various locomotive designs Robinson is perhaps best remembered for his highly successful GCR '8K' class of 0-8-0 freight engines (LNER '04' class), of which over 400 examples were built. Robinson was responsible for the GCR '9N' class of Pacific Tank locomotives (BR 'A5'). After leaving the LNER Robinson became a director of Beyer Peacock & Company.

John George Robinson, CBE died in retirement at Bournemouth on 7 December 1943.

Worsdell ex-NER Gateshead-built (1908) 'A6' class 4-6-2T No 69794 was pictured whilst stored out of use at Starbeck depot Harrogate (50D), in June 1951. This loco was withdrawn and cut up in August 1951. *Rail Photoprints Collection*

Wilson Worsdell – North Eastern Railway

Wilson Worsdell was born at Monks Coppenhall, Crewe, on 7 September 1850; he was a younger brother of locomotive engineer William Worsdell.

Brought up in the Quaker faith he was educated at Ackworth, a boarding school in Yorkshire.

Wilson followed in the footsteps of his brother William by spending a short time learning the ways of locomotive construction at Crewe. Also in keeping with the chosen career path of his brother he worked for a period at the Altoona Works of the Pennsylvania Railroad USA.

Returning to Britain in 1871 he at first joined the London & North Western Railway (LNWR) before taking up the post of Assistant Locomotive Superintendent (to his brother) at the North Eastern Railway. On William's retirement in 1890, the younger Worsdell became Locomotive Superintendent (that title changed to Chief Mechanical Engineer in 1902) and he served as CME until his retirement in 1910. Wilson was an advocate of the 'Big Engine Policy' and his period at the NER was a highly productive one; perchance he should also be remembered for being at the forefront of 4-6-0 passenger engine development in Britain. Worsdell's NER 'W' class 4-6-0T class locos (colloquially known as 'Whitby Tanks') were later converted to 4-6-2T engines by Raven (LNER 'A6' class).

Wilson Worsdell died at South Ascot in 1920.

Urie London & South Western Railway 'H16' class 'Pacific Tank' Southern Railway No 520 (BR No 30520) pictured at Feltham circa 1928. Note the 'E' prefix letter above the tank side number. This loco came into BR stock in 1948; it was withdrawn in November 1962 but not cut up until October 1963. *Rail Photoprints Collection*

Robert Wallace Urie – London & South Western Railway

Robert Wallace Urie was born at Ardeer in Ayrshire on 22 October 1964. After a formal education he undertook an apprenticeship in 1869 with the Glasgow engineering firm of Gauldie, Marshall & Co, who built a variety of steam engines for both land and marine use. He then had spells of employment in the capacity of draughtsman at Glasgow firms Messrs Dübs & Company and Messrs William King & Company. Urie moved to the Caledonian Railway (CR) in the 1880s, where he continued to hone his skills at the drawing board. Urie was in 1890 promoted to Chief Draughtsman under St Rollox Works' CME, Drummond, who later promoted him to the post of Works Manager. The pair became close work colleagues.

In 1897 both men moved south of the border to work at the London & South Western Railway (LSWR), where Drummond became Locomotive Superintendent and Urie Works Manager at the railway's Nine Elms Works in London. In 1909 the pair moved to the newly built LSWR Eastleigh Works. In 1912 Dugald Drummond died 'in service' and Urie succeeded him as CME, remaining in that post until his own retirement at the time of the 1923 'Groupings'. Amongst Urie's locomotive design achievements was the LSWR 'H16' class of Pacific Tank locomotives.

Robert Wallace Urie died in his native Scotland at Largs, Ayrshire, on 6 January 1937.

Pickersgill 'Wemyss Bay Tank', Caledonian Railway '944' class 4-6-2T loco BR No 55359 is pictured at Beattock from where during the 1950s these engines were regularly deployed on banking duties. This engine came into BR stock in 1948; it was withdrawn in October 1953 and cut up two months later. *David Anderson*

William Pickersgill – Caledonian Railway

William Pickersgill was born in the Nantwich area of Cheshire in 1861. Following his formal education Pickersgill took up an apprenticeship with the Great Eastern Railway (GER) at Stratford, London, in 1876, and thereafter went into full-time employment with that company. He became firstly a Locomotive and Technical Inspector and then moved to Norwich in 1891, taking up the post of District Locomotive Superintendent.

Pickersgill moved to the Great North of Scotland Railway (GNoSR) in 1894, where he succeeded James Johnson as Locomotive Superintendent. He further developed the railway's 4-4-0 types and importantly oversaw the commissioning of the new locomotive works at Inverurie, which was completed in 1903 and delivered its first new locomotive in April 1909. In 1912 he served as Chairman of the Association of Railway Locomotive Engineers.

In March 1914 Pickersgill moved to the Caledonian Railway to take over the post of Locomotive, Carriage & Wagon Superintendent, a position he held until 'Grouping' in 1923 when he was appointed Mechanical Engineer of the Northern Division of the London Midland & Scottish Railway (LMS), and he fulfilled that role until his retirement in 1925. Amongst his locomotive designs was the CR '944' class of 4-6-2T engines which were colloquially known as 'Wemyss Bay Tanks'.

William Pickersgill died in Bournemouth on 2 May 1928.

Gresley Pacific 'A1' class, loco No 4470 GREAT NORTHERN, the first of the designer's 4-6-2 express locomotives seen in original condition, this is the locomotive Thompson rebuilt as his prototype Pacific. Pictured in an unknown northern location and in the front of a period *Daily Mirror* hoarding! *Rail Photoprints Collection*

Dr Sir Herbert Nigel Gresley, CBE – Great Northern Railway/London & North Eastern Railway

Although his family was from Netherseal, Derbyshire, Herbert Nigel Gresley was actually born in Edinburgh on 19 June 1876, that location being due to his mother's ante-natal complications.

Gresley was educated at a school in Sussex and thereafter at Marlborough College (1890–1893).

After leaving college Gresley joined the London & North Western Railway (LNWR) at Crewe Works, where he was an apprentice under F.W. Webb. On the completion of his indentures, in 1897, he became employed by the company and worked on the shop floor for a year.

Gresley moved to the Lancashire & Yorkshire Railway (L&YR) in 1898, where he worked under the engineer J.A.F. Aspinall. At the L&YR he served at the Blackpool depot as foreman of the running sheds and also worked in the L&YR Carriage & Wagon Department.

Gresley left to join the Great Northern Railway (GNR) in 1905, in order to take up the post of Superintendent in the Carriage & Wagon Department. In 1911 he was appointed Chief Mechanical Engineer (CME) of the GNR. Following 'Grouping' Gresley was appointed to the post of CME with the London & North Eastern Railway (LNER). He was responsible for the design/modification of 10 GNR steam locomotive classes, which included one Pacific type. For the LNER Gresley designed/rebuilt 18 locomotive classes, which included 3 Pacific tender engine types and 2 Pacific Tank types.

Gresley was awarded the C.B.E. in 1920, knighted in 1936 and made an honorary Doctor of Science by Manchester University in that same year.

Dr Sir Herbert Nigel Gresley, CBE died 'in service' after a short illness on 5 April 1941, at his Hertfordshire home.

Stanier streamlined Pacific heading a down 'Coronation Scot' working is pictured taking water on Moore Troughs (WCML) in this stunning 1938 LMS image. *Dr Ian C. Allen/Transport Treasury*

Sir William Stanier, FRS – London Midland & Scottish Railway

William Arthur Stanier was born 27 May 1876 in Swindon, Wiltshire, where his father was employed by the Great Western Railway (GWR) as Chief Clerk to William Dean.

Stanier was educated at Swindon High School and thereafter for just one year at Wycliffe College.

In 1891 Stanier joined the GWR, initially as an office boy and then took up a five-year apprenticeship in the workshops (1892–1897). In 1904 he was appointed to the post of Divisional Locomotive Superintendent at London, returning to Swindon in 1912 to take up the post of Assistant Works Manager and moving up to Swindon Works Manager in 1920.

Stanier was famously 'headhunted' in late 1931 by the London Midland & Scottish Railway (LMS) when that railway's chairman Sir Josiah Stamp recognised his burgeoning talents. The fact that early career promotion chances for Stanier at the GWR were limited is worthy of note (in fact GWR CME Collett stayed in post until 1941). Stanier thus left Swindon to become Chief Mechanical Engineer (CME) of the LMS on 1 January 1932. Employing the benefit of hindsight it is easy to see that Swindon's loss was very much Crewe's gain! Stanier was responsible for the design/conversion of 14 LMS steam locomotive classes, of which 2 were Pacific types.

Stanier was knighted in 1943 and was elected a Fellow of the Royal Society (FRS) on his actual retirement in 1944, although following his advisory wartime (Second World War) work, having been seconded to the Ministry of Production, Stanier effectively ceased working for the LMS in 1939.

Sir William Stanier, FRS died on 27 September 1965, at Rickmansworth.

Bulleid 'West County' class 4-6-2 No 21C101 (BR 34001) EXETER in original 'air smoothed casing' form, the first of the designer's light Pacifics, is pictured leaving Semley with an up LSWR route service in 1948. Rebuilt in November 1967, loco No 34001 was withdrawn in July 1967 and cut up in the October of that year. *Rail Photoprints Collection*

Dr Oliver Vaughan Snell Bulleid, CBE – Southern Railway/British Railways

Oliver Vaughan Snell Bulleid was born in New Zealand on 19 September 1882; his parents were British immigrants to that country. On the death of William Bulleid the family returned to Llanfyllin, Wales (1889).

After a formal education Bulleid attended Accrington Technical College, and at the age of 18 (1901) joined the Great Northern Railway (GNR) and served an apprenticeship under H.A. Ivatt, after which he was appointed to the post of assistant to the Locomotive Running Superintendent, and a year later promoted to Doncaster Works Manager. Bulleid left Britain in 1908 to work in Paris for the French division of Westinghouse Electric Corporation as a test engineer. However, he retained a tie with Doncaster, as in that year he married Ivatt's youngest daughter.

Returning to Britain in 1910 he served a brief period with the British Board of Trade, where amongst his duties was the organisation of trade exhibitions etc., a job which brought him into contact with Gresley, Stanier and Hawksworth.

Bulleid rejoined the GNR in 1912 and worked as Personal Assistant to Nigel Gresley. At the start of the First World War (1914) Bulleid joined the British Army rail transport arm, where he attained the rank of Major. In 1918 he returned to the GNR to become Manager – Wagon & Carriage Works. At the LNER in 1923 he became Gresley's assistant, and as such worked on several locomotive designs, including the 'A4' Pacific class.

In 1937 Bulleid joined the Southern Railway (SR) as CME and served there until 1948. He designed 4 steam locomotive classes for the SR and British Railways Southern Region (BRSR), which included 2 Pacific types, the Merchant Navy 'MN' class and the West Country 'WC'/Battle of Britain 'BB' class.

In 1949 Bulleid left BRSR to join Córas Iompair Éireann (CIÉ), in the Republic of Ireland, on a consultancy basis, becoming their CME in 1951; he retired in 1958.

He was awarded the CBE in 1949 and made an honorary Doctor of Science by the University of Bath in 1967.

Dr Oliver Vaughan Snell Bulleid, CBE died on 25 April 1970, in Malta.

Thompson's prototype rebuild of Gresley's prototype 'A1' is depicted here at York motive power depot in its rebuilt form as 'A1/1' Pacific No 60113 GREAT NORTHERN. The loco's livery of BR blue with broad black and narrow white lining was worn for only the brief period from January 1950 until May 1951. The rather conspicuous headboard was carried on the centenary of the Great Northern Railway (GNR) on 16 July 1950; the portrait on the headboard depicts Edmund Denison, the driving force behind the creation of the Great Northern Railway. Withdrawn in December 1962 this loco was cut up in February 1963, despite its historical importance. *W.J. Wyse/Mike Morant Collection*

Edward Thompson – London & North Eastern Railway

Edward Thompson was born the son of an assistant master at Marlborough College in 1881. He was educated first at the aforementioned college and thereafter he took the Mechanical Science Tripos (honours examination for a BA) at Pembroke College, Cambridge.

After graduating from Cambridge, Thompson worked in both manufacturing industry and the railways for a period. In 1910 he joined the North Eastern Railway (NER) as Assistant Divisional Locomotive Superintendent, where he served for two years. In 1912 he left that employ in order to take up the position of Carriage & Wagon Superintendent with the Great Northern Railway (GNR). Thompson had a long association with that company and subsequently the London & North Eastern Railway (LNER) and he became Workshop Manager at Stratford in 1930.

On the death of Nigel Gresley, in 1941, Thompson left Stratford to take up the post of Chief Mechanical Engineer (CME) with the LNER at Doncaster. It is well known that Thompson was not the greatest admirer of Gresley's design work and immediately on taking up the post of CME he set about changing things to suit his steam locomotive engineering preferences, whilst in addition he commenced on overseeing a much needed standardisation process at the LNER. Thompson was the son-in-law of Sir Vincent Raven.

Thompson designed the highly successful 'B1' class of locomotives and 4 Pacific types/variants, which included the rebuilding of Gresley's prototype Pacific loco Great Northern, as his prototype 4-6-2 designated class 'A1/1'.

Thompson retired from the LNER in 1946.

Edward Thompson died in 1954.

Peppercorn redesigned the last 15 Pacific locos of Thompson's 'A2' class, which were built to his specification and designated 'A2/3' class. Engine No 60533 HAPPY KNIGHT is pictured at London Kings Cross station on 17 September 1956. This loco was withdrawn in June 1963 and cut up in the November of that year. *M.J. Reade/Colour Rail*

Arthur Henry Peppercorn, OBE – London & North Eastern Railway/British Railways

Arthur Henry Peppercorn was born in Leominster, Herefordshire, on 29 January 1889. He was educated at Hereford Cathedral School and thereafter in 1905 started upon his railway career by serving an apprenticeship at the Great Northern Railway (GNR) under Henry Alfred Ivatt.

Peppercorn's early railway career was interrupted by the First World War, when he joined the British Army and served with the Royal Engineers throughout that conflict, later returning to the GNR and after 'Grouping' staying on to serve the London & North Eastern Railway (LNER) under Edward Thompson. He became Chief Mechanical Engineer (CME) of the LNER on 1 July 1946 following Thompson's retirement. He was, by all accounts, a popular appointment, the Doncaster design staff perceiving that he was in his ways more like Gresley than his predecessor. Indeed he included in the makeup of his team some of Gresley's former assistants. Peppercorn was the last CME of the LNER before 'Nationalisation' and therefore only served in that role for some 18 months. Subsequently he continued to work at Doncaster with British Railways (BR) as Chief Mechanical Engineer, Eastern and North Eastern Regions. Although responsible for other steam locomotive build projects, Peppercorn is best known for his 'A1' class and 'A2' class Pacifics.

He retired from BR at the end of 1949; accordingly he was an active CME for three and a half years.

Arthur Henry Peppercorn, OBE died on 3 March 1951.

Ivatt-modified Stanier 'Princess Coronation/Duchess' class Pacific No 46257 CITY OF SALFORD, the last of the class to be built, is pictured passing Weaver Junction on the West Coast Main Line (WCML) a few months after being put into traffic during 1949. Note the plain BRITISH RAILWAYS name style on the tender and large cabside number. Withdrawn in October 1964 this loco was cut up in January 1965. *R.A. Whitfield/Rail Photoprints Collection*

Henry George Ivatt – London Midland & Scottish Railway/British Railways

Henry George Ivatt was born on 4 May 1886 in Dublin, Ireland; he was the son of GNR railway engineer Henry A. Ivatt; Ivatt junior was educated at Uppingham School.

He joined the London & North Western Railway (LNWR) at Crewe in 1904, where he served an apprenticeship under George Whale. In the years that followed he worked in several departments including the drawing office, as Assistant Foreman Crewe North Shed and the Experimental Locomotive Department. During the First World War (1914–18) he served in France on the staff of the Director of Transportation; at the end of hostilities Ivatt was appointed Assistant Locomotive Superintendent of the North Staffordshire Railway (NSR) in 1919; that company became part of the London, Midland & Scottish Railway (LMS) in 1923.

Ivatt was transferred to Derby Works in 1928 and became Works Superintendent there in 1931. He then moved to Glasgow, taking up the post of Divisional Mechanical Engineer Scotland in 1932, returning to England in 1937 to become Principal Assistant to CME William A. Stanier. In 1944 Stanier retired and was succeeded by Charles Fairburn; however, that gentleman's sudden death in October 1945 again created a vacancy for the top locomotive engineering job at the LMS. Accordingly Henry George Ivatt was promoted to the post on 1 February 1946; he was of course the last person to hold the post of CME at the LMS. Ivatt served in the post until 1948 and when Riddles became CME of British Railways (BR) in 1948 Ivatt became CME of the London Midland Region, a post he held until his retirement from BR in 1951. Amongst his many steam locomotive engineering achievements Ivatt oversaw the production and modification of the last two Stanier 'Princess Coronation/Duchess' class Pacific locomotives.

Henry George Ivatt died on 4 October 1976.

Riddles 'Clan' class Pacific No 72009 CLAN STEWART was the last of the ten 'Clans' to be built and is depicted here outside Crewe works on 9 March 1952. The loco is newly painted, with BR crest affixed but unlined. Note that the newly built engine was at that time temporarily minus two driving axles and valve gear. This loco was withdrawn in August 1965 and cut up in the December of that year. *Mike Morant Collection*

Robert Arthur Riddles, CBE – British Railways

Robert Arthur Riddles was born on 23 May 1892 and trained as an apprentice with London & North Western Railway (LNWR) at Crewe Works between 1909 and 1913.

At the onset of the First World War he joined the Royal Engineers, serving until 1919. His first two senior positions with the London Midland & Scottish Railway (LMS) were as 'Assistant to the Works Manager' Crewe and thereafter as 'Progress Assistant to the Works Manager' Crewe, between 1920 and 1928. Riddles then served at Derby Works in the position of Assistant Works Superintendent before later returning to Crewe in order to fulfil the same role. In 1933 he became Locomotive Assistant to Stanier (CME, LMS) and progressed to become Principal Assistant to the CME, a role he continued in until 1937 when for a two-year spell he became Mechanical and Electrical Engineer, LMS Scotland.

In 1939, just prior to the start of the Second World War, Riddles was in the United States of America as leader of the LMS contingent accompanying the 'Coronation Scot' exhibition train on its eventful tour of that country. R.A. Riddles was awarded the CBE in 1943.

Upon the creation of the Railway Executive in 1947, in preparation for the nationalisation of the railways in 1948, he was appointed Member of the Railway Executive for Mechanical and Electrical Engineering. He was subsequently chosen to lead the team set up in order to create the 'Standard' class locomotives.

Amongst the Riddles-inspired BR locomotives were three Pacific types. Riddles retired from BR on 30th September 1953.

Robert Arthur Riddles, CBE died on 18 June 1983.

'Britannia' class Pacific No 70004 WILLIAM SHAKESPEARE is pictured storming through Folkestone Warren with the up 'Golden Arrow', in this atmospheric 1953 image. This loco was withdrawn in December 1967 and cut up in April 1968.
Rail Photoprints Collection

Chapter 3

1908

Great Western Railway '111' Class 4-6-2, designed by Churchward

In January 1907 the GWR board made an initial allocation of £4,400 for the construction of the Churchward Pacific, the first 4-6-2 steam locomotive to be constructed in Britain. They subsequently voted for a further amount of £860 to be awarded in order to cover what was described as additional expenses, associated with the project.

This groundbreaking locomotive was built with a massive 23ft-long Swindon No 6 boiler and incorporated the new 'No 1' superheater with an appropriately wide Belpaire firebox in order to accommodate a firegrate area of 41.79sq ft. Churchward was greatly interested in the potential of the wide firebox concept and in that regard THE GREAT BEAR can rightly be considered as a test-bed engine. In some respects the loco was, except for its 15"-diameter cylinders, similar to a conventional 'Star' class engine. Loco No 111's high weight (145.04 tons with tender) meant an axle load of 20 tons which restricted its route availability severely and the engine was as a consequence mainly operated over the London to Bristol route.

Churchward-designed Pacific No 111 THE GREAT BEAR is pictured on shed at Old Oak Common circa 1915; the locoman seen is thought to be Thomas Blackhall, an Oxfordshire footplateman who was a regular driver of this loco in its 4-6-2 configuration. This image was taken after the locomotive boiler had been fitted with a boiler top feed. *Mike Bentley Collection*

THE GREAT BEAR was considered by its designer to be a test-bed project for GWR Pacific locomotive design; however, the railway built only one 4-6-2. *Drawing reproduced by kind permission of the Great Western Society http://www.gws mainline.org/*

The GWR route availability code of No 111 was Red and although the loco's tractive effort (27,800lbf) actually placed it within power classification 'D' the engine was given a rating of 'Special' on account of its weight characteristics, and that was indicated by a black plus sign on the cabside red disc.

During a 1913 upgrade the loco was given a new Swindon No 3 superheater. Commentators of the time concluded that the Great Western Railway (GWR) Pacific, although up to all the tasks it was asked to perform in traffic, was never really pushed to the limits. Occasional reports suggested that the loco could in certain circumstances be a poor steamer.

As a test-bed locomotive Churchward and his team would almost certainly have desired to take the development of the 4-6-2 wide firebox locomotive further, but they were not asked by the GWR management to do so.

In January 1924 the loco was listed as being in need of heavy repairs and subsequently withdrawn from traffic by the GWR. The amount of available work was not considered to be sufficient to justify repairing the Pacific and so it was alternatively converted into a 'Castle' class (4073) 4-6-0. The total distance ran in revenue-earning service by the GWR Pacific was approximately 527,272 miles. In the guise of a 4 cylinder 4-6-0 the formerly unique engine retained its 111 number but received a change of name, becoming VISCOUNT CHURCHILL; as a 'Castle' class engine the loco clocked up a further 1,989,628 miles.

Churchward, who had retired from the GWR on 31 December 1921, even so he did not receive the withdrawal and conversion news of Pacific No 111 at all well. It is said that when he later learned of the Great Northern Railways (GNR) intention to built a Pacific to a Gresley design he pointedly remarked "what did that young man want to build that for? We could have sold him ours."

Number	Name	Built	Date	Withdrawn
111*	THE GREAT BEAR	Swindon	02/1908	1924*

This locomotive rebuilt as 4073 'Castle' class 4-6-0 No 111 Viscount Churchill (withdrawn 08/1953)

The GREAT BEAR is pictured waiting to depart from Paddington station in 1910; note the engineman keeping a watchful eye on the tank loco shunting on the adjacent track. This image helps to give a good indication of the loco's overall size; note also the lack of a boiler top-feed arrangement. *Robert Brookman Collection*

GWR 4-6-2 No 111 THE GREAT BEAR

Introduced: 1908

Power Classification: Special Red

Built: Swindon Works – 1 locomotive

Designer: G.J. Churchward

Company: Great Western Railway

Driving Wheel: 6ft 8½ins

Boiler Pressure: 225psi superheated

Cylinders: 4 – 15ins diameter x 26ins stroke

Tractive Effort @ 85%: 27,800lbf

Valve Gear: Inside Walschaerts with rocking shafts (piston valves)

Water Capacity: 4000 gallons

Coal Capacity: 6 tons

From this angle the 4-6-2 wheel arrangement can be clearly appreciated; with the benefit of hindsight some railway historians were of the opinion that a larger cab, perhaps with the inclusion of a side window, would have greatly improved the look of this originally unique machine. *Mike Bentley Collection*

Loco No 111 seen when rebuilt as a 'Castle' class 4-6-0; VISCOUNT CHURCHILL is pictured at speed circa 1925. *Mike Bentley Collection*

Chapter 4

1910

London Brighton & South Coast Railway
'J1' Class 4-6-2T, designed by Marsh

Marsh had successfully designed and built a class of 4-4-2 tank engines designated the 'I3' class and on the back of that decided to provide the LBSCR with a more powerful type of tank engine which would be capable of hauling the railway's heavy London–Brighton express trains. His new design, which was designated 'J1', was a 4-6-2T locomotive and it was built at Brighton Works, being completed in December 1910.

A superb image of the original Marsh 'J1' Pacific Tank loco LBSCR No 325 ABERGAVENNY (SR 2325, BR 32365); built at Brighton Works and introduced into traffic in December 1910 this loco became the first 4-6-2T specifically built for express passenger work in Britain. In this circa 1912 image the loco is pictured whilst parked on the 'through road' at East Croydon and is facing in the direction of London. *Mike Morant Collection*

The impressive Pacific tank incorporated a Schmidt superheater and Stephenson valve gear and with 6ft 7½in-diameter wheels it certainly looked to be an express locomotive. When first in service the loco performed well and lived up to its 4P power rating; however, after modifications to the firebox (which improved coal consumption figures) it proved to be an even more successful engine.

The railway then placed an order for another locomotive in May 1911 but soon afterwards Marsh left the companies employ, under what some deduced to be strange circumstances. His leaving was officially described as 'prolonged sick leave' and as a consequence all work on what would have been the second loco in the class was halted.

This loco ran in several liveries, which included lined grey, LBSCR standard umber, SR pre-war green-lined white and black, plain black during the Second World War, and express locomotive SR malachite green lined in yellow and black. Initially the loco name was carried on the side tanks with the LBSCR number on the side of the tender. Later the word SOUTHERN was applied to the side tanks with number B325 below; under the SR the engine was renumbered 2325, still in that style. In wartime black livery the word SOUTHERN was carried on the sidetanks with the number being removed to the tender. From June 1946 the loco again had the word SOUTHERN on the side tanks and the number on the tender. From the time of 'Nationalisation' the engine carried the number 32325 on the tender side but the side tank was plain. At some time during the BR period this loco also carried its number on the rear of the tender and at some period also had a smokebox number plate.

Number	Name	Built	Date	Withdrawn
LBSCR 325	ABERGAVENNY	Brighton	12/1910	06/1951
SR B325 and 2325	Name removed 03/1924			
BR 32325				

The engine was cut up at Brighton Works

LBSCR 4-6-2T 'J1' class

Introduced: 1910

Power Classification: 4P

Built: Brighton Works – 1 loco built

Designer: Douglas Earle Marsh

Company: London Brighton & South Coast Railway

Driving Wheel: 6ft 7½ins

Boiler Pressure: 170psi superheated

Cylinders: 2 – 21ins diameter x 26ins stroke

Tractive Effort @ 85%: 20,840lbf

Valve Gear: Stephenson (piston valves)

Water Capacity: 2300 gallons

Coal Capacity: 3 tons

The Marsh-designed 'J1' class is in this image portrayed in Southern Railway livery at the south end of New Cross Gate shed in the 1930s. Note the absence of a smokebox number plate. *Mike Morant Collection*

There is so much of interest in this picture. Marsh 'J1' 4-6-2T No 32325 seen here carrying the ornate version of early BR numbering and wearing fully lined malachite livery, but with no stamp of ownership on the tank side and with a number on the rear of the tender. Bunker first shots are never amongst viewers' favourites but this one shows the unusual application of the number on the bunker, to say nothing of that enormous pile of coal within it. Add to that the SECR birdcage set of coaches, what more could we ask of an archive steam era image? The location is Tunbridge Wells West just a few yards from the end of the platforms. *Mike Morant Collection*

Marsh 'J1' class 4-6-2T 2325 passes the entry point for New Wandsworth Goods depot, just south of Clapham Junction. Note the name SOUTHERN on the side tank and the four digit number on the tender side. *Mike Morant Collection*

London Brighton & South Coast Railway 'J1' class 4-6-2T No 325 seen in 'as built' condition.

Chapter 5

1910–1911

North Eastern Railway 'Y' Class 4-6-2T (BR 'A7') designed by Worsdell/Raven

Ex-North Eastern Railway (NER) 'Y' class (BR 'A7' class) No 69773 (which is in fact an 'A7/1' variant) is pictured between shunting duties in the Hull area circa 1951. Note the shunter's pole on the buffer beam and also how some coal has lodged itself on the loco's cab roof. *Author's Collection*

The 'A7' class of Pacific tank engines were the only purpose-built 4-6-2T type on that railway as the other two classes of Pacific tanks ('A6' and 'A8') were in reality locomotives converted to that configuration from other types. The 'A7' class was designed for the railway during the period of Wilson Worsdell's reign as Chief Mechanical Engineer (CME) but built during the time in that post of Vincent Raven, his predecessor. The class was designed to haul heavy goods trains, and intentionally not passenger traffic. This powerful design was intended primarily as motive power for coal trains between the many colliery lines within the railway's operating area and rail-connected 'shipping staithes' (piers).

In line with other Raven designs the engines had three cylinders which drove the leading coupled axle and incorporated three independent sets of Stephenson link motion.

One batch of 20 engines was built at Darlington in the period 1910/11 and all of the class passed into BR ownership (1948). At the time of construction two spare boilers were also fabricated and in 1916 they were fitted with Schmidt superheaters; those steam raising units then replaced the boilers on locos No 1126 and 1175. The two displaced boilers were fitted to other members of the class and also during various rebuilds superheating was fitted to eventually 17 members of the class. Rebuilds under Robinson, circa 1932, included the fitting of that engineer's own design of superheater, necessitating longer smokeboxes than those incorporated in the saturated-type boilers. In 1935 further modifications to the 'A7' boilers were carried out making them interchangeable with the 'A6', 'A8', 'H1' and 'T1' LNER class engines. Over the years certain engines of the class carried various designs of chimneys, steam domes and smokeboxes.

Under LNER ownership the class was relegated to shunting duties in the region's bigger marshalling yards; at those locations the engines' power was invaluable especially when heavy trains needed to be 'hump shunted'. As heavy mineral traffic declined in the immediate post-war years the 'A7' class were less in demand, with the first member of the class being withdrawn in May 1951. By the end of 1952 some 17 engines remained in service; however, none of the class remained in service after the end of 1957.

NER 4-6-2T 'Y' class, LNER/BR 'A7' class, BR numbers 69770–69789

Introduced: 1910–11

Power Classification: 5F (reclassified 3F in 1953)

Built: Darlington Works – 20 locomotives

Designer: Originally Wilson Worsdell but built under CME Vincent Raven

Company: North Eastern Railway

Driving Wheel: 4ft 7¼ins

Boiler Pressure: 180psi original build

   160psi rebuilt boiler superheated

   175psi rebuilt as A7/1 Robinson boiler superheated

   175psi rebuilt as A7/1 Robinson boiler not superheated

Cylinders: 3 – 16½ins diameter x 26ins stroke

Tractive Effort @ 85%: Variously 29,405lbf, 26,140lbf, 28,585lbf

Valve Gear: Stephenson (piston valves)

Water Capacity: 2300 gallons

Coal Capacity: 5 tons

Number	Built	Completed	Withdrawn	Variant
NER 1113, LNER 1113 and 9770, BR 69770	Darlington	10/1910	10/1954	A7/1
NER 1114, LNER 1114 and 9771, BR 69771	Darlington	11/1910	11/1954	A7/1
NER 1126, LNER 1126 and 9772, BR 69772	Darlington	11/1910	12/1957	
NER 1129, LNER 1129 and 9773, BR 69773	Darlington	12/1910	03/1955	A7/1
NER 1136, LNER 1136 and 9774, BR 69774	Darlington	12/1910	08/1954	A7/1
NER 1170, LNER 1170 and 9775, BR 69775	Darlington	12/1910	04/1952	
NER 1174, LNER 1174 and 9776, BR 69776	Darlington	01/1911	06/1954	A7/1
NER 1175, LNER 1175 and 9777, BR 69777	Darlington	01/1911	05/1952	
NER 1176, LNER 1176 and 9778, BR 69778	Darlington	02/1911	05/1955	
NER 1179, LNER 1179 and 9779, BR 69779	Darlington	02/1911	11/1954	A7/1
NER 1180, LNER 1180 and 9780, BR 69780	Darlington	02/1911	11/1954	A7/1
NER 1181, LNER 1181 and 9781, BR 69781	Darlington	03/1911	11/1956	A7/1
NER 1182, LNER 1182 and 9782, BR 69782	Darlington	03/1911	12/1957	
NER 1183, LNER 1183 and 9783, BR 69783	Darlington	03/1911	12/1956	A7/1
NER 1185, LNER 1185 and 9784, BR 69784	Darlington	04/1911	03/1956	A7/1
NER 1190, LNER 1190 and 9785, BR 69785	Darlington	04/1911	11/1955	
NER 1191, LNER 1191 and 9786, BR 69786	Darlington	05/1911	12/1957	A7/1
NER 1192, LNER 1192 and 9787, BR 69787	Darlington	05/1911	08/1954	A7/1 'n'
NER 1193, LNER 1193 and 9788, BR 69788	Darlington	05/1911	11/1955	A7/1
NER 1195, LNER 1195 and 9789, BR 69789	Darlington	06/1911	05/1951	A7/1 variant, engines rebuilt with Robinson-type superheated boilers

A7/1 note 'n', engine rebuilt as A7/1 but not superheated
The whole class was cut up at Darlington Works

Chapter 6

1911–1916

London & North Western Railway 4-6-2 'Superheater Tanks', designed by Bowen-Cooke

This 'LNWR Pacific Tank' design class of 47 engines was built at Crewe Works in three batches and the first locomotive completed carried the No 2665 when outshopped from the works on 10 January 1911 by the LNWR. The 4-6-2 design was also described as a 5'-6" Six Coupled Side Tank Engine (Fitted with Superheater) or the '2665' class.

The class titles are interesting to say the least; take for example the general use of the word 'Superheater', which may in fact have been accorded to the class retrospectively because 'as built' some of these engines were superheated but others were not. However, over time all of the class was fitted with superheaters. Secondly the descriptive use of the measurement 5' 6" in the alternative class title does not refer to the size of the driving wheels, which were actually 5' 8½" in diameter.

In common with other London & North Western Railway (LNWR) engines Bowen-Cooke's Pacific tanks utilised the Schmidt system of superheating and thus were initially fitted with 'Superheater Dampers' in order to allow the driver an option to close off steam flow through the superheater elements when the loco's regulator was closed. The cab-located control for the damper moved the appropriate handrail horizontally, thereby operating a

London & North Western Railway Bowen-Cooke-designed 4-6-2 tank No 917 is pictured when almost new; the location is Shrewsbury shed. Note the LNWR cabside crest, roof vent, parallel boiler and distinctive Belpaire firebox. This finely detailed image was taken by Mr P.W. Pilcher, who used to be a music teacher at Shrewsbury School. *Edward Talbot Collection*

LNWR/LMS '5ft 6ins Superheater 4-6-2 Tank'

Introduced: 1910–16

Power Classification: 3P

Built: Crewe Works – 47 locomotives (built in 3 batches)

Designer: C.J. Bowen-Cooke

Company: London & North Western Railway

Driving Wheel: 5ft 8½ins

Boiler Pressure: 175psi superheated (first 12 not superheated but later modified)

Cylinders: Inside – 20ins diameter x 26ins stroke

Tractive Effort @ 85%: 27,800lbf

Valve Gear: Joy, inside gear

lever on the side of the smokebox. In later years the dampers were found to be unnecessary, and judged as 'adding no benefit to the performance of the engines' they were removed.

In addition to being very useful suburban tank engines, and often employed on West Coast mainline duties, these sturdy locos also banked (or double headed) trains over Shap, and because of their relatively low axle loading frequently worked trains over the Central Wales line.

The LNWR 'Pacific Tanks' had a coal-carrying capacity of 3 tons and a water capacity of 1700 gallons. The LMS scrapped most of the class at Crewe Works between 1936 and 1938; however, 3 locos remained in traffic into the early 1940s, and the last example is recorded as having been cut up on 26 November 1941.

LNWR 4-6-2T as LMS No 6960 is seen leaving Oxenholme on the main line. An interesting picture, as it shows the Saturdays-only 'Market Train' from Ingleton to Kendal – i.e. which ran to take people from Ingleton to Kendal for the market. The engine was an Oxenholme allocated loco which first ran light from Oxenholme to Low Gill and reversed there to take the down line on the branch to Ingleton, in order to pick up the train (in this period image you can see that the train is comprised of Midland stock). Thereafter it took the train to Low Gill, where the loco again ran round the train before proceeding down to Oxenholme where it ran round the train again, before proceeding to Kendal. On the way back the engine crew carried out similar manoeuvres, but of course in the reverse order. *H. Gordon Tidey/Edward Talbot Collection*

LNWR 4-6-2T 'Superheater Tank' No 6992, with a very full coal bunker, is pictured in LMS plain black livery whilst waiting to depart with a four-coach local train at Rugeley Trent Valley station in the 1930s, possibly a Nuneaton service or a train to Walsall via the Cannock Line. This delightfully period image was taken by Mr P.S. Kendrick, a mining surveyor who at that time lived in nearby Hednesford. *Edward Talbot Collection*

The date is circa 1914 and an LNWR 4-6-2T (number undecipherable) is seen in charge of an up 'Irish Mail' train (worked from Rugby during that period by one of these locos); the location is south of Watford. Note the three vans at the front of the seven-vehicle train. The permanent way seen under construction in the foreground of the picture is a section of the Watford Electric lines (officially opened 1922). *Edward Talbot Collection*

Chapter 7

1912

London Brighton & South Coast Railway 'J2' Class 4-6-2T, designed by Marsh

Marsh left the LBSCR before the building of the second 'J1' class 4-6-2T loco was completed and so his successor as CME, Lawson Billinton, took over the responsibility for completing the loco. However, he made several changes including importantly incorporating Walschaerts valve gear in place of the Marsh-specified Stephenson gear. Accordingly, what should have been the second 'J1' class Pacific tank engine was designated 'J2' class; that loco was completed in March 1912.

Both locomotives performed well, although No 326 was considered by engine crews to be the faster of the two. The 'J1' and 'J2' were used on the LBSCR's heaviest trains, up until the formation of Southern Railway (SR) in January 1923.

Ex-London Brighton & South Coast Railway Marsh 'J2' class 4-6-2T No 2326 pictured in Southern livery (malachite green) at Tunbridge Wells West in September 1947, note this Southern livery style did not have a smokebox number plate. *J.M. Jarvis/Colour Rail*

Number	Name	Built	Completed	Withdrawn
LBSCR 326	BESSBOROUGH	Brighton	03/1912	06/1951
SR B326 and 2326	Name removed 04/1925			
BR 32326				

During 1925 and 1926, the two classes were gradually replaced on the heaviest London–Brighton express trains by more powerful newly introduced tender locomotives, but the 'J1' and 'J2' tanks were still used on lighter express services until the completion of the London to Brighton line electrification, in 1935. Thereafter they were transferred to Eastbourne and used on express services between that town and London right up to the outbreak of the Second World War.

The two locomotives spent the early months of the War in store but were later transferred to Tunbridge Wells depot. Both survived into British Railways (BR) ownership in 1948, being withdrawn in June 1951, when they were both replaced by new LMS Fairburn-designed 2-6-4T locomotives.

This loco ran in several liveries, which included LBSCR standard umber, SR pre-war green-lined white and black, plain black during the Second World War, and express locomotive SR malachite green lined in yellow and black. Initially the loco name was carried on the side tanks with the LBSCR number on the side of the tender. Later the word SOUTHERN was applied to the side tanks with number B326 below, under the SR the engine was renumbered 2326, still in that style. In wartime black livery the word SOUTHERN was carried on the side tanks with the number being removed to the tender. From June 1946 the loco again had the word SOUTHERN on the side tanks and the number on the tender. From the time of 'Nationalisation' the engine carried the number 32326 on the tender side but the side tank was plain. At some time during the BR period this loco (unlike No 32325) is not thought to have carried a smokebox number plate.

This loco was cut up at Brighton Works.

LBSCR 4-6-2T 'J2' class

Introduced: 1912

Power Classification: 4P

Built: Brighton Works – 1 loco built

Designer: Douglas Earle Marsh, modified and built by Lawson Billinton

Company: London Brighton & South Coast Railway

Driving Wheel: 6ft 7½ins

Boiler Pressure: 170psi superheated

Cylinders: 2 – 21ins diameter x 26ins stroke

Tractive Effort @ 85%: 20,840lbf

Valve Gear: Walschaert (piston)

Water Capacity: 2300 gallons

Coal Capacity: 3 tons

Marsh 'J2' class 4-6-2T No 2326 waiting to enter the works for attention, pictured at Eastleigh in April 1934. *Mike Morant Collection*

The superbly turned out Marsh 'J2' class LBSCR 4-6-2T No 2326 pictured in this delightfully detailed study, with the Southern Railway loco crew looking on from the footplate. The location is thought to be Brighton and the date circa 1926. Note the Billinton-inspired Walschaerts valve gear. *Rail Photoprints Collection*

Chapter 8

1914–1916

Great Central Railway '9N' Class 4-6-2T (LNER/BR 'A5/1'), designed by Robinson

This was Robinson's last passenger tank design for the Great Central Railway (GCR); it was built with the haulage of suburban passenger services in mind and in particular the testing routes over GCR metals out of London Marylebone station to Aylesbury and High Wycombe, on which it gave over 30 years of faultless service.

The 'A5/1' class engines were built by the GCR in two batches between 1911 and 1917, with a third batch of the Pacific Tanks being built by the LNER in 1923, all at Gorton Works. The last ten built (after grouping) received side window cabs and accordingly the earlier-built members of the class were modified to suit as they entered the works for overhaul. The boilers were interchangeable with the GCR 'D9' class of 4-4-0 locos.

The 'A5' class engines were amongst the first GCR engines to incorporate superheating using firstly Schmidt equipment and later Robinson-designed units. Initially there were various superheater variants but between 1915 and 1917 they were all modified to a standard Robinson pattern, which became generally referred to as the 'Robinson Superheater'. Robinson's design expanded the superheater elements into the smokebox header, and had a combined blower and circulating valve, to protect the elements from the firebox gases when

British Railways Eastern Region 4-6-2T 'A5/1' class No 69828 (originally GCR '9N' class) is seen near Bollington, Cheshire, with a local service for Macclesfield, in June 1957. This loco was GCR No 156, thereafter LNER Nos 5156 and 9828. *Colour Rail*

Numbers	Built	Completed	Withdrawn
GCR 165, LNER 5165 and 9800, BR 69800	Gorton	03/1911	08/1959
GCR 166, LNER 5166 and 9801, BR 69801	Gorton	04/1911	04/1960
GCR 167, LNER 5167 and 9802, BR 69802	Gorton	05/1911	02/1959
GCR 168, LNER 5168 and 9803, BR 69803	Gorton	05/1911	07/1959
GCR 169, LNER 5169 and 9804, BR 69804	Gorton	05/1911	04/1958
GCR 170, LNER 5170 and 9805, BR 69805	Gorton	06/1911	09/1959
GCR 23, LNER 5023 and 9806, BR 69806	Gorton	06/1911	06/1960
GCR 24, LNER 5024 and 9807, BR 69807	Gorton	06/1911	07/1958
GCR 447, LNER 5447, BR N/A	Gorton	1911	1942
GCR 448, LNER 5448 and 9809, BR 69808	Gorton	08/1911	11/1960
GCR 449, LNER 5449 and 9809, BR 69809	Gorton	10/1912	05/1959
GCR 450, LNER 5450 and 9810, BR 69810	Gorton	11/1912	10/1958
GCR 451, LNER 5451 and 9811, BR 69811	Gorton	11/1912	10/1958
GCR 452, LNER 5452 and 9812, BR 69812	Gorton	11/1912	07/1959
GCR 128, LNER 5128 and 9813, BR 69813	Gorton	12/1912	04/1960
GCR 129, LNER 5129 and 9814, BR 69814	Gorton	12/1912	11/1960
GCR 371, LNER 5371 and 9815, BR 69815	Gorton	06/1917	07/1957
GCR 372, LNER 5372 and 9816, BR 69816	Gorton	07/1917	01/1959
GCR 373, LNER 5373 and 9817, BR 69817	Gorton	08/1917	04/1960
GCR 374, LNER 5374 and 9818, BR 69818	Gorton	09/1917	12/1958
GCR 411, LNER 5411 and 9819, BR 69819	Gorton	10/1917	03/1958
GCR 3, LNER 5003 and 9820, BR 69820	Gorton	01/1923	11/1960
GCR 6, LNER 5006 and 9821, BR 69821	Gorton	02/1923	05/1960
GCR 7, LNER 5007 and 9822, BR 69822	Gorton	02/1923	11/1958
GCR 30, LNER 5030 and 9823, BR 69823	Gorton	03/1923	04/1960
GCR 45, LNER 5045 and 9824, BR 69824	Gorton	04/1923	12/1958
GCR 46, LNER 5046 and 9825, BR 69825	Gorton	04/1923	11/1959
GCR 88, LNER 5088 and 9826, BR 69826	Gorton	05/1923	07/1958
GCR 154, LNER 5154 and 9827, BR 69827	Gorton	05/1923	11/1959
GCR 156, LNER 5156 and 9828, BR 69828	Gorton	06/1923	05/1958
GCR 158, LNER 5158 and 9829, BR 69829	Gorton	06/1923	05/1960

Loco No 69800 cut up at Gorton Works, all other members of the class at Darlington Works

GCR/LNER 4-6-2T '9N' class, LNER/BR 'A5/1' class, BR numbers 69800–69829

Introduced: 1911/23

Power Classification: 4P (reclassified 3P in 1953)

Built: Gorton Works, 31 locomotives (1 loco scrapped pre-BR)

Designer: John G Robinson

Company: Great Central Railway

Driving Wheel: 5ft 7ins

Boiler Pressure: 180psi superheated

Cylinders: Inside – 20ins diameter x 26ins stroke

Tractive Effort @ 85%: 23,750lbf

Valve Gear: Stephenson (piston valves)

Water Capacity: 2280 gallons

Coal Capacity: 4 tons 3cwts

the driver closed the locomotive's regulator.

The highly successful 'A5/1' class engines were never rebuilt but some changes aside from the superheater developments were made and they included the fitting of Ross pop safety valves circa 1920.

All of the class were fitted with water pick-up apparatus, which being little used in traffic was removed between 1948 and 1949. A number of the class were fitted with experimental Automatic Train Control equipment known as 'Reliostop'.

With the arrival of the newer 1923 batch of engines some of the earlier allocated ones were transferred to the Bradford area where they greatly improved the reliability of local passenger services. In 1928 six of the Bradford batch of engines was moved south to operate out of

Great Central Railway Robinson-designed '9N' class engine is seen as BR Eastern Region 'A5/1' class No 69804 in July 1955. The location is Langwith Junction (then 40E, changed to 41J in July 1958); the loco is fully coaled up and ready for its next turn of duty. This loco was formerly GCR No 169, LNER Nos 5169 and 9804. *K.C.H. Fairey/Colour Rail*

Robinson '9N' class 'Pacific Tank' BR No 69817 (LNER A5/1 class) is seen on shed at Gorton (then 39A) in April 1955, original GCR No 373, LNER Nos 5373 and 9817. *Mike Stokes Collection*

Kings Cross on the services to Hitchin and Baldock; during that period a member of the class was by all accounts clocked with a train at 70mph, a speed believed to be a class record. After the LNER took over the former London Transport line between Rickmansworth and Aylesbury they replaced the aging 'H2' class 4-4-0T locos with 'A5' types. From 1948, Thompson 'L1'class replaced the 'A5/1s' on their original Marylebone services. The surplus 'A5s' were then moved to Lincolnshire. From 1950 onwards, some moved north to work the Darlington–Saltburn services, and in 1951 some moved to Hull, again to undertake suburban passenger workings.

The first of the 'A1/1' class to be withdrawn was No 5547 (LNER No) with cracked frames in 1942, this loco never coming into BR ownership. BR inherited thirty of the class in 1948. None survived in service beyond November 1960.

Heading tender first away from Macclesfield with a local service to Manchester is LNER 4-6-2T No 69828, seen in the summer of 1955; loco's original GCR No 156, LNER numbers 5156 and 9828. Note the wisp of steam from the inside Stephenson piston valve gear, emitting from under the boiler. The advertising hoardings tell their 'own' story of the era; for example comedian Nat Jackley is advertised as 'coming soon' to the local theatre, Persil was even then 'Washing Whiter' and there was, as always, 'A Glass and a Half of Milk in a bar of Cadbury's Dairy Milk Chocolate'. *Mike Stokes Collection*

Chapter 9

1914–1916

North Eastern Railway 'W' Class as 4-6-0T 'Whitby Tanks', designed by Worsdell, rebuilt as 4-6-2T by Raven (BR 'A6' class)

Wilson Worsdell introduced a class of 10 tank engines specifically for use on the stiffly graded line between Whitby and Scarborough on the Yorkshire coast. They were built as 4-6-0T engines and were designated 'W' class, built to replace the aging 0-4-4T previously in use over that route. The 'W' class became colloquially known as 'Whitby Tanks'. They were the first class of six-coupled tank locomotives introduced by the North Eastern Railway (NER).

When first taken into service the 'W' class was put to work temporarily between Harrogate and Leeds, whilst infrastructure-imposed restrictions on the coastal route were resolved. On moving to their intended location the engines proved to be extremely sure-footed performers; however, as traffic on the popular seaside route increased they were found to be lacking in coal- and water-carrying capacities.

To rectify those shortcomings the locos were suitably modified between 1914 and 1916 to the design of the then NER CME, Worsdell. The enlargement modifications required the fitting of a trailing axle and accordingly the Worsdell 4-6-0T locomotives became Raven 'Pacific Tanks'.

North Eastern Railway (NER) Worsdell-designed 4-6-2 (Pacific) 'Whitby Tank', LNER No 69791, is seen in ex-works condition at Starbeck shed (50D) in June 1950, original NER No 687, LNER Nos 687 and 9791. *T.B. Owen/Colour Rail*

NER 4-6-2T 'W' class, LNER/BR 'A6' class, BR numbers 69791–69799

Introduced: 1907–08 as 4-6-0T, rebuilt 1914–16 as 4-6-2T

Power Classification: 4P

Built: Gateshead Works – 10 locomotives

Designer: Wilson Worsdell

Rebuilt Vincent Raven

Company: North Eastern Railway

Driving Wheel: 5ft 1¼ins

Boiler Pressure: 175psi, 6 locos later superheated

Cylinders: Inside – 19ins diameter x 26ins stroke

Tractive Effort @ 85%: 23,750lbf

Valve Gear: Stephenson (piston valves)

Water Capacity: 1893 gallons

Coal Capacity: 4 tons

In 1932 seven of the class were given modified boilers, work which involved the removal of tube stays and the addition of further boiler tubes, the work increased the tube heating surface from 1168sq ft to 1204sq ft. Following further modifications in 1936 those 'A6' class boilers became interchangeable with those of the 'A6', 'A7', 'A8', 'H1', and 'T1' class engines (i.e. all diagram sixty-three boilers).

In line with that work superheaters were fitted between 1937 and 1944. Three of the class retained saturated boilers for all of their working lives.

As the Gresley-rebuilt 'A8' class 4-6-2T engines entered service they started to replace 'A6' engines on the Whitby route, as a consequence the 'A6s' were seen additionally working in the Leeds, Northallerton and Darlington areas.

BR took into stock eight 'A6' class locos into stock (1948) and only one of those engines lasted into 1953.

Numbers	Built	Completed	Rebuilt 4-6-2	Withdrawn
NER 686, LNER 686 and 9790, BR N/A	Gateshead	1907	1914–16 S	1947
NER 687, LNER 687 and 9791, BR 69791	Gateshead	12/1907	1914–16 S	08/1951
NER 688, LNER 688 and 9792, BR 69792*	Gateshead	12/1907	1914–16 S	12/1948
NER 689, LNER 689 and 9793, BR 69793	Gateshead	01/1908	1914–16 S	04/1951
NER 690, LNER 690 and 9794, BR 69794	Gateshead	02/1908	1914–16	08/1951
NER 691, LNER 691 and 9795, BR 69795	Gateshead	03/1908	1914–16	07/1950
NER 692, LNER 692 and 9796, BR 69796	Gateshead	03/1908	1914–16 S	03/1953
NER 693, LNER 693 and 9797, BR 69797	Gateshead	03/1908	1914–16 S	08/1951
NER 694, LNER 694 and 9798, BR 69798	Gateshead	04/1908	1914–16	02/1951
NER 695, LNER 695 and 9799, BR 69799*	Gateshead	04/1908	1914–16 S	02/1950

* Number allocated but not applied to loco
S – Superheated locomotives
All 'A/6' class locomotives were cut up at Darlington Works

Chapter 10

1917

Caledonian Railway '944' Class 4-6-2T 'Wemyss Bay Tanks', designed by Pickersgill

This twelve-locomotive class was built for the Caledonian Railway to a Pickersgill design by North British Locomotive Co Ltd at their Glasgow Hyde Park Works to order No L672, and the engines were allocated the NBL works numbers 21480–91. Confusingly, some listings show the class as being an 'in-house build' by the Caledonian Railway at St Rollox Works. The engines were basically a smaller tank loco version of the CR '54630' class tender engines.

The large passenger tanks were the only engines of that type ever built for the Caledonian Railway and they were specifically designed for use on the semi-fast services out of Glasgow to the Clyde coast. For that reason the powerful Pacific Tanks were referred to colloquially as 'Wemyss Bay Tanks'. Following their removal from passenger duties the remaining members of the class were allocated to banking duties at Beattock, a roster they easily coped with.

Locos allocated LMS numbers 15357 and 15358 were withdrawn prior to nationalisation and of the remaining ten taken into BR stock only eight were given their allocated BR numbers with loco Nos 55351 and 55355 being cut up in 1948 and 1949 respectively. Loco No 55356 fared little better, it being withdrawn in June 1950, the last loco in service being 55359, which survived until October 1953.

A former suburban passenger loco after being transferred to banking duties at Beattock, Caledonian Railway '944' class 4-6-2T loco (BR No 55359) is pictured at the top of the incline with a string of other 'Beattock Bankers', in this instance a pair of 2-6-4T Fairburn tanks and a former CR 0-6-0, all awaiting their return to the foot of the bank to resume the rear assistance of northbound trains, in April 1953. *David Anderson*

CR 4-6-2T '944' class, BR numbers 55350–55361

Introduced: 1917

Power Classification: 4P

Built: North British Locomotive Co Ltd – 12 locomotives

Designer: William Pickersgill

Company: Caledonian Railway

Driving Wheel: 5ft 9ins

Boiler Pressure: 180psi superheated

Cylinders: Outside – 19½ins diameter x 26ins stroke

Tractive Effort @ 85%: 21,920lbf

Valve Gear: Stephenson (piston valves)

Numbers	Built	Completed	Withdrawn
CR 951, LMS 15357, BR N/A	North British Locomotive Co Ltd	02/1917	07/1946
CR 952, LMS 15358, BR N/A	North British Locomotive Co Ltd	02/1917	06/1946
CR 944, LMS 15350, BR 55350	North British Locomotive Co Ltd	03/1917	04/1952
CR 945, LMS 15351, BR 55351*	North British Locomotive Co Ltd	03/1917	12/1948
CR 946, LMS 15352, BR 55352	North British Locomotive Co Ltd	01/1917	03/1952
CR 947, LMS 15353, BR 55353	North British Locomotive Co Ltd	01/1917	07/1951
CR 948, LMS 15354, BR 55354	North British Locomotive Co Ltd	01/1917	08/1949
CR 949, LMS 15355, BR 55355*	North British Locomotive Co Ltd	01/1917	01/1948
CR 950, LMS 15356, BR 55356	North British Locomotive Co Ltd	01/1917	06/1950
CR 953, LMS 15359, BR 55359	North British Locomotive Co Ltd	04/1917	10/1953
CR 954, LMS 15360, BR 55360	North British Locomotive Co Ltd	05/1917	02/1952
CR 955, LMS 15361, BR 55361	North British Locomotive Co Ltd	05/1917	06/1952

* Number allocated but not applied to loco

Caledonian Railway '944' class 4-6-2T loco BR No 55355 is pictured having taken water at Glasgow Central station in the early 1950s, note the Caledonian Bow Tie (on the middle lamp bracket) is set with both arms pointing upwards denoting Glasgow services to and from Gourock and also Dumbarton or Balloch. Originally this Pacific Tank carried Caley No 949 and LMS No 15355. *Colour Rail*

The sturdy appearance of the Pickersgill-designed Caledonian Railway '944' class 4-6-2T locos is clearly illustrated in this shot of BR No 55352, seen between duties in June 1951 at Beattock (then 68D), original CR No 946 and LMS No 15352. *K.C.H. Fairey/Colour Rail*

Time for a chat! An engineman from another loco finds time to chat to the crew of 4-6-2T No 55359 whilst that loco waits to return 'downhill'. The South Lanarkshire location for this image was adjacent to the summit signal box, which was in steam days located at 1015 feet above sea level, and thus wide open to the elements. *David Anderson*

'Wemyss Bay Tank' Caledonian Railway '944' class 4-6-2T loco, BR No 55359, pictured at Beattock Summit prior to returning downhill after a banking turn and after taking water, during April 1953. It should be remembered that steam locomotives frequently required assistance in order to get their trains up the incline, particularly in the northbound direction, which had steeper gradients. The Beattock engine shed (68D) had enough steam locomotives allocated in order to provide a 24-hour standby 'banking' service, thus minimising train delays. *David Anderson*

Chapter 11

1921–1922

London & South Western Railway 'H16' Class 4-6-2T, designed by Urie

Urie had previously built a very successful class of 'Hump Shunters' for working the then newly opened Feltham Marshalling Yard; they were the 'G16' class of 4-8-0T engines constructed at Eastleigh Works in 1921, just prior to grouping. To complement those engines and to also primarily work heavy transfer freight trains between the freight yards at Feltham, Brent (Midland Railway) and Willesden (London & North Western Railway) Urie then designed the 'H16' class of 4-6-2 tank engines.

There were five locomotives in the class and they were also built at Eastleigh Works between 1921 and 1922, again prior to the railway company grouping which came into force on 1 January 1923. The new class of freight engines had many features in common with the 'G16' locos; for example, identical boiler, motion and bogies and very similar cylinders. However their driving wheels were larger (5ft 7ins in diameter).

Preserved Un-Rebuilt Bulleid Battle of Britain light pacific No 34081 92 SQUADRON is based at the Nene Valley Railway but often visits other heritage railway centres. The loco is seen in the yard at Sheffield Park on the Bluebell Railway during a 2007 visit. *Paul Pettitt*

LSWR 4-6-2T 'H16' class, BR numbers 30516–30520

Introduced: 1921

Power Classification: 5F (reclassified 6F in 1953)

Built: Eastleigh Works – 5 locomotives

Designer: Robert Urie

Company: London & South Western Railway

Driving Wheel: 5ft 7ins

Boiler Pressure: 180psi superheated

Cylinders: Outside – 21ins diameter x 28ins stroke

Tractive Effort @ 85%: 28,200lbf

Valve Gear: Walschaerts (piston valves)

Water Capacity: 2000 gallons

Coal Capacity: 3 tons 10cwts

By employing the Pacific configuration Urie was able to design an extra-large bunker, carried on the associated radial trailing truck. By enlarging the side tanks (effectively removing the downward sloping top common to the 'G16' class) he was also able to increase the water-carrying capacity of the 'H16' class, therefore allowing the engines to range much further between servicing stops. Other than a change of superheaters to a Maunsell pattern the locos remained mainly unaltered throughout their service lives.

As freight traffic around the marshalling yards declined, and modern traction began to take over what were previously steam duties, work for rostered turns for the 'H16' class changed. Although designated freight locos they were occasionally pressed into passenger-train service and in particular that work would have included special trains during Royal Ascot Week. They were not ideally suited to passenger work due to their limited water-carrying capacity and a propensity for rough riding when travelling bunker first.

Unlike the plain black livery of the 'G16s', the 'H16' class were given the standard Southern passenger livery of lined olive green. That was changed to a plain black livery during the Second World War and that livery was retained by most of them during the British Railways steam era. During the 1950s the 'H16s' were regularly employed on Clapham Junction–Waterloo empty stock duties (ECS workings) and in their final years they found regular employment on the Fawley branch oil trains. The whole of the class were withdrawn during November 1962; however, none were cut up immediately, with four engines resisting the cutting torches until July to October 1963 and one until April 1964 (30518).

Numbers	Built	Completed	Withdrawn
LSWR 516, SR E516, BR 30516	Eastleigh	11/1921	11/1962
LSWR 517, SR E517, BR 30517	Eastleigh	11/1921	11/1962
LSWR 518, SR E518, BR 30518	Eastleigh	12/1921	11/1962
LSWR 519, SR E519, BR 30519	Eastleigh	01/1922	11/1962
LSWR 520, SR E520, BR 30520	Eastleigh	02/1922	11/1962

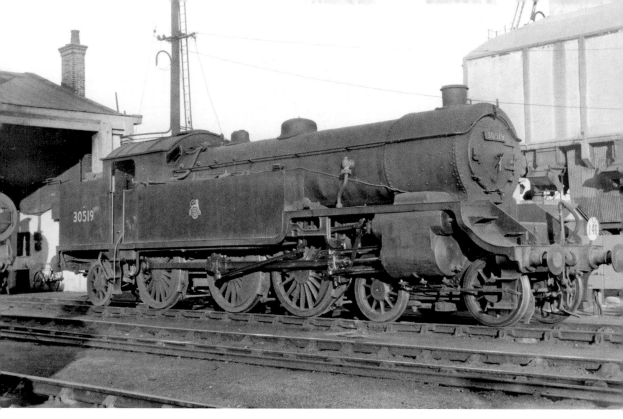

London & South Western Railway 'H16' class 'Pacific Tank' BR No 30519 'on shed' at Feltham (70B) in 1961. Note the addition of a smokebox door number plate. *Richard Lewis/Rail Photoprints Collection*

LSWR 'H16' class 'Pacific Tank' BR No 30517 is pictured in light steam and on shed at Eastleigh (then 71A) in May 1961. *K.C.H. Fairey/Colour Rail*

LSWR 'H16' class 'Pacific Tank' BR No 30517 is again pictured on shed; this time the loco is seen at Feltham (70B) during 1961. During the 1950s, all five locos of the class were allocated to Feltham shed in South West London, from where they worked on shunting duties, local goods trains and occasionally empty coaching stock workings. In their final years, several were used on Fawley branch oil trains. *Mike Stokes Collection*

The Urie-designed 4-6-2T 'H16' class engines were originally built for the London & South Western Railway (LSWR). BR No 30517 is pictured in light steam at Nine Elms shed (70A) in June 1959. *K.C.H. Fairey/Colour Rail*

A superb profile shot of LSWR 'H16' class 'Pacific Tank' BR No 30520 'on shed' at Feltham (70B) in September 1962. The Urie-designed 4-6-2T has a full tender of coal and being at working boiler pressure is just lifting the valves. *Rail Photoprints Collection*

Super power for the 5.12pm Fawley–Southampton stopper as H16 4-6-2T No 30516 and Ivatt 2 No 41319 are seen between Marchwood and Totton, 4/6/60. It may be that the H16 was being worked back to Eastleigh unbalanced after arriving with an oil tank train. *Hugh Ballantyne/Rail Photoprints Collection*

Chapter 12

1922–1925

Great Northern Railway 'A1' Class 4-6-2, designed by Gresley

In April 1922 NER loco No 1470 (LNER 4470) became the first example of the Gresley 'A1' class to enter service. The second Pacific No 1471 followed in July 1922 whilst at the same time an order for a further batch of nine engines was placed. At the time of their introduction Gresley had stated that the 'A1' class 4-6-2 engines were designed to pull 600-ton trains at express speeds, and in September 1922 the second example built, No 1471 (LNER 4471), proved that claim by pulling such a train under test conditions, thus confirming the ability of this new class to undertake express passenger work on the routes between London and the North.

London & North Eastern Railway (LNER) ex-Great Northern Railway (GNR) Gresley 'A1' class Pacific No 4470 GREAT NORTHERN is pictured passing Saltersford in July 1926. Note that in this LNER apple-green livery style the loco number is carried under the LNER initials on the tender, and also on the buffer beam. *Mike Bentley Collection*

Immediately following his appointment as Chief Mechanical Engineer (CME) of the GNR Gresley began work to improve that railway's motive power availability by providing the company with large express passenger locomotives. Gresley had observed firsthand the performance of the four-cylinder compound 'Atlantic' (4-4-2) types built by his predecessor (H.A. Ivatt); those engines had high pressure boilers and wide grate areas.

His experimentation led him to modify an old Ivatt-built 'Atlantic' locomotive in 1915, whilst at that time considering the merits of two new types of Pacific design, one of which was simply a refined version of his modified 'Atlantic' design. Gresley's ongoing work included the investigation of three-cylinder engine configuration which in turn fuelled his great interest in valve gear, and accordingly he introduced his new design of 'Conjugated Valve Gear'. That system was subsequently patented in November 1915; however, Gresley freely admitted that its origin lay in a lapsed Holcroft* patent. Simply put, the conjugated system worked by operating the valve for the middle cylinder from the motion of the two outside units.

During the period of the First World War Gresley was obliged to temporarily suspend his development of express passenger locomotives in favour of the then more urgently required goods engines. However he did test his patented valve gear with other 3-cylinder loco classes including the 'O2' 2-8-0 and the express goods 'K3' 2-6-0 designs. At the end of the war Gresley recommenced work on his three-cylinder Pacific design, which of course by that time included the use of his famous (perchance infamous) conjugated valve gear.

The first two Gresley three-cylinder Pacifics were totally different from the GNR's Ivatt 'Atlantics' and accordingly they caused quite a stir amongst the railway fraternity. Their subsequent performance in traffic justified the designer's claims for them and the engines, which rode well, were hailed as being excellent locomotives.

The introduction of the 'A1' class set Gresley on the road to later gaining his deserved reputation as a designer of great Pacific locomotives; remember that he was appointed CME of the LNER when that company took over the GNR in 1922. Compared with other locomotives of the time the 'A1' class engines had comparatively large cabs, which for the first time in British locomotive building history boasted padded seats for the enginemen!

The newly introduced Pacifics had three-cylinders all driving on the second coupled axle; they incorporated two outside sets of Walschaerts valve gear working in conjunction with Gresley's patent conjugated valve gear, which acted on the centre valve and was located in front of the cylinder. This hybrid valve arrangement has long been considered as being the Achilles Heel of Gresley Pacific designs as they experienced problems with 'middle valve over-running' which in turn led to instances of 'middle big-end' failure.

* Harold Holcroft (1882–1973) was a locomotive engineer who saw service with several railway companies including the Great Western and the Southern Railways. He developed his own type of conjugated valve gear, and reportedly assisted Gresley during the design of the GNR version.

Numbers	Name	Built	Completed	Rebuilt as A1/1**
GNR 1470, LNER 4470	GREAT NORTHERN	Doncaster	04/1922	09/1945

** Rebuilt Edward Thompson 1945

GNR/LNER 4-6-2 Gresley 'A1' class

Introduced: 1922 onwards

Power Classification: 7P

Designer: Nigel Gresley

Company: Great Northern Railway/London & North Eastern Railway

Driving Wheel: 6ft 8ins

Boiler Pressure: 180psi, superheated (525 square feet)

Total Heating Surface: 3455 square feet

Cylinders: 3 – 20ins diameter x 26ins stroke

Tractive Effort @ 85%: 29,835lbf

Valve Gear: Outside Walschaerts, inside Gresley derived motion (piston valves)

Water Capacity: 5000 gallons

Coal Capacity: 8 tons

In this later image of GREAT NORTHERN the loco's number is still carried on the front buffer beam but now on the cabside, and not the tender. Perchance the LNER decided that carrying specific loco numbers on the tender sides prevented those tenders from being interchangeable! *Mike Bentley Collection*

Chapter 13

1922–1924

North Eastern Railway/London & North Eastern Railway 'A2' Class 4-6-2, designed by Raven

In keeping with other companies the North Eastern Railway's development of new express passenger locomotive types was held up by the need to reprioritise engineering requirements during the period of the First World War. The company urgently required more powerful locomotives to cope with the then increasing passenger loadings on the East Coast Main Line (ECML). At the end of hostilities the company's Chief Mechanical Engineer (CME), Vincent Raven, lost no time in developing one of his successful 'Atlantic' (4-4-2) 'C7'

Ex-North Eastern Railway, LNER 'A2' class Raven Pacific No 2403 CITY OF DURHAM (with large tender) is pictured leaving Darlington on 29 May 1936. *Mike Bentley Collection*

class into a 4-6-2 design. Indeed some observers were of the opinion that the NER hurried the building of their Pacific locomotive in order to get it into traffic before that railway company ceased to exist. The timescale employed would seem to support that theory!

Building authorisation for the first two (of five) Pacifics to Raven's design was given on 30th March 1922 and line drawings for the class were completed and published in the following July. Both were recorded as having been delivered by December 1922, in time for 'Grouping' (January 1923). However, in reality the first engine, No 2404 CITY OF NEWCASTLE, was presented to the watching railway public still in paint-shop grey whilst the second of the class, No 2402 CITY OF KINGSTON UPON HULL, did not actually run until January 1923, and was therefore strictly speaking an LNER engine.

The resultant stretched 'Atlantic' was a very long engine with increased cylinder and boiler diameter. The three cylinders of the 'A2' design (like its 'C7' predecessor) drove on the front coupled axle, in association with three independent sets of Stephenson valve gear. A large firebox was fitted and the weight of that was spread out over the 4-6-2's trailing truck. In order to counter the adverse effects experienced by the use of longer boiler tubes some were increased in diameter, and boiler pressure was increased from 175psi to 200psi. The locomotives' length proved to be restrictive in terms of route availability. Indeed these lengthened engines reportedly attracted the colloquial nickname 'Skittle Alleys'.

Following successful results in traffic with the first two engines the other three locomotives of the class were built by the LNER and they entered service in March 1924, but with a Gresley-designed 'A1' style rear bogie (trailing truck). By all accounts there was little difference between the Raven Pacifics and the 'A1' locos when they were subjected to comparison testing in 1923; however the 'A2' class engines were a little more successful in maintaining full boiler pressure than the 'A1' class locos. When in October 1923 the LNER placed an order for a further large quantity of Gresley Pacifics the fate of the Raven Pacifics was settled.

Originally allocated to Gateshead, the five members of the 'A2' class moved to York in 1934. With the exception of a few visits to London Kings Cross in 1923 for the aforementioned comparison trials, they spent their first ten years operating between Grantham and Edinburgh,

NER/LNER 4-6-2 Raven 'A2' class, NER/LNER numbers 2400–2404

Introduced: 1922–23

Built: Darlington Works – 5 locomotives (2 for NER, 3 for LNER)

Designer: Vincent Raven

Company: North Eastern Railway/London & North Eastern Railway

Driving Wheel: 6ft 8ins

Boiler Pressure: 200psi

Cylinders: 3 – 19ins diameter x 26ins stroke

Tractive Effort @ 85%: 29,918lbf

Valve Gear: Stephenson (piston valves)

Water Capacity: 4125 gallons

Coal Capacity: 5 ton 10cwt

Numbers	Names	Built	Completed	Withdrawn
NER-LNER 2400	CITY OF NEWCASTLE	Darlington	12/1922	04/1937
NER-LNER 2401	CITY OF KINGSTON UPON HULL	Darlington	12/1922	07/1936
LNER 2402*	CITY OF YORK	Darlington	03/1924	07/1936
LNER 2403	CITY OF DURHAM	Darlington	03/1924	05/1937
LNER 2404	CITY OF RIPON	Darlington	03/1924	02/1937

* No 2402 was the first LNER-built locomotive to be scrapped

with occasional runs to Leeds. Whilst at York, they mainly hauled heavy secondary express passenger trains on the ECML, although the free-steaming Raven Pacifics were also rostered to fast freight and mail trains.

Circa November 1929 loco No 2404 was fitted with a modified 'A1' type boiler as it was considered unpractical to specifically build new boilers for such a small class of engines; to accommodate that type of boiler the loco, firebox and boiler were suitably modified. The original NER six-wheel tenders were replaced with standard Gresley eight-wheel non-corridor tenders towards the end of 1934.

The class remained in traffic until 1936/37 when it was withdrawn as the need for replacement boilers approached, and that work, coupled with their restricted route availability, meant the end of the Raven Pacifics.

Worthy of note is the fact that whilst developing his 4-6-2 steam locomotive class Vincent Raven was also working on a design of 4-6-4 electric locomotive which he envisaged hauling 450-ton trains at express train speeds along the ECML. Should Raven's proposed electrification plans for the East Coast Main Line have come to fruition in the early 1920s remains one of the biggest 'what ifs' in railway history!

Livery colours included fully lined and lettered grey, 'Saxony' green and LNER green.

LNER 'A2' class Raven Pacific No 2403 CITY OF DURHAM is pictured taking water at York on 25 May 1936; note the Gresley eight-wheel tender. *Mike Bentley Collection*

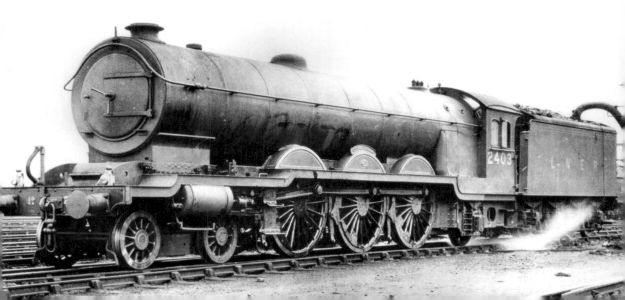

LNER 'A2' class Raven Pacific No 2404 CITY OF RIPON is pictured after the fitting of a modified 'A1' type boiler; note that the loco is coupled to an original NER six-wheel tender. *Mike Bentley Collection*

Chapter 14

1922–1935

London & North Eastern Railway 'A1' ('A10') and subsequently 'A3' Class 4-6-2, designed by Gresley

In 1948 British Railways inherited a class of seventy-eight Gresley-designed three-cylinder un-streamlined Pacific locomotives comprised of:

- 'A1' class locomotives at 'Grouping' built 1922–1923, Nos 4470 (became BR 60113 'A1/1' class) and 4471 (BR 60102)
- 'A1' class locomotives built after 'Grouping' (between 1924 and 1925) Nos 2543–2582 BR 60044–60083), 4472–4481 (BR 60103–60112)
- 'A3' class locomotives built after 'Grouping' (between 1928 and 1935) Nos 2500–2508 (BR 60035–60043), 2595–2599 (BR 60084–60088), 2743–2752 (BR 60089–60098), 2795–2797 (BR 60099–60101)

Following the creation of the London & North Eastern Railway (LNER) the ex-GNR Gresley Pacifics continued to be introduced into service and they were in the main described as good performers and were both popular with engine crews and well received by the travelling public. 'A3' loco building took place at two equally famous steam locomotive manufacturing centres, Doncaster Works (NER & LNER) and North British Locomotive Co Ltd, Glasgow (for LNER). Improvements/modifications to the class continued to be made and the major ones are detailed herewith.

Modifications made in 1925 included loco No 4477 GAY CRUSADER having its steam lap setting increased. In the same year Gresley Pacific No 4474 VICTOR WILD was performance tested against the Great Western Railway (GWR) 4-6-0 'Castle' class loco No 4079 PENDENNIS CASTLE. The outcome of which resulted in the 'A1' class engines then in service being rebuilt, as the GWR 4-6-0 was proved to be the superior engine. The rebuilding of the class included the fitting of long travel, long lap valves which had the desired effect and greatly improve the performance of the 'A1s'. In 1927 loco No 2555 CENTENARY had its valve travel set at 5¾ inches in full gear. In traffic conditions the alterations showed a reduction in coal consumption from 50lb/mile to 39lb/mile. That huge saving resulted in all of the 'A1' class being similarly modified between that year and 1931.

During that period the class were fitted with corridor tenders allowing them to be regularly used hauling long distance high-speed express passenger trains. A study of the engines' names, coupled with a little knowledge of the so called 'Sport of Kings', serves to confirm that the majority of the class were named after famous racehorses. GREAT NORTHERN was of course named after the famous railway company, FLYING SCOTSMAN after the Anglo

The first Gresley ex-Great Northern Railway (GNR) Pacific pictured carrying the LNER number No 1470E (thus dating the image of 1923 vintage); note the engine number was at that time carried on the tender sides under the letters LNER and on the front buffer beam. GREAT NORTHERN is pictured in full cry when passing New Southgate with a Kings Cross to Leeds service; observe also that the loco was not carrying a nameplate. *Mike Bentley Collection*

Scottish train of the same name whilst other names used included those of high-ranking railway officials.

In 1927 loco No 4480 ENTERPRISE was rebuilt with a larger superheater unit added and the boiler pressure increased from 180psi to 220psi; at the same time it was converted to a left-hand-drive engine.

That loco effectively became the first 'A3' engine and together with locos Nos 2573 HARVESTER, 2578 BAYARDO and 2580 SHOTOVER (after those engines were rebuilt) was designated variant 'A3/1'. At around the same time loco No 2544 LEMBERG was similarly rebuilt and it additionally had the size of its cylinders reduced from 20-inch diameter to 18¼-inch diameter, that loco being reclassified variant 'A3/2'.

A batch of twenty-seven 'A3s' built in 1935 had a new type of boiler with the famous LNER 'Banjo Dome', an addition which could simply be described as an oval-shaped steam collector located on top of the rear boiler ring. The last batch of nine newly built 'A3' Pacifics (1935) were also fitted with that distinctive feature, which by that time had became a standard fitting on all LNER large wide firebox boilers and also replacement 'A3' boilers.

In 1945 LNER CME Thompson rebuilt the original engine No 4470 (60113) and that loco, as previously stated, became the prototype for his own class of Pacific express passenger

Gresley LNER 'A3' 4-6-2 No 60088 BOOK LAW, in as-built condition and complete with 'Banjo Dome', is pictured at Grantham shed (35B) in March 1959. *D.H. Beecroft/Ron White Collection*

engine; designated variant 'A1/1' it subsequently became the first locomotive in the class later known as Thompson/Peppercorn 'A1' Pacifics. All of the other surviving Gresley 'A1' engines were at that time designated by the LNER as 'A10' class engines. To complete the history of classification it is important to note that on the introduction of the new Peppercorn-designed 'A1' engines (in 1948) the Gresley 'A1' and 'A10' Pacifics (after rebuilding) were all designated as 'A3' class locos. Only one 'A10' engine came into BR ownership, that being No 60068 SIR VISTO; that loco was rebuilt in December 1948, thus also becoming an 'A3'. Some of the locomotives were fitted with GNR-type tenders with added coal rails whilst others were fitted with LNER-type tenders.

Loco No 2571 (BR 60097) HUMORIST was the first of the class to be fitted with an experimental set of smoke deflectors, Kylchap blastpipe and double chimney in 1947. Between 1958 and 1960 all the other engines in the class were fitted with Kylchap blastpipes and double chimneys which improved performance but the associated softer exhaust caused smoke to drift around the boiler and as a result impair the driver's forward vision. To counteract that effect the locos were fitted with small 'Wing' deflectors on either side of the chimney, a modification which helped but did not completely eliminate the drifting smoke

Loco No 4472 FLYING SCOTSMAN after arrival at York with the Alrinchamian Railway Excursion Society 'Elizabethan' railtour from Kings Cross; note the two tenders. Bulleid Pacific No 35026 LAMPORT & HOLT LINE waits to take over for the run to Newcastle on 22 October 1966. *John Chalcraft/Rail Photoprints Collection*

'A3' Pacific No 60097 HUMORIST is pictured in ex-works condition at Doncaster in 1948; the loco was resplendent in newly applied BR blue livery with black smoke deflectors and smokebox and carried a smokebox number plate; the principal livery colour changed to BR green in November 1952. Loco No 2571 (BR 60097) HUMORIST was the first of the class to be fitted with an experimental set of smoke deflectors, Kylchap blastpipe and double chimney, in 1947. The loco retained that style of smoke deflectors for the remainder of its working life. *Mike Stokes Archive*

LNER 4-6-2 Gresley 'A1', 'A10' and subsequently 'A3' class, BR numbers 60035–60112

Introduced: 1922–23, 1924–25, 1928–30, 1934–35

Power Classification: 7P

Built: Doncaster Works 60102–60112 (1922–23), 60044–60063 (1924–25), 60084–60101 (1928–30) 60035–60043 (1934–35). North British Locomotive Co Ltd, 60064–60083 (1924)

Designer: Nigel Gresley

Company: London & North Eastern Railway

Driving Wheel: 6ft 8ins

Boiler Pressure: 'A1' and 'A10' 180psi, 'A3' 220psi superheated

Cylinders: 3 20ins x 26ins, 18¼ins x 26ins, 19ins x 26ins

Tractive Effort @ 85%: 'A3' 36,465lbf 30,362lbf 32,909lbf – 'A1'and'A10' 29,835lbf

Valve Gear: Walschaerts with derived motion (piston valves)

Water Capacity: 5000 gallons

Coal Capacity: 8 tons (Corridor tender 9 tons)

effect. In a later modification, designed to eliminate that problem, 'German' type (otherwise referred to as 'Trough' type) were later fitted to fifty-eight of the class between 1961 and 1962.

Liveries used included NER lined green; LNER lined green and black; wartime and BR black and in the post war/BR period lined blue, also experimental purple and BR green.

The first 'A3' class loco was withdrawn in 1959, as the Deltics replaced steam haulage on the East Coast Main Line in 1961. The 'A3s' moved to other duties, most notably the expresses to Scotland on the Midland Route out of Leeds. The last 'A3' to be withdrawn, No 60052 PRINCE PALATINE, was withdrawn in January 1966. All were scrapped except for No 4472, FLYING SCOTSMAN, which was withdrawn in January 1963 and sold into preservation.

Batch of nine locomotives, LNER Order No 331

Numbers	Name	Built	Completed	Modifications	Withdrawn
LNER 2500 and 35, BR 60035	WINDSOR LAD	Doncaster	07/1934	D 02/1959	09/1961
LNER 2501 and 36, BR 60036, G 07/1962	COLOMBO	Doncaster	07/1934	D 11/1958	11/1964
LNER 2502 and 37, BR 60037, G 05/1962	HYPERION	Doncaster	07/1934	D 10/1958	12/1963
LNER 2503 and 38, BR 60038	FIRDAUSSI	Doncaster	08/1934	D 08/1959	11/1963
LNER 2504 and 39, BR 60039, G 06/1961	SANDWICH	Doncaster	09/1934	D 07/1959	03/1963
LNER 2505 and 40, BR 60040, G 03/1962	CAMERONIAN	Doncaster	10/1934	D 10/1959	07/1964
LNER 2506 and 41, BR 60041, G 01/1963	SALMON TROUT	Doncaster	12/1934	D 07/1959	11/1965
LNER 2507 and 42, BR 60042, G 09/1962	SINGAPORE	Doncaster	12/1934	D 09/1958	07/1964
LNER 2508 and 43, BR 60043	BROWN JACK	Doncaster	02/1935	D 02/1959 G 02/1962	05/1964

D – Double Chimney G – German-style smoke deflectors

Disposal: 60035–60039–60044 Doncaster Works, 60036 Drapers, Hull, 60037–60041/42 Arnott Young, Carmyle, 60038 Darlington Works, 60040 Hughes Bolckows, North Blyth, 60043 Motherwell Machinery & Scrap, Wishaw

Gresley 'A3' class 4-6-2 No 60035 WINDSOR LAD pictured adjacent to the turntable at Haymarket shed (64B). Note the prominent 'Banjo Dome', double chimney but the absence of small smoke deflectors in this August 1958 study. *David Anderson*

Gresley 'A3' class 4-6-2 No 60036 COLOMBO with original-style single chimney and small-type 'Wing' smoke deflectors storms away from Darlington with 'The North Briton' on 22 June 1953 (double chimney November 1959). 'The North Briton' ran between Leeds City and Glasgow Queen Street via York. The train first ran on 26 September 1949 and last ran on 4 May 1968. *Mike Morant Collection*

Gresley 'A3' class 4-6-2 No 60038 FIRDAUSSI in a very clean condition pauses at Doncaster station in September 1959 (double chimney fitted August 1959); the loco then carried BR green livery. *Mike Stokes Archive*

Gresley 'A3' class 4-6-2 No 60038 FIRDAUSSI is seen at Doncaster in near original condition in this April 1959 image. *Mike Stokes Archive*

Gresley 'A3' class 4-6-2 No 60041 SALMON TROUT in BR green, is pictured between turns at Carlisle Canal (68E) in September 1955. *K.C.H. Fairey/Colour Rail*

Gresley 'A3' class 4-6-2 No 60043 BROWN JACK pictured at Dalmeny Junction with an Edinburgh Waverley–Dundee Tay Bridge special. The train was rostered in order to transport display team members of the RCMP, their horses and equipment, hence the reason for the unique smokebox adornment. The date of the special was 15 June 1957. *David Anderson*

Gresley 'A3' class 4-6-2 No 60043 BROWN JACK seen near to Haymarket Central Junction with an early morning Edinburgh Waverley–Dundee–Aberdeen express passenger service on 8 Sept 1957. *David Anderson*

Batch of ten locomotives, LNER Order No 301

Numbers	Name	Built	Completed Re-built	Modifications	Withdrawn
LNER 2543 and 44, BR 60044	MELTON	Doncaster	06/1924 R 09/1947	D 10/1959 G 08/1961	06/1963
LNER 2544 and 45, BR 60045	LEMBERG	Doncaster	07/1924 R 12/1927	D 10/1959 G 11/1961	11/1964
LNER 2545 and 46, BR 60046	DIAMOND JUBILEE	Doncaster	08/1924 R 08/1941	D 07/1958 G 12/1961	06/1963
LNER 2546 and 47, BR 60047	DONOVAN	Doncaster	08/1924 R 01/1948	D 07/1959 G 12/1961	04/1963
LNER 2547 and 48, BR 60048	DONCASTER	Doncaster	08/1924 R 05/1946	D 05/1959 G 12/1961	08/1963
LNER 2548 and 49, BR 60049	GALTEE MORE	Doncaster	09/1924 R 10/1945	D 03/1959 G 10/1960	12/1962
LNER 2549 and 50, BR 60050	PERSIMMON	Doncaster	10/1924 R 12/1943	D 04/1959 G 10/1961	06/1963
LNER 2550 and 51, BR 60051	BLINK BONNY	Doncaster	11/1924 R 11/1945	D 08/1959 G 03/1962	11/1964
LNER 2551 and 52, BR 60052	PRINCE PALATINE	Doncaster	11/1924 R 08/1941	D 11/1959 G 10/1962	01/1966
LNER 2552 and 53, BR 60053	SANSOVINO	Doncaster	11/1924 R 09/1943	D 11/1958 G 11/1960	06/1963

D – Double Chimney, G – German-style smoke deflectors, R–Rebuilt
Disposal: 60044–60046/47/48/49/50–60053 Doncaster Works, 60051 Hughes Bolckows, North Blyth, 60052 McLellans, Langloan, 60045 Drapers, Hull

Gresley 'A3' class Pacific No 60044 MELTON is seen at an unknown location on the ECML circa 1962. The German-style smoke deflectors may not, in the opinion of many, have looked fitting on such a handsome class of engines but they did by all accounts do the job which they were intended to do. *Mike Stokes Archive*

Gresley 'A1' class Pacific No 2544 emerged from the works in July 1924 but wasn't named LEMBERG until August 1925; in this superb earlier portrait the loco is seen without nameplates. The location is almost certainly Doncaster. Loco No 2544 was subsequently rebuilt and then classified as an 'A3'; this loco became BR 60045. *Mike Morant Collection*

Gresley 'A3' Pacific No 60045 LEMBERG, in BR green livery, seen when on standby for southbound ECML services at Darlington, on 31 July 1965; in fact some 41 years after the ex-works image of this loco (pictured as No 2544) in a previous image. *Brian Robbins/Rail Photoprints Collection*

Gresley 'A3' class 4-6-2 No 60046 DIAMOND JUBILEE seen on the ECML whilst over the water troughs at Wiske Moor; note the very filthy condition of the loco in this early 1963 image. *Mike Stokes Archive*

The 'A3' class German-style smoke deflectors can be seen in detail on this 1963 image of No 60046 DIAMOND JUBILEE taken on shed at Doncaster (36A). *Mike Stokes Archive*

Gresley 'A1' class Pacific No 2547 emerged from Doncaster Works in August 1924 but wasn't named DONCASTER until March 1926, dating this superb image prior to that occasion. Note that the loco number is on the tender under the LNER initials and also on the buffer beam preceded by a No symbol. The location is almost certainly the turntable at Doncaster; interestingly the loco was named after the 1873 Derby winner of that name. Loco No 2547 was subsequently rebuilt and then classified as an 'A3'; it became BR 60048. *Mike Morant Collection*

Gresley 'A1' class Pacific No 2548 GALTEE MORE (became 'A3' class and BR 60049). The Doncaster-built loco in original condition looks splendid in this 1937 image which was taken adjacent to the coaling plant at York shed. *Ron White Collection*

Gresley 'A3' class 4-6-2 No 60052 PRINCE PALATINE waits to depart from Sheffield Victoria station in this September 1952 image. *Mike Stokes Archive*

Gresley 'A3' class 4-6-2 No 60052 PRINCE PALATINE is seen 'hard up to the buffer stops' at Colwick shed yard (then 38A) in this June 1950 image. *Colour Rail*

Gresley 'A3' class 4-6-2 No 60053 SANSOVINO pictured hard at work passing Bentley in June 1959. The problem of drifting smoke, created by a softer exhaust after fitting an 'A3' with a Kylchap blastpipe and double chimney arrangement, is partially illustrated in dramatic action shot which also shows to good effect the LNER-style non-corridor tender with rounded top. *Mike Stokes Archive*

Sir Nigel Gresley's FLYING SCOTSMAN is perhaps the most well known of preserved steam locomotives. As such the preserved 'A3' class Pacific has always been in great demand and in addition to making numerous mainline runs the engine has visited a whole host of preserved railways. In the black and white image the loco is seen during a 1960s visit to an open day at Stockport (with single chimney); note that the young enthusiasts have made themselves comfortable on the engine's buffer beam. The colour image shows the iconic loco on duty at Llangollen Railway in 1995 (with double chimney); at that time the loco was owned by music producer and railway enthusiast Pete Waterman; however the engine is now part of the national collection and is often based at the National Railway Museum York. *Both images Keith Langston*

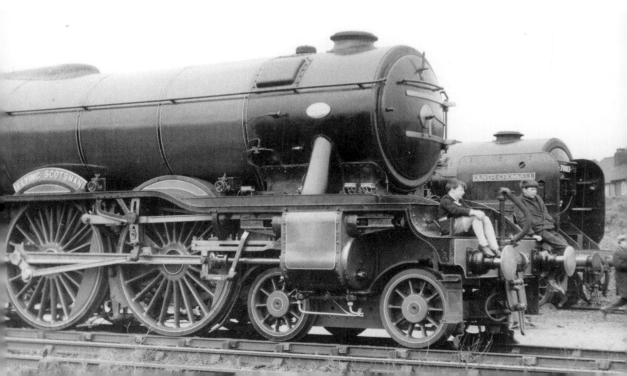

Gresley 'A3' class 4-6-2 No 60052 PRINCE PALATINE seen in action at Hawick, this time with a fitted fast freight train diagrammed to travel over the long lamented Waverley route on 28 August 1965. *Rail Photoprints Collection*

Batch of ten locomotives, LNER Order No 302

Numbers	Name	Built	Completed Re-built	Modifications	Withdrawn
LNER 2553 and 54, BR 60054	PRINCE OF WALES pre 1926 MANNA	Doncaster	12/1924 R 07/1943	D 08/1958 G 05/1962	06/1964
LNER 2554 and 55, BR 60055	WOOLWINDER	Doncaster	12/1924 R 06/1942	D 06/1958	09/1961
LNER 2555 and 56, BR 60056	CENTENARY	Doncaster	02/1925 R 08/1944	D 07/1959 G 08/1961	05/1963
LNER 2556 and 57, BR 60057	ORMONDE	Doncaster	02/1925 R 01/1947	D 10/1958 G 09/1961	10/1963
LNER 2557 and 58, BR 60058	BLAIR ATHOL	Doncaster	02/1925 R 12/1948	D 10/1958	06/1963
LNER 2558 and 59, BR 60059	TRACERY	Doncaster	03/1925 R 12/1945	D 07/1958 G 09/1961	12/1962
LNER 2559 and 60, BR 60060	THE TETRARCH	Doncaster	03/1925 R 01/1942	D 03/1959	09/1963
LNER 2560 and 61, BR 60061	PRETTY POLLY	Doncaster	04/1925 R 05/1944	D 10/1958 G 02/1962	09/1963
LNER 2561 and 62, BR 60062	MINORU	Doncaster	05/1025 R 06/1944	D 02/1959 G 07/1961	12/1964
LNER 2562 and 63, BR 60063	ISINGLASS	Doncaster	06/1925 R 04/1946	D 02/1959 G 08/1961	06/1964

D – Double Chimney, G – German style smoke deflectors, R – Rebuilt
Disposal: 60054–60062/63 Kings, Norwich, 60055/56–60058/59, 60061 Doncaster Works, 60057 Arnott Young, Carmyle, 60060 Darlington Works

Gresley 'A3' class 4-6-2 wearing its pre-nationalisation colours and 1946 allocated LNER No 56 CENTENARY (BR 60056) starts away from Doncaster to the delight of the two enthusiasts, one of whom realises that they are in the photographer's viewfinder. Note the ex-GNR-style tender with coal rails, in this circa 1948 image. *Rail Photoprints Collection*

Gresley 'A3' class Pacific No 60061 PRETTY POLLY gets a 'polish up' at Kings Cross depot (34A) on 23 March 1961. It can clearly be seen that the loco is fitted with the larger-size LNER-style 'Wing' smoke deflectors on each side of the double chimney. Note the electric lamps and full plate smoke deflectors on the Peppercorn 'A1' No 60122 CURLEW, behind the Gresley loco. *Rail Photoprints Collection*

Having received its German-style smoke deflectors Gresley 'A3' class 4-6-2 No 60063 ISINGLASS is pictured fresh from overhaul at Doncaster works in this August 1961 image. *Mike Morant Collection*

Batch of twenty locomotives, LNER Order No L787

Numbers	Name	Built	Completed Re-built	Modifications	Withdrawn
LNER 2563 and 64, BR 60064	TAGALIE, pre 1941 WILLIAM WHITELAW	NBL	08/1924 R 11/1942	D 08/1959	09/1961
LNER 2564 and 65, BR 60065	KNIGHT OF THISTLE*	NBL	07/1924 R 03/1947	D 10/1958 G 11/1961	06/1964
LNER 2565 and 66, BR 60066	MERRY HAMPTON	NBL	07/1924 R 12/1945	D 10/1958 G 10/1961	09/1963
LNER 2566 and 67, BR 60067	LADAS	NBL	08/1924 R 11/1939	D 04/1959 G 04/1961	12/1962
LNER 2567 and 68, BR 60068*	SIR VISTO	NBL	08/1924 R 12/1948*	D 04/1959	08/1962
LNER 2568 and 69, BR 60069	SCEPTRE	NBL	09/1924 R 05/1942	D 08/1959	10/1962
LNER 2569 and 70, BR 60070	GLADIATEUR	NBL	09/1924 R 01/1947	D 04/1959 G 09/1961	05/1964
LNER 2570 and 71, BR 60071	TRANQUIL	NBL	09/1924 R 10/1944	D 06/1958 G 11/1961	10/1964
LNER 2571 and 72, BR 60072	SUNSTAR	NBL	09/1924 R 07/1941	D 07/1959	10/1962
LNER 2572 and 73, BR 60073	ST. GATIEN	NBL	10/1924 R 11/1945	D 07/1958 G 07/1961	08/1963
LNER 2573 and 74, BR 60074	HARVESTER	NBL	10/1924 R 04/1928	D 03/1959	04/1963
LNER 2574 and 75, BR 60075	ST FRUSQUIN	NBL	10/1924 R 06/1942	D 09/1959 G 04/1962	01/1964
LNER 2575 and 76, BR 60076	GALOPIN	NBL	10/1924 R 06/1941	D 06/1959	10/1962
LNER 2576 and 77, BR 60077	THE WHITE KNIGHT	NBL	10/1924 R 07/1943	D 04/1959 G 07/1961	07/1964
LNER 2577 and 78, BR 60078	NIGHT HAWK	NBL	10/1924 R 01/1944	D 02/1959 G 03/1962	10/1962
LNER 2578 and 79, BR 60079	BAYARDO	NBL	10/1924 R 05/1928	D 04/1960	09/1961
LNER 2579 and 80, BR 60080	DICK TURPIN	NBL	11/1924 R 11/1942	D 10/1959 G 11/1961	10/1964
LNER 2580 and 81, BR 60081	SHOTOVER	NBL	11/1924 R 11/1942	D 10/1958 G 08/1961	10/1962
LNER 2581 and 82, BR 60082	NEIL GOW	NBL	11/1924 R 01/1943	D 08/1959 G 08/1961	09/1963
LNER 2582 and 83, BR 60083	SIR HUGO	NBL	12/1924 R 12/1941	D 08/1959 G 02/1962	05/1964

* The only 'A10' class loco to come into BR stock. Loco No 60065 originally carried the its name as KNIGHT OF THE THISTLE
NBL – North British Locomotive Co Ltd, D – Double Chimney, G – German-style smoke deflectors, R – Rebuilt
Disposal: 60064–60066/67/68/69–60072–60074–60076–60078/79, 60081 Doncaster Works, 60065 Kings, Norwich, 60070/71–60080 Drapers, Hull, 60073–60075–60082 Darlington Works, 60077 Arnott Young, Carmyle, 60083 Hughes Bolckows, North Blyth

Gresley 'A3' Pacific No 60073 ST GATIEN is pictured passing Princes Street Gardens whilst heading from Haymarket shed to Edinburgh Waverley station in order to work a southbound express. The loco has a double chimney and German style smoke deflectors in this early 1960s image. *David Anderson*

Gresley 'A3' Pacific No 60071 TRANQUIL looks exactly that, standing as she does in the early evening light at Darlington shed yard (51A) in this September 1954 image. Note that the loco is still coupled to an ex-NER-style tender with coal rails. *Colour Rail*

Gresley 'A3' Pacific No 60072 SUNSTAR pictured in ex-works condition at York in BR blue livery and with an LNER tender in September 1949. *Ernest Sanderson/Ron White Collection*

Apple-green liveried Gresley 'A3' Pacific No 60073 ST GATIEN pictured with BRITISH RAILWAYS in full on the tender at stands at York station in this delightfully period image. *Mike Morant Collection*

Gresley 'A3' Pacific No 60075 ST FRUSQUIN is pictured passing Doncaster at speed with an up express circa 1953. *Mike Stokes Archive*

Gresley 'A3' Pacific No 60083 SIR HUGO leads 'A4' Pacific No 60011 EMPIRE OF INDIA off shed at Haymarket. Note that the Gresley pair have full tenders of quality Lanarkshire coal as they head down to Waverley station, in order to work separate southbound services, in this splendidly evocative 1956 image. *David Anderson*

This stunning image of North British Locomotive Co Ltd-built 'A3' class 4-6-2 No 60080 DICK TURPIN shows clearly the then important, and always busy, Haymarket depot (64B) to the rear of the light engine which was working its way down to Waverley station. *David Anderson*

Gresley 'A3' Pacific No 60081 SHOTOVER in a very grimy condition pictured hard at work on the ECML in 1954. *M.J. Reade/Colour Rail*

'Apple green' Gresley 'A3' class Pacific pictured carrying LNER No 2582 in August 1946, which it only did for a total of two months before becoming No 83 and then under BR No 60083. *C.C.B. Herbert/Ron White Collection*

Batch of five locomotives from LNER Order No 317 (for eight locomotives in total)

Numbers	Name	Built	Completed	Modifications	Withdrawn
LNER 2595 and 84, BR 60084	TRIGO	Doncaster	02/1930	D 06/1959 G 01/1962	11/1964
LNER 2596 and 85, BR 60085	MANNA	Doncaster	02/1930	D 11/1959 G 04/1962	10/1964
LNER 2597 and 86, BR 60086	GAINSBOROUGH	Doncaster	04/1930	D 06/1959	11/1963
LNER 2598 and 87, BR 60087	BLENHEIM	Doncaster	04/1930	D 07/1958 G 02/1962	10/1963
LNER 2599 and 88, BR 60088	BOOK LAW	Doncaster	07/1930	D 07/1959 G 06/1961	10/1963

D – Double Chimney, G – German style smoke deflectors
Disposal: 60084 Hughes Bolckows, North Blyth, 60085 Drapers, Hull, 60086–60088 Darlington Works, 60087 Arnott Young, Carmyle

Gresley 'A3' Pacific No 60085 MANNA was in ex-works condition when photographed outside Doncaster Works in April 1962. The loco was waiting to return to its home depot of Heaton (52B) after having been 'shopped' for the fitting of German-style smoke deflectors and evidently a repaint in BR green. *Rail Photoprints Collection*

Gresley 'A3' Pacific No 60089 FELSTEAD (with an ex-NER tender) was being admired by two gentlemen whilst halted by adverse signals at the north end of Inverkeithing station; the loco was awaiting a clear road with the 2.30pm Edinburgh Waverley–Dundee–Aberdeen express, in July 1955. *David Anderson*

The setting for this fascinating Scottish steam era image is the outskirts of Craiglockhart on the Edinburgh Suburban Line and the spur to the west (in the foreground) was newly laid and not at that time in use. The date was July 1955 and the Gresley 'A3' Pacific No 60090 GRAND PARADE is in charge of an Empty Coaching Stock (ECS) working. *David Anderson*

Batch of ten locomotives, LNER Order No 314

Numbers	Name	Built	Completed	Modifications	Withdrawn
LNER 2743 and 89, BR 60089	FELSTEAD	Doncaster	08/1928	D 10/1959 G 11/1961	10/1963
LNER 2744 and 90, BR 60090	GRAND PARADE	Doncaster	08/1928	D 08/1959 G 01/1963	10/1963
LNER 2745 and 91, BR 60091	CAPTAIN CUTTLE	Doncaster	09/1928	D 03/1959 G 10/1961	10/1964
LNER 2746 and 92, BR 60092	FAIRWAY	Doncaster	10/1928	D 10/1959 G 10/1961	10/1964
LNER 2747 and 93, BR 60093	CORONACH	Doncaster	11/1928	D 12/1958	05/1962
LNER 2748 and 94, BR 60094	COLORADO	Doncaster	12/1928	D 08/1959 G 08/1961	02/1964
LNER 2749 and 95, BR 60095	FLAMINGO	Doncaster	01/1929	D 02/1959	04/1961
LNER 2750 and 96, BR 60096	PAPYRUS	Doncaster	02/1929	D 07/1958 G 09/1961	09/1963
LNER 2751 and 97, BR 60097*	HUMORIST	Doncaster	03/1929	D 08/1957	08/1963
LNER 2752 and 98, BR 60098	SPION KOP	Doncaster	04/1929	D 07/1959	10/1963

* Carried a different pattern of smoke deflectors and was the first to be fitted with a double chimney
D – Double Chimney, G – German-style smoke deflectors
Disposal: 60089–60098 Inverurie Works, 60090 Cowlairs Works, 60091/92 Drapers, Hull, 60093–60095–60097 Doncaster Works, 60094 Hendersons, Airdrie, 60096 Arnott Young, Carmyle

Gresley 'A3' Pacific No 60095 FLAMINGO pictured at Haymarket depot in this summer 1955 image; the loco had been fitted with a double chimney in the February of that year. *David Anderson*

Gresley 'A3' Pacific No 60098 SPION KOP pictured leaving Dalmeny station with an Aberdeen–Dundee–Edinburgh Waverley express in this 1955 image. *David Anderson*

Batch of three locomotives, LNER Order No 317 (for eight locomotives)

Numbers	Name	Built	Completed	Modifications	Withdrawn
LNER 2795 and 99, BR 60099	CALL BOY	Doncaster	04/1930	D 07/1958 G 07/1961	10/1963
LNER 2796 and 199, BR 60100	SPEARMINT	Doncaster	05/1930	D 09/1958 G 08/1961	06/1965
LNER 2797 and 101, BR 60101	CICERO	Doncaster	06/1930	D 02/1959	04/1963
D – Double Chimney, G – German-style smoke deflectors					
Disposal: 60099–60101 Arnott Young, Carmyle, 60100 Darlington Works					

Gresley 'A3' Pacific No 60099 CALL BOY heading an Aberdeen–Dundee Tay Bridge–Edinburgh service. The train is waiting in order to give the passengers from a Glasgow Queen Street-bound express the opportunity to change trains. *David Anderson*

Gresley 'A3' Pacific No 60100 SPEARMINT pictured on the shed road at Doncaster (36A) in 1960. *Mike Stokes Archive*

This locomotive is one of two original Gresley prototype Pacifics GNR Order No 293 (see also Peppercorn 'A1' class)

Numbers	Name	Built	Completed Re-built	Modifications	Withdrawn
GNR 1471, LNER 4471 and 102, BR 60102	SIR FREDERICK BANBURY	Doncaster	07/1922 R 10/1942	D 04/1959	11/1961
Disposal: 60102 Doncaster Works					

Gresley 'A3' Pacific No 60102 SIR FREDERICK BANBURY in immaculate condition, pictured at Grantham shed (34F) in June 1960. *K.R. Pirt/Ron White Collection*

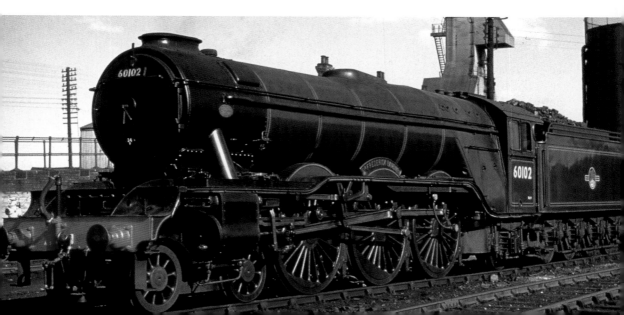

Batch of ten locomotives, LNER Order No 297

Numbers	Name	Built	Completed Re-built	Modifications	Withdrawn
LNER 4472 and 103, BR 60103	FLYING SCOTSMAN	Doncaster	02/1923 R 01/1947	D 01/1959 G 12/1961	01/1963 Preserved
LNER 4473 and 104, BR 60104	SOLARIO	Doncaster	03/1923 R 10/1941	D 04/1959	12/1959
LNER 4474 and 105, BR 60105	VICTOR WILD	Doncaster	03/1923 R 10/1942	D 03/1959 G 12/1960	06/1963
LNER 4475 and 106, BR 60106	FLYING FOX	Doncaster	04/1923 R 03/1947	D 04/1959 G 10/1961	12/1964
LNER 4476 and 107, BR 60107	ROYAL LANCER	Doncaster	05/1923 R 10/1946	D 06/1959 G 02/1962	09/1963
LNER 4477 and 108, BR 60108	GAY CRUSADER	Doncaster	06/1923 R 01/1943	D 04/1959 G 11/1961	10/1963
LNER 4478 and 109, BR 60109	HERMIT	Doncaster	06/1923 R 11/1943	D 03/1959 G 01/1961	12/1962
LNER 4479 and 110, BR 60110	ROBERT THE DEVIL	Doncaster	07/1923 R 08/1942	D 05/1959 G 06/1961	05/1963
LNER 4480* and 111, BR 60111	ENTERPRISE	Doncaster	08/1923 R 07/1927	D 06/1959 G 04/1962	12/1962
LNER 4481 and 112, BR 60112	ST SIMON	Doncaster	09/1923 R 08/1946	D 07/1958 G 10/1962	12/1964

* LNER No 4480 was effectively the first 'A3' engine
D – Double Chimney, G – German-style smoke deflectors, R – Rebuilt
Disposal: 60104/5/7/9/10/11 Doncaster Works, 60106–60112 Kings, Norwich, 60108 Darlington Works

Gresley Pacific 'A3' No 60082 NEIL GOW is pictured making its way down to Edinburgh Waverley Station from Haymarket shed (64B). *David Anderson*

The only Gresley 'A3' class Pacific to be preserved, BR No 60103 FLYING SCOTSMAN 'on shed' at London Kings Cross depot (34A), pictured in BR green livery, June 1960. *Ian Turnbull/Rail Photoprints Collection*

Gresley 'A1' class Pacific No 4474 VICTOR WILD (this loco as an 'A3' class carried BR number 60105) was pictured at London Kings Cross in 1925 during the period that the loco was performance tested against the Great Western Railway (GWR) 4-6-0 'Castle' class loco No 4079 PENDENNIS CASTLE. *Colour Rail*

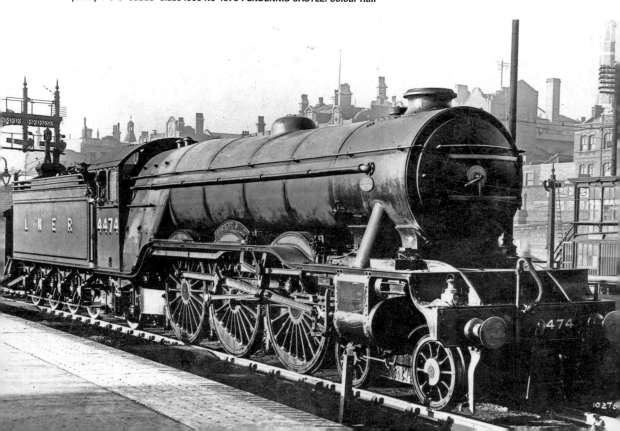

Gresley Pacific No 60105 VICTOR WILD in 'A3' condition is pictured heading an ECML express service at Crow Park on 12 May 1959. This loco was fitted with its double chimney in the preceding March and was fitted with German-style smoke deflectors in 1960. *A. Durant/Mike Morant Collection*

Gresley Pacific No 60107 ROYAL LANCER was preparing to depart from York in this March 1962 image. *Mike Stokes Archive*

Gresley Pacific No 60111 ENTERPRISE at London Marylebone station pre double chimney (1959). This loco received German-style smoke deflectors in April 1962 but was withdrawn only five months later! *Mike Stokes Archive*

BR green Gresley Pacific No 60112 ST. SIMON pictured with a double chimney and small 'Wing' smoke deflectors was photographed entering York station with an up parcels working circa 1959. *W. Smith/Colour Rail*

Chapter 15

1925–1928

Great Central Railway '9N' Class 4-6-2T (LNER/BR 'A5/2') designed by Robinson, modified by Gresley

The Robinson Great Central Railway design '9N' 4-6-2T, which became LNER/BR 'A5/2', so impressed Gresley that he decided to have a further batch built. He had recognised that the class represented a useful addition to the LNER fleet and the additional thirteen engines were designated 'A5/2' variant and built by Hawthorn Leslie & Co for the LNER and were initially intended for use in the North Eastern area, around Middlesbrough.

In comparison to the original Robinson engines the Gresley 'A5/2' designed Pacific Tanks had cut down chimneys, reduced boiler mountings and were fitted with Westinghouse and vacuum brakes.

LNER 4-6-2T No 69837, a Gresley-modified Hawthorn Leslie & Co-built A5/2 class loco is seen between duties at Doncaster St James' Park station* in September 1955 double heading with an Ivatt 2-6-0, LNER Nos 1767 and 9837. *David Anderson*

* The single island platform station was built by the LNER to serve excursion traffic, principally special trains in connection with the St Leger horse racing festival held each September; it was also used for seaside excursions.

The engines gave good service and were popular with footplate crews. The first loco withdrawn was No 69833 in April 1957, the scrapping no doubt hastened by the anticipated introduction of Diesel Multiple Units (DMUs) on the services they previously had charge of. All the remaining members of the class were withdrawn in 1958, and thus outlasted in service by many of the original Robinson 'A5' 4-6-2 class.

LNER 4-6-2T 'A5/2' class, BR numbers 69830–69842

Introduced: 1926

Power Classification: 4P (reclassified 3P in 1953)

Built: Hawthorn Leslie & Co, 13 locomotives

Designer: Nigel Gresley modified from Robinson original design

Company: London & North Eastern Railway

Driving Wheel: 5ft 7ins

Boiler Pressure: 180psi superheated

Cylinders: Inside 20ins diameter x 26ins stroke

Tractive Effort @ 85%: 23,750lbf

Valve Gear: Stephenson (piston valves)

Water Capacity: 2280 gallons

Coal Capacity: 4 tons 3cwts

Numbers	Built	Completed	Withdrawn
LNER 9830, BR 69830	Hawthorn Leslie & Co	09/1925	11/1958
LNER 9831, BR 69831	Hawthorn Leslie & Co	10/1925	11/1958
LNER 9832, BR 69832	Hawthorn Leslie & Co	10/1925	10/1958
LNER 9833, BR 69833	Hawthorn Leslie & Co	10/1925	04/1957
LNER 9834, BR 69834	Hawthorn Leslie & Co	11/1925	10/1958
LNER 9835, BR 69835	Hawthorn Leslie & Co	11/1925	11/1958
LNER 9836, BR 69836	Hawthorn Leslie & Co	12/1925	08/1958
LNER 9837, BR 69837	Hawthorn Leslie & Co	12/1925	12/1958
LNER 9838, BR 69838	Hawthorn Leslie & Co	12/1925	11/1958
LNER 9839, BR 69839	Hawthorn Leslie & Co	01/1926	09/1958
LNER 9840, BR 69840	Hawthorn Leslie & Co	01/1926	09/1958
LNER 9841, BR 69841	Hawthorn Leslie & Co	02/1926	09/1958
LNER 9842, BR 69842	Hawthorn Leslie & Co	03/1926	10/1958

All 'A5/2' class locomotives were cut up at Darlington Works

Chapter 16

1931–1936

North Eastern Railway 'D' Class 4-4-4T (LNER 'H1'/'A8' Class and BR 'A8'), designed by Raven and converted to 4-6-2T by Gresley

Raven designed North Eastern Railway (NER) 'D' class (originally built as 4-4-4T engines, the whole class was rebuilt as 4-6-2T by Gresley 1931–36) became LNER 'H1' class and subsequently BR 'A8' class. BR loco No 69861 (formerly LNER 2154 and 9861) makes a fine sight as the Pacific Tank passes Beckhole with a three coach Whitby–Malton local service in 1956; note that the leading coach is an ex-NER brake composite in teak. *J.M. Jarvis/Colour Rail*

The LNER 'A8' Pacific Tanks started life as North Eastern Railway (NER) 4-4-4T locos designated 'H1' class; they were Raven-designed engines and all were built at Darlington Works between 1913 and 1922. These two-cylinder locos worked mainly on fast passenger trains between Darlington and Newcastle, and Newcastle and the North East Coast. In traffic it was found that the 'H1s' had a tendency to roll excessively at high speed, an undesirable phenomenon created by their double bogie construction.

During the mid 1920s the London & North Eastern Railway (LNER) introduced the 'A5' class of 4-6-2T engines which, intended for similar diagrams and routes as the 'H1s', were recognised as being much more sure-footed performers. Accordingly in 1931 Gresley ordered that 'H1' No 2162 (became BR 69869) be converted to the Pacific configuration. Thereafter the converted engine was subjected to a series of trial runs throughout the North East which in turn proved that the modifications had cured the excessive rolling problems. The whole class of LNER 'H1' engines were then converted to 4-6-2T during the period 1933 to 1936.

During the rebuilds Robinson superheaters were fitted in place of the existing Schmidt type and as a result of further boiler modifications (introduced in 1935) the 'A8' boilers became interchangeable with those of the 'A6' and 'A7' Pacific Tanks. There was some variety in the types of chimneys, steam domes and smokeboxes used, and many were fitted with larger coal bunkers, some with additional hoppers.

The new class of 4-6-2Ts were ideally suited to working heavy suburban passenger services and also medium-distance passenger services on the North Eastern and Yorkshire coastal routes. Originally the allocation of the forty-five 'A8' class engines was split between the North East area, Newcastle, Whitby, Scarborough, Hull and Leeds.

The introduction of Diesel Multiple Units (DMUs) during the 1950s led to the withdrawal of the class, the first engine withdrawn being No 69876 in October 1957, and none of the class made it through to the end of 1960.

NER 4-6-2T 'A8' class, originally NER 'D' class and LNER 'H1' class built as 4-4-4T locos (1913–22). BR numbers 69850–69894

Introduced: 1913–22 as 4-4-4T

Power Classification: 4P (reclassified 3P in 1953), forty-five locomotives

Built: Darlington Works

Designer: Raven design, modified and converted to 4-6-2T by Gresley 1931–36

Company: North Eastern Railway

Driving Wheel: 5ft 9ins

Boiler Pressure: 175psi superheated

Cylinders: 3 – 16½ins diameter x 26ins stroke

Tractive Effort @ 85%: 22,890lbf

Valve Gear: Stephenson (piston valves)

Water Capacity: 2000 gallons

Coal Capacity: 4 tons

Numbers	Built	Completed as 4-6-2T	Withdrawn
LNER 2143 and 9850, BR 69850	Darlington	12/1933	06/1960
LNER 2144 and 9851, BR 69851	Darlington	03/1935	11/1958
LNER 2145 and 9852, BR 69852	Darlington	02/1936	11/1959
LNER 2146 and 9853, BR 69853	Darlington	05/1935	01/1960
LNER 2147 and 9854, BR 69854	Darlington	08/1933	05/1960
LNER 2148 and 9855, BR 69855	Darlington	03/1936	02/1960
LNER 2149 and 9856, BR 69856	Darlington	09/1934	12/1959
LNER 2150 and 9857, BR 69857	Darlington	06/1935	02/1960
LNER 2151 and 9858, BR 69858	Darlington	06/1936	05/1960
LNER 2152 and 9859, BR 69859	Darlington	03/1936	02/1960
LNER 2153 and 9860, BR 69860	Darlington	08/1934	09/1960
LNER 2154 and 9861, BR 69861	Darlington	08/1935	08/1960
LNER 2155 and 9862, BR 69862	Darlington	01/1933	09/1958
LNER 2156 and 9863, BR 69863	Darlington	09/1935	02/1959
LNER 2157 and 9864, BR 69864	Darlington	06/1936	02/1959

'A8' class 4-6-2T BR No 69854 (formerly LNER 2147 and 9854) is seen in profile at Scarborough shed (50E) in August 1955 note the turntable pit in the foreground. Note the grated hopper on top of the coal bunker. *David Anderson*

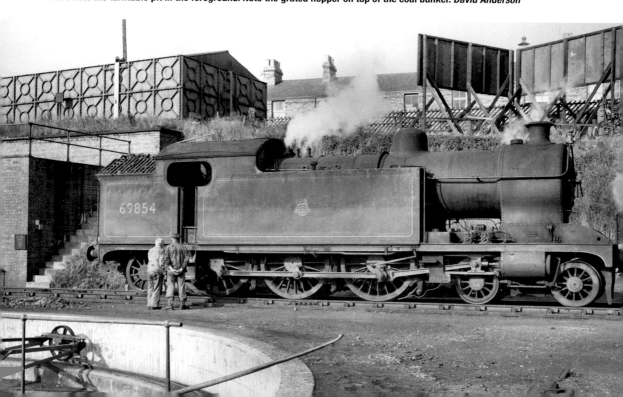

'A8' class 4-6-2T BR No 69855 (formerly LNER 2148 and 9855) pictured between services at Eaglescliffe during September 1955. *Mike Stokes Collection*

'A8' class 4-6-2T BR No 69860 (formerly LNER 2153 and 9860) pictured in the company of LNER Thompson-designed 'L1' class 2-6-4T No 67754 at Thornaby (51L) in April 1960. Note it can just be seen that the loco has a rag 'in the form of a scarf' wrapped around the base of the chimney! *Mike Stokes Collection*

Numbers	Built	Completed as 4-6-2T	Withdrawn
LNER 2158 and 9865, BR 69865	Darlington	05/1935	04/1958
LNER 2159 and 9866, BR 69866	Darlington	08/1934	12/1958
LNER 2160 and 9867, BR 69867	Darlington	07/1936	12/1959
LNER 2161 and 9868, BR 69868	Darlington	01/1936	11/1957
LNER 2162 and 9869, BR 69869	Darlington	07/1931	06/1960
LNER 1517 and 9870, BR 69870	Darlington	08/1936	06/1960
LNER 1518 and 9871, BR 69871	Darlington	05/1933	11/1958
LNER 1519 and 9872, BR 69872	Darlington	09/1934	10/1958
LNER 1520 and 9873, BR 69873	Darlington	04/1935	02/1960
LNER 1523 and 9874, BR 69874	Darlington	04/1935	08/1959
LNER 1528 and 9875, BR 69875	Darlington	01/1933	05/1960
LNER 1529 and 9876, BR 69876	Darlington	05/1934	10/1957
LNER 1531 and 9877, BR 69877	Darlington	02/1934	12/1959
LNER 1499 and 9878, BR 69878	Darlington	06/1936	06/1960
LNER 1500 and 9879, BR 69879	Darlington	01/1934	02/1959

'A8' class 4-6-2T BR No 69865 (formerly LNER 2158 and 9865) pictured between trains at Whitby in June 1957. *Hugh Ballantyne/Rail Photoprints Collection*

Scarborough (50E) allocated 'A8' class 4-6-2T BR No 69867 (formerly LNER 2160 and 9867) waits to depart from Scarborough station with a local service to Malton in August 1955. *David Anderson*

A couple of Gresley rebuild 'A8 class Pacific Tanks' are seen on shed at Saltburn (51K) in the mid 1950s. The loco in the foreground is BR No 69869, previous LNER Nos 2162 and 9869. Note that loco No 69869 was the experimental 'H1' class 4-4-4T conversion engine. *K.C.H. Fairey/Colour Rail*

'Pacific Tanks' pictured inside the Scarborough depot roundhouse during June 1959, they are A8 class 2-6-2T locos Nos 69867 (LNER 2160 and 9867) and 69877 (LNER 1531 and 9877); the locos are in the company of another unidentified member of the forty-five-strong class. *K.C.H. Fairey/Colour Rail*

Numbers	Built	Completed as 4-6-2T	Withdrawn
LNER 1501 and 9880, BR 69880	Darlington	04/1934	07/1960
LNER 1502 and 9881, BR 69881	Darlington	02/1936	07/1958
LNER 1503 and 9882, BR 69882	Darlington	08/1936	11/1958
LNER 1504 and 9883, BR 69883	Darlington	06/1934	11/1958
LNER 1525 and 9884, BR 69884	Darlington	05/1933	11/1958
LNER 1526 and 9885, BR 69885	Darlington	05/1936	06/1960
LNER 1527 and 9886, BR 69886	Darlington	01/1936	06/1960
LNER 1327 and 9887, BR 69887	Darlington	05/1934	12/1960
LNER 1329 and 9888, BR 69888	Darlington	05/1934	05/1960
LNER 1330 and 9889, BR 69889	Darlington	10/1934	05/1960
LNER 1521 and 9890, BR 69890	Darlington	05/1935	01/1958
LNER 1328 and 9891, BR 69891	Darlington	05/1934	09/1958
LNER 1326 and 9892, BR 69892	Darlington	01/1935	11/1958
LNER 1522 and 9893, BR 69893	Darlington	02/1934	11/1958
LNER 1530 and 9694, BR 69894	Darlington	03/1935	06/1960

Disposal: all 'A/8' class locomotives were cut up at Darlington Works

'A8' class 4-6-2T BR No 69881 (formerly LNER 1502 and 9881) pictured double heading with 'D49' 4-4-0 No 62731 SELKIRKSHIRE (formerly LNER 2756 and 2731). The LNER / BR Eastern Region pairing was seen in this superbly detailed image at Whitby West Cliff station in June 1957, whilst heading the RCTS 'Yorkshire Coast' railtour. *Hugh Ballantyne/Rail Photoprints Collection*

Chapter 17

1933–1952

London Midland & Scottish Railway 'Princess Royal' Class 4-6-2, designed by Stanier

Almost the very first task facing William Stanier when he joined the London Midland & Scottish Railway (LMS) in order to take up the post of Chief Mechanical Engineer (CME) was to provide the then West Coast Mainline (WCML) operators with a new design of large express locomotive, specifically for use on their Anglo-Scottish route.

It was no surprise to the railway fraternity that when Stanier in 1933 unveiled his first two Pacific locomotives (from the eventual class of thirteen) they exhibited some distinctly Great Western Railway (GWR) design features, for Stanier had learned his craft at the famous

LMS 'Princess Royal' class Pacific No 46200 THE PRINCESS ROYAL stands resplendent under the Camden coaling tower, on 3 June 1962, the occasion of the 'Aberdeen Flyer' charter. *Dave Cobbe Collection/Rail Photoprints Collection*

Swindon Works, firstly under pioneer designer G.J. Churchward and thereafter as Principal Assistant to the great standardising innovator C.B. Collett, during the last ten years of his forty-year-long GWR career. A widely held belief is that, before leaving for Crewe, Stanier packed into his work chest not only his personal belongings but also several sets of drawings including those relating to tapered boiler design, a feature of steam locomotive building hitherto untried by the LMS.

Perchance, in a not too unkindly manner, some commentators of the time partly credited the success of the newly introduced LMS 'Princess Royal' 4-6-2 engines on a Crewe adherence to Swindon locomotive building principles. Indeed it was famously banded about amongst railway folk (away from the earshot of Crewe personnel of course) that if you wanted to see the epitome of a GWR express locomotive design at work you would need to look no further than Stanier's first LMS Pacific class!

In addition to the use of a tapered boiler the initial two engines of the class also included a Stanier design of low temperature superheater. They first saw service on the famous 'Royal Scot' services between London Euston and Glasgow Central stations.

Following the success of the first two engines, and after a period of evaluating the performance statistics, Stanier made some modifications before Crewe Works commenced on building the rest of the class; notably the design of superheater was changed for a 32-element unit which dramatically improved performance.

In 1935 production of the remainder of the engines in the class commenced with the first conventional example (No 6203) being completed in July of that year and the last (No 6212) in the November following. However, a month before No 6203 was outshopped an experimental turbine-driven example No 6202 was made available to the LMS traffic department. That locomotive gained its motive power from steam turbines, and not conventional cylinders and associated valve gear.

Each locomotive was named after a Princess and the official name of the class was chosen because at the time Mary, Princess Royal, was Commander in Chief of the Royal Scots. The second member of the class was named PRINCESS ELIZABETH after the princess who of course went on to become HRH Queen Elizabeth II of England, Northern Ireland and Wales,

Preserved ex-LMS 'Princess Royal' class Pacific No 6201, in LMS guise, has become a firm favourite with mainline charter passengers. Loco No 6201 is seen here with a 'Thames-Clyde Express' recreation on the famous Settle & Carlisle route. The original 'Thames Clyde Express', introduced September 1927 and last ran 3 May 1975 (with an enforced break during the war years), ran between London St Pancras and Glasgow St Enoch and thereafter Glasgow Central after the closure of St Enoch station. *Fred Kerr*

and accordingly Queen Elizabeth I of Scotland. Because of the class's royal association (Princess Elizabeth was crowned Queen 2 June 1953) railwaymen almost always referred to the class as 'Lizzies'.

Loco No 6201 (BR 46201) PRINCESS ELIZABETH set up two record runs between London and Glasgow. Firstly on 16 November 1936 the loco hauled a test train between London Euston and Glasgow Central at an average speed of 68.2mph, and on the following day the loco made the return non-stop run at a remarkable average speed of 70mph with a journey time of only 5 hours and 53 minutes for the 401½ mile journey. Those charged with timing special train '703' recorded several instances of speeds over 90mph and that a top speed of 95.75mph was attained and held for more than a mile.

Famously the third 'Princess Royal' class Pacific became known as 'The Turbomotive' and as such it was a radically different design than its sister locomotives. The boiler and wheels of No 6202 were identical to all the other 'Princess Royal' class 4-6-2 engines but the two round-topped elongated fabrications carried on top of the running plates, also the lack of outside motion and cylinders and the addition of a double chimney, set it well and truly aside from the rest. They covered the steam turbines, two in total with the one located on the nearside (and being by far the larger unit) housing the forward drive turbine (with eighteen rows of blades) whilst the smaller unit on the locomotive's off side housed the reversing turbine (with four rows of blades). Loco No 6202 was also fitted with smoke deflectors during the later period of its time in service 'The Turbomotive' was the only successful steam turbine powered railway engine to be built in Britain, and thereafter used extensively in traffic.

Perhaps like all prototypes this loco suffered from a great many instances of downtime, spending long periods in the works whilst the engineers further refined the system. But when it did work it worked extremely well, and its performance was by all accounts at least equal to those others of the class.

In service 'The Turbomotive' covered over 458,000 miles before being 'retired' in 1949 (pending rebuilding to a conventional specification). The locomotive's perhaps premature withdrawal from traffic was hastened by the need to replace the forward turbine which had failed, and BR finances at the time coupled with the fact that Stanier was no longer in charge of the new nationalised railway system led to No 6202 being temporarily laid up in Crewe Works.

For all railway enthusiasts there were specific defining line-side moments, especially during the steam era when not all motive power looked boringly familiar. Naively hoping, against all hope, that the Crewe bosses would allow a repaired 'Turbomotive' a last fling on the WCML, this train-mad schoolboy kept up a summer-holiday-long vigil at a favourite spot just north of Hartford station. Of course it never happened, but during the occasions of my ever hopeful 'Turbomotive' watch I did see my first mainline diesel; it was no real substitute and I can even today recall the, then, almost alien smell as it thundered past heading north!

Back to the matter of No 6202, as British Railways became established in the early 1950s the management embarked upon a long overdue (because of wartime conditions) review of its motive power and, in addition to considering additions to the nation's diesel and electric traction fleets, they embarked upon a steam locomotive building programme. So whilst Crewe Works was tooling up for the construction of BR Standard locomotives the powers that be also decided to rebuild 'The Turbomotive' as a conventional engine.

BR loco No 46202 was actually rebuilt with some of the design features which had been incorporated in Stanier's next Pacific type, the 'Princess Coronation/Duchess' class. Retaining its 6-foot-6-inch-diameter driving wheels No 46202 was built with new frames which accommodated the same axle spacing and cylinders as the class's successors. The new loco, later named PRINCESS ANNE, had a tractive effort (@ 85%) of 41,538flb making it

LMS 4-6-2 'Princess Royal' class, BR numbers 46200–46212

Introduced: 1933–35

Power Classification: 7P (reclassified 8P in 1951)

Built: Crewe Works

Designer: William Stanier

Company: London Midland & Scottish Railway

Driving Wheel: 6ft 6ins

Boiler Pressure: 250psi superheated

Cylinders: 4 – 16¼ins diameter x 28ins stroke

(LMS 6202) Turbine rebuilt 4 – 16½ins x 28ins stroke

Tractive Effort @ 85%: 40,285lbf – Turbine loco 41538lbf

Water Capacity: 4000 gallons

Coal Capacity: 10 tons

theoretically the most powerful steam locomotive on British Railways. The engine returned to service on 28 August 1952, and on that day was observed working the 8.30am Euston–Liverpool express resplendent in BR express locomotive green livery.

However, the newly built 4-6-2 PRINCESS ANNE was to be the holder of BRs 'most powerful' claim for only a few short weeks, as on 8 October 1952 the engine was seriously damaged (and later judged to be beyond economical repair) in the horrific Harrow & Wealdstone railway disaster. The scrapping of No 46202 indirectly led to the creation of another Pacific type, more of that later.

Leaving aside the forced retirement of No 46202 the initial members of the class to be withdrawn from traffic were Nos 46201 and 46203 (the first preserved examples), both withdrawn October 1962. At the end of 1961 six members of the class were still in service but none of them made it beyond the end of 1962.

The 'Princess Royal' class carried many changes of colour and varying livery styles over their long service lives including LMS maroon, wartime black, BR blue, green, red and black whilst incorporating varied styles of lettering.

Locos 6200/1LMS Crewe Works Lot, No 99

Numbers	Names	Built	Completed	Withdrawn
LMS 6200, BR 46200	THE PRINCESS ROYAL	Crewe	07/1933	11/1962
LMS 6201, BR 46201	PRINCESS ELIZABETH	Crewe	11/1933	10/1962 Preserved

LMS 'Princess Royal' class Pacific no 46200, ready for the 'off' at Crewe with the 'Aberdeen Flyer' railtour which took place on 2 and 3 June 1962. This loco was one of four engines of the class turned out in BR red livery in 1958. The mainline sections of this comprehensive tour ran London Kings Cross via York and Newcastle to Edinburgh Waverley with 'A4' loco 60022 MALLARD, Edinburgh Waverley via Dundee Tay Bridge to Aberdeen with loco 'A4' No 60004 WILLIAM WHITELAW and returned south, hauled Aberdeen to Carlisle by 'Princess Royal' No 46201 PRINCESS ELIZABETH and Carlisle–Crewe–London Euston by 'Princess Royal' No 46200 THE PRINCESS ROYAL. *David Anderson*

The author would like to acknowledge and thank the website 'Six Bells' Junction (http://www.sixbellsjunction.co.uk) for all the railtour information used in this publication.

Ex LMS 'Princess Royal' class loco No 46200 THE PRINCESS ROYAL prepares to depart from Crewe with the return leg of the 'Aberdeen Flyer' railtour. Note the inspector in a traditional 'Blocker' (bowler hat). *David Anderson*

In this image No 46200 THE PRINCESS ROYAL is pictured reversing the ECS stock out of Euston Station; note that the man with the 'Blocker' is still on the footplate! This train was, unfortunately due to delays en-route, approx. three hours late arriving at London Euston. *David Anderson*

Stanier 'Princess Royal' class Pacific No 46200 THE PRINCESS ROYAL was relegated to freight duties during the last few months of her working life, and is depicted here near Forteviot, which lies between Gleneagles and Perth, on 11 June 1962, just five months before withdrawal from active service. *Mike Morant Collection*

Stanier 'Princess Royal' class Pacific No 46201 PRINCESS ELIZABETH pictured working hard to climb Beattock Bank with a Birmingham New Street–Glasgow Central express in the summer of 1958. *David Anderson*

Stanier 'Princess Royal' class Pacific No 46201 PRINCESS ELIZABETH seen near Greskine whilst descending Beattock Bank with the up 'Mid-Day Scot' on 18 July 1959. *David Anderson*

Pacific No 46201 PRINCESS ELIZABETH getting to grips with the ascent of Beattock Bank with a Birmingham New Street–Glasgow Central express in August 1955; note the SIPHON bogie van directly behind the engine. *David Anderson*

In this July 1958 image Stanier Pacific No 46201 PRINCESS ELIZABETH is seen leaving Carstairs Junction after a halt to detach the Edinburgh coaches from a Birmingham New Street–Glasgow Central service. *David Anderson*

Experimental turbine-driven locomotive commonly referred to as 'The Turbomotive'

Loco No 6202, Lot No 100

Numbers	Name	Built	Completed	Withdrawn
LMS 6202, BR 46202	Not carried until 08/1952	Crewe	06/1935	1949

** Converted to a conventional locomotive and put back into traffic 08/1952

The experimental non-condensing steam turbine-driven locomotive No 6202 entered service in June 1935. The loco is pictured with a domed boiler as fitted in 1936, but without smoke deflectors which were a 1939 addition. *Author's Collection*

Commonly referred to as 'The Turbomotive' the LMS turbine powered Pacific locomotive No 46202 is pictured near to Halton Junction with an up Liverpool–Euston service, circa 1949. In this image the smaller reversing turbine located on the 'off side' of the boiler can be clearly seen. This loco was the only member of the class to be fitted with smoke deflectors for a period of its time in traffic. *R.A. Whitfield/Rail Photoprints Collection*

LMS turbine-powered Pacific locomotive No 46202 is seen at speed with the 8.30 Euston–Liverpool near Sutton Weaver on the WCML; in this image the main forward drive turbine is visible, circa 1949. *R.A. Whitfield/Rail Photoprints Collection*

Rebuilt as a conventional 'Princess Royal' class locomotive in 1952 No 46202 PRINCESS ANNE was fitted with slightly larger cylinders than the other members of the class which were set further forward. The engine also sported a raised section of running plate over the leading and second set of driving wheels, a new design of motion bracket and a large cover over the cylinder steam pipes. This engine never really had the opportunity to show if the modification improved performance as No 46202 was damaged and deemed as being 'beyond economical repair' in the tragic Harrow & Wealdstone railway disaster which occurred on 8 October 1952, only a matter of months after the loco had returned to traffic. The image shows the newly built Pacific lying over at Shrewsbury shed (then 84G) following an August 1952 'running in' turn from Crewe. *Author's Collection*

Locos 6203–6206, Lot No 120

Number	Name	Built	Date	Withdrawn
LMS 6202, BR 46202	PRINCESS ANNE	Crewe	08/1952*	06/1954
LMS 6203, BR 46203	PRINCESS MARGARET ROSE	Crewe	07/1935	10/1962 Preserved
LMS 6204, BR 46204	PRINCESS LOUISE	Crewe	07/1935	11/1961
LMS 6205, BR 46205	PRINCESS VICTORIA	Crewe	07/1935	11/1961
LMS 6206, BR 46206	PRINCESS MARIE LOUISE	Crewe	08/1935	10/1962

* As a conventional locomotive

Stanier Pacific No 46203 PRINCESS MARGARET ROSE seen at Glasgow Polmadie (66A) depot; this Crewe North (5A) allocated engine was being serviced before its next southbound run. *David Anderson*

Stanier 'Princess Royal' class 4-6-2 No 46203 PRINCESS MARGARET ROSE was the first conventional locomotive of the 1935 batch of ten engines which carried a new design of 32-element superheater, also at Glasgow Polmadie depot prior to working a southbound express. *David Anderson*

Stanier 'Princess Royal' No 46203 PRINCESS MARGARET ROSE accelerates away from Carstairs Junction with a Birmingham New Street–Glasgow Central express. *David Anderson*

PRINCESS MARGARET ROSE is pictured whilst stopped at Carstairs Junction in order to allow the Edinburgh (Princess Street) portion of the 11.05 Birmingham New Street–Glasgow Central service to be shunted off the back of the train. *David Anderson*

'Princess Royal' class 4-6-2 No 46203 PRINCESS MARGARET ROSE hurries past Camden motive power depot with the Merseyside Express in July 1959. 'The Merseyside Express' was introduced in March 1928 and last ran on 16 April 1966 (with an enforced break during the war years). The popular service connected London Euston with Liverpool Lime Street and contained a portion for Southport Chapel Street. *A.E. Durant/Mike Morant Collection*

'Princess Royal' class 4-6-2 No 46204 PRINCESS LOUISE pictured when carrying the early version of BR red livery, lined black and orange. The loco is backing off Crewe Works towards the North shed (5A), 1958. *Ron White Collection*

Stanier Pacific No 46204 PRINCESS LOUISE is seen hard at work on the WCML near to Hartford with the up Merseyside Express in 1958. *R.A. Whitfield/Rail Photoprints Collection*

Stanier Pacific No 46205 PRINCESS VICTORIA is pictured with a clear road travelling southbound on the WCML near to Weaver Junction, circa 1950. Note the 'Y' frame (tripod shape) motion bracket which was added to only this member of the class in 1938. *Author's Collection*

Stanier Pacific No 46206 PRINCESS MARIE LOUISE, under the then encroaching (but as yet not energised) overhead wires, is pictured whilst waiting to take over an up express at Crewe in 1962. *Colour Rail*

Stanier Pacific No 46206 PRINCESS MARIE LOUISE passes Tebay with a southbound express in April 1953. *Rail Photoprints Collection*

Locos 6207–6212, Lot No 120

Numbers	Name	Built	Completed	Withdrawn
LMS 6207, BR 46207	PRINCESS ARTHUR OF CONNAUGHT	Crewe	08/1935	11/1961
LMS 6208, BR 46208	PRINCESS HELENA VICTORIA	Crewe	08/1935	10/1962
LMS 6209, BR 46209	PRINCESS BEATRICE	Crewe	08/1935	09/1962
LMS 6210, BR 46210	LADY PATRICIA	Crewe	09/1935	10/1961
LMS 6211, BR 46211	QUEEN MAUD	Crewe	09/1935	10/1961
LMS 6212, BR 46212	DUCHESS OF KENT	Crewe	10/1935	10/1961

* As a conventional 4-cylinder Pacific. Although damaged beyond repair at Harrow & Wealdstone on 8 October 1952, No 46202 was not officially deleted from the BR stock list until June 1954. Disposal: 46200 Connels, Coatbridge, 46202–46204/12 Crewe Works

Pure nostalgia! Well at least for those of 'an age'. Young enthusiasts at London Euston station seen admiring Stanier 'Princess Royal' Pacific No 46207 PRINCESS ARTHUR OF CONNAUGHT, which had newly arrived with the 'Merseyside Express'. It seemed back then that at least two out of every three youngsters wore Clarks sandals! I know that this author certainly did, furthermore they were bought annually from the local Co-op using the family 'Divi', now that dates me! As for the little guy on the right he can't have been any more than three years old when *David Anderson* took this wonderful image in July 1960. Were you one of the lads in this picture?

LMS 'Princess Royal' class Pacific No 6207 PRINCESS ARTHUR OF CONNAUGHT pictured leaving Carlisle with the Glasgow portion of the down 'Mid-Day Scot' on 8 July 1936. *George Barlow/Transport Treasury*

'Princess Royal' class Pacific No 46208 PRINCESS HELENA VICTORIA. Note the red (not maroon) livery lined orange and black in a panel on the cabside. The loco was in need of a clean when photographed at Camden shed (1B) in February 1959. *T.B. Owen/Colour Rail*

'Princess Royal' class Pacific No 46208 PRINCESS HELENA VICTORIA picks up water on the move, from Moore Troughs, whilst heading south with an up express in 1949. *R.A. Whitfield/Rail Photoprints Collection*

LMS 'Princess Royal' class Pacific No 6208 PRINCESS HELENA VICTORIA storms towards Shap summit circa 1948. *Mike Morant Collection*

LMS 'Princess Royal' class Pacific No 6209 PRINCESS BEATRICE also climbing towards Shap Summit circa 1948. *Mike Morant Collection*

'Princess Royal' class Pacific No 46209 PRINCESS BEATRICE on Beattock Bank with a relief Birmingham New Street–Glasgow Central express on 9 July 1960.
David Anderson

'Princess Royal' class Pacific No 46210 LADY PATRICIA pictured on shed at Polmadie depot circa 1955. Note the loco was in BR blue livery with black and white lining. *David Anderson*

'Princess Royal' class Pacific No 46210 LADY PATRICIA pictured at Elvanfoot, between Carstairs and Beattock on the WCML with the up 'Mid-Day Scot' on 16 April 1955. The following year locos No 46210 and No 46207 were transferred on loan to the BR Western Region during an express locomotive shortage caused by defective 'King' class engines. *David Anderson*

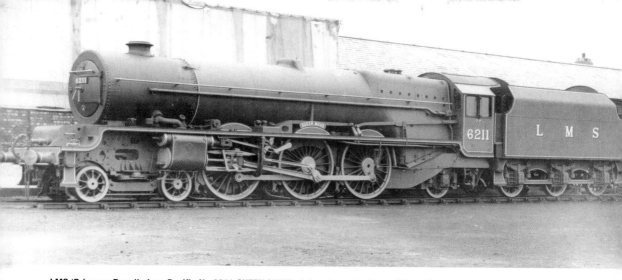

LMS 'Princess Royal' class Pacific No 6211 QUEEN MAUD pictured outside Crewe Works liveried in photographic grey for this official LMS publicity image, or is it No 6211? It is not! In truth this is an image of loco No 6203 (PRINCESS MARGARET ROSE) dressed up as No 6211 which was taken at the works on 1 January 1937, crafty people those LMS publicity boys! *Mike Bentley Collection*

This is really 'Princess Royal' No 46211 QUEEN MAUD, pictured at Crewe with a down 'Mid-Day Scot' working in the winter of 1955. *Mike Bentley Collection*

Another fine 'Princess Royal' class 4-6-2 study, this time No 46212 DUCHESS OF KENT on shed at Glasgow Polmadie (66A) in 1960. *David Anderson*

Another fine 'Princess Royal' class 4-6-2 study, this time DUCHESS OF KENT, a Crewe North (9A) engine, is seen whilst being serviced at Glasgow Polmadie shed (66A). This loco entered service in October 1935, approximately two years and six months after the first of the class, No 46200. *David Anderson*

LMS 'Princess Royal' class Pacific No 46212 DUCHESS OF KENT battles towards Beattock Summit with the morning Birmingham New Street to Glasgow Central express on an overcast day in the summer of 1960. *David Anderson*

Chapter 18

1935–1938

London & North Eastern Railway 'A4' Class 'Streamlined' 4-6-2, designed by Gresley

O f all the London & North Eastern Railways (LNER) Pacific locomotives the Gresley 'A4' class streamlined engines were undoubtedly the most well known and certainly amongst the most popular with both rail travellers and enthusiasts alike. In the early 1930s the management of the LNER were well aware of the increasing competition from road and air travel for the then lucrative Anglo Scottish and Yorkshire/North Eastern passenger business. To help compete, and indeed even increase their market share, the LNER board realised that three factors would be all important; those they identified as being speed, passenger comfort and reliability.

Of course the LNER was not just in competition with the newly emerging methods of travel; there was, as there always had been, their old rival the London Midland & Scottish Railway (LMS) to consider. Under their then newly appointed Chief Mechanical Engineer (CME) William A. Stanier they had in 1933 introduced a new class of Pacific locomotives, the 'Princess Royal' class, which was specifically designed to capture a bigger share of the Anglo Scottish passenger business. The gauntlet had been well and truly thrown down! Accordingly LNER Chief Mechanical Engineer (CME) Nigel Gresley was well aware of the task in hand.

Gresley 'A4' class Pacific No 4489 DOMINION OF CANADA (BR 60010) carried a bell in front of the chimney and that addition was presented to the London & North Eastern Railway (LNER) by the Canadian Pacific Railway in 1938. The loco is one of four engines turned out in 'Silver Jubilee' livery to match the express train service of the same name. When first introduced the 'A4' class locomotives were fitted with valances over the driving wheels (as seen below); however, in order to facilitate maintenance the valances were removed during the period of the Second World War. *Rail Photoprints Collection*

Outside these shores locomotive development had seen greatly increased speeds; in Germany the diesel-electric powered 'Fliegende Hamburger' ('Flying Hamburger') had been put into service in 1933 with a timetable that required long stretches being travelled at 85mph. In America by 1934 the US Burlington Zephyr reportedly travelled at speeds of 112.5mph during its 1015-mile scheduled run. Gresley went to Germany specifically to travel on the 'Flying Hamburger' and he was said to have been impressed by the use of streamlining, instantly realising its advantage at high speeds. Of course both the aforementioned trains were only usually formed of two or three carriage units respectively but Gresley gleaned enough information to be able to calculate that his 'A3' Pacific steam locomotive design could perhaps be modified to haul trains of a greater weight (nine coaches) at higher average speeds than they currently did.

It is often said that the Second World War hastened the development of aircraft and air travel at a rate which would never have been achieved under peacetime conditions. Perchance the fierce rivalry between the railway companies during their aggressive campaigns to attract travellers, in the period between the two world wars, similarly hastened the advance of express locomotive design in general and Pacific design in particular.

Gresley and his team carried out trials intended to prove that a modified 'A3' class locomotive design would be suitable. During those trials Gresley 'A1' class 4-6-2 FLYING SCOTSMAN broke the 100mph barrier whilst sister engine PAPYRUS went on to set a speed record of 108mph. Armed with the results of those trials Gresley went to the LNER board for approval, and was instantly given the green light to go ahead and develop what he had termed the 'Silver Jubilee' streamlined train project.

In passing it is prudent to mention the then state of the art seven-coach trains as they are very much a part of the British Pacific story. The 'Silver Jubilee' was designed as a complete streamlined concept, i.e. a fully streamlined locomotive and seven matching streamlined coaches. The train had a capacity for 198 passengers who would be carried in coaches built with valances between the bogies and flexible covers over the coach ends; each set comprised twin articulated brake thirds, triple articulated restaurant sets and twin articulated first class units. Four sets of coaches were put into service, with four matching locomotives, and all were resplendent in an eye-catching silver livery; the 'Silver Jubilee' trains covered the journey between London and Newcastle in only four hours.

The first of the new three-cylinder locomotives was No 2509 (BR No 60016) and SILVER LINK was completed at Doncaster Works in September 1935. The look of the loco took the railway world by surprise and by all accounts caused somewhat of a furore, it was by the standard of those times different, to say the very least. The Gresley 'A4' class was in steam engineering terms a development of the 'A3' class but it could not possibly have looked more dissimilar! Whilst in France Gresley had seen a wedge-shaped Bugatti design of railcar and that was said to be the inspiration for the form of the 'A4'.

The LNER design team had refined their model of the intended new body shape during wind tunnel tests at the National Physical Laboratory at Teddington Middlesex. By employing the science of aerodynamics the streamlining would, it was claimed, 'aid the efficient conversion of energy into forward motion and thus permit the achievement of higher speeds'. Importantly in the case of a steam engine the new body shape would also need to lift smoke clear of the cab.

Therein reportedly hangs a tale! During the early tests the benefits of streamlining soon became evident but the problem of lifting smoke clear of the loco for a while remained unsolved. During the tests it was noticed that a thumbprint (slight depression) had accidentally been made to the plasticine model just behind the chimney. Purely, it is said on impulse, the engineers decided to run another test with the thumbprint still in place; as they did the simulated wind tunnel smoke lifted clear of the loco!

Gresley 'A4' Pacific No 4468 MALLARD, a preserved locomotive in the National Collection, took the world steam locomotive speed record on 7 July 1938. The stunning streamlined form (including valences over the driving wheels) can be fully appreciated in this picture taken at the National Railway Museum, York. *Fred Kerr*

Whilst the design of course carries the Gresley name it must be said that in practice the choice of streamlining for new engine design was firmly championed by Sir Ralph Wedgwood, the company chairman at that time. He was supported in that regard by the input of Gresley's assistant, one Oliver Bulleid, an engineer who would later play his own part in the Pacific story.

A great many highly qualified engineers have since argued the benefits to performance or otherwise of streamlined 'A4' locomotives but notwithstanding that the effect of the design on the media was outstanding from the moment they first saw SILVER LINK they were hooked. In the 'A4' the LNER had delivered a sure-fire publicity winner.

There were also of course tangible results to savour. During a demonstration run from Kings Cross to Grantham on 27 September 1935 a speed of 112.5mph was achieved twice, thus taking the record away from 'A3' class loco PAPYRUS. The first service run of the 'Silver Jubilee' took place on 1 October 1935 with loco No 2509 in charge of the seven-coach train.

Apart from the obvious streamlining, some of the other main differences between the 'A3' and new 'A4' design were streamlined steam passages, increased boiler pressure (225psi to 250psi) and also the cylinders of the 'A4' were cast slightly smaller at 18½ inches in diameter so that the valves could be increased to 9 inches in diameter. As with the 'A3' design Walschaerts valve gear was used on the outside cylinders, and Gresley's own design of conjugated gear used for the inside cylinder.

The success of the first four engines heralded the building of other batches between 1936 and 1939, as the design had proved itself more than capable of hauling the fastest trains over the ECML routes of the LNER. As confirmation of reliability it was said that the good folk of York would set their clocks against the characteristic chime whistle of the 'Silver Jubilee' as it passed the station!

As first built the 'A4' class engines were fitted with valences over the driving wheels, but during the war years they were adjudged to hinder maintenance and were removed. Four of the class were built with Kylchap blast pipes and double chimneys (60005, 60022, 60033 and 60034), which considerably improved their running characteristics at high speeds; all of the others were built with single chimneys. Some of the class were attached to corridor tenders in order to allow a change of locomotive crew during long non-stop runs.

British Railways (BR) rebuilt the whole of the class as double-chimney engines and also carried out modifications to the middle big ends in order to overcome what had been a persistent problem of 'over running'. Locos No 60003, 60014 and 60031 were originally built with reduced 17-inch diameter cylinders and those engines were later converted to normal cylinder size by BR.

The 'A4' Pacifics became regarded as Gresley's masterpiece and they surely proved that when No 4468 (BR 60022) broke the World speed record for steam locomotives. On 7 July

LNER 4-6-2 'A4' class, BR numbers 60001–60034

Introduced: 1935/38

Power Classification: 7P (reclassified 8P in 1951), 34 locomotives

Built: Doncaster Works

Designer: Nigel Gresley

Company: London & North Eastern Railway

Driving Wheel: 6ft 8ins

Boiler Pressure: 250psi superheated

Cylinders: 3 – 18½ins diameter x 26ins stroke*

Tractive Effort @ 85%: 35,455lbf

Valve Gear: Outside Walschaerts with inside Gresley derived motion (piston valves)

Water Capacity: 5000 gallons

Coal Capacity: 8 tons

* Loco Nos 60003, 60012, 60014, 60020 and 60031 had their inside cylinder dimensions reduced to 17ins diameter x 26ins stroke this reduced the tractive effort figure to 33616lbf. No's 60003, 60014 and 60031 were later reconverted by BR.

1938 a speed of 126mph was famously reached on Stoke Bank, and that occasion has been well documented. Nigel Gresley was never entirely happy with the 126mph timing and expressed an opinion that it was 'misleading'; in the event the LNER claimed a peak average of 125mph and that was enough to beat the then German-held record speed of 124.5mph. However the commemorative plaque fixed upon the locomotive shows the record speed as 126mph.

With the exception of No 4469, which was destroyed in a the Second World War air raid all 34 Gresley 'A4' class engines came into BR stock in 1948. Scrapping started in 1962 when six engines were withdrawn in the October of that year. By the end of 1964 only twelve 'A4' Pacifics remained in service and that total was halved by the end of 1965; none of the class made it beyond the end of 1966, the now preserved engines No 60019 BITTERN being one of the last to be retired by BR.

Numbers	Names	Built	Completed	Withdrawn
LNER 4469	GADWALL SIR RALPH WEDGWOOD (03/1939)	Doncaster Lot No 1871	03/1935	06/1942

Loco renamed; No 4469 was extensively damaged by German bombs whilst at York shed on 29 April 1942, and was subsequently cut up at Doncaster Works. The name was reassigned to loco No 4466 (BR 60006) in January 1944.

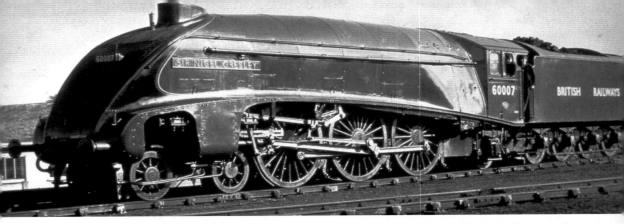

Gresley 'A4' class Pacific No 60007 SIR NIGEL GRESLEY was looking resplendent in freshly applied garter blue livery with red wheels and lettered BRITISH RAILWAYS on the tender when pictured outside Rugby Testing Station on the occasion of that facilities opening in October 1948. *J.M. Jarvis/Colour Rail*

Of all the LNER locomotives the 'A4' class carried the most livery combinations of colour and style. The colours included silver and grey, garter blue, wartime NE black, white lined express blue and BR purple, but, however, the last livery of the class was BR green with orange and black lining, which was applied from 1951 onwards.

Numbers	Names	Built	Completed	Double Chimney	Withdrawn
LNER 4500 and 1, BR 60001	SIR RONALD MATTHEWS	Doncaster 1873	04/1938	04/1958	10/1964
LNER 4499 and 2, BR 60002	POCHARD pre 04/1939 SIR MURROUGH WILSON	Doncaster 1872	04/1938	07/1957	05/1964
LNER 4494 and 3, BR 60003	OSPREY pre 10/1942 ANDREW K. MCCOSH	Doncaster 1859	08/1937	07/1957	12/1962
LNER 4462 and 4, BR 60004	GREAT SNIPE pre 07/1941 WILLIAM WHITELAW	Doncaster 1864	11/1937	01/1958	07/1966
LNER 4901 and 5, BR 60005	CAPERCAILLIE pre 09/1942 SIR CHARLES NEWTON	Doncaster 1875	06/1938	06/1938*	03/1964
LNER 4466 and 6, BR 60006	HERRING GULL pre 01/1944 SIR RALPH WEDGWOOD	Doncaster 1868	01/1938	09/1957	09/1965
LNER 4498 and 7, BR 60007	SIR NIGEL GRESLEY	Doncaster 1863	11/1937	01/1958	02/1966 Preserved
LNER 4496 and 8, BR 60008	GOLDEN SHUTTLE pre 09/1945 DWIGHT D. EISENHOWER	Doncaster 1861	09/1937	08/1958	07/1963 Preserved
LNER 4488 and 9, BR 60009	OSPREY pre 06/1937 UNION OF SOUTH AFRICA	Doncaster 1853	06/1937	11/1958	06/1966 Preserved
LNER 4489 and 10, BR 60010	DOMINION OF CANADA	Doncaster 1854	05/1937	01/1958	05/1965 Preserved

* Built with Kylchap blastpipe and double chimney, also name changed from Charles H. Newton to correspond with his knighthood
Disposal: 60001 Hughes Bolckows, North Blyth, 60002 Cohens Cargo Fleet, 60003 Doncaster Works, 60004–60006 Motherwell Machinery & Scrap, Wishaw, 60005 Campbells, Airdrie

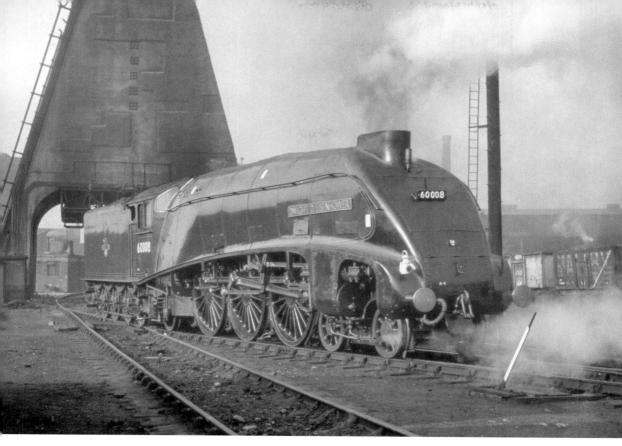

Gresley 'A4' class Pacific 60008 DWIGHT D. EISENHOWER seen outside the coaling plant at Kings Cross shed (34A) in October 1961. *J.P. Mullett/Colour Rail*

Gresley 'A4' class Pacific 60008 DWIGHT D. EISENHOWER was pictured whilst departing from Grantham in 1955. *Mike Stokes Archive*

Gresley 'A4' class Pacific 60009 UNION OF SOUTH AFRICA is one of several 'A4' class engines which have carried other names during their working lives. Then Scottish based 'No 9' is pictured storming past Edinburgh Haymarket with a northbound excursion. *David Anderson*

Gresley 'A4' class Pacific 60010 1949 DOMINION OF CANADA, pictured whilst on the turntable at Grantham circa 1949. *Rail Photoprints Collection*

Gresley 'A4' class Pacific 60011 EMPIRE OF INDIA pictured heading down to Edinburgh Waverley station from Haymarket shed (64B) in order to haul a southbound express. Note that the loco has the headboard reversed, an LNER tradition. The headboard will be turned the correct way only after the engine is attached to its train. *David Anderson*

Numbers	Names	Built	Completed	Double Chimney	Withdrawn
LNER 4490 and 11, BR 60011	EMPIRE OF INDIA	Doncaster 1855	06/1937	01/1958	05/1964
LNER 4491 and 12, BR 60012	COMMONWEALTH OF AUSTRALIA	Doncaster 1856	06/1937	07/1958	08/1964
LNER 4492 and 13, BR 60013	DOMINION OF NEW ZEALAND	Doncaster 1857	06/1937	07/1958	04/1963
LNER 2509 and 14, BR 60014	SILVER LINK	Doncaster 1818	09/1935	12/1958	12/1962
LNER 2510 and 15, BR 60015	QUICKSILVER	Doncaster 1819	09/1935	08/1957	04/1963
LNER 2511 and 16, BR 60016	SILVER KING	Doncaster 1821	11/1935	08/1957	03/1965
LNER 2512 and 17, BR 60017	SILVER FOX	Doncaster 1823	12/1935	05/1957	10/1963
LNER 4463 and 18, BR 60018	SPARROW HAWK	Doncaster 1865	12/1937	01/1958	06/1963
LNER 4464 and 19, BR 60019	BITTERN	Doncaster 1866	12/1937	09/1957	09/1966 Preserved
LNER 4465 and 20, BR 60020	GUILLEMOT	Doncaster 1867	12/1937	01/1958	03/1964

Disposal: 60011–60020 Darlington Works, 60012–60016 Motherwell Machinery & Scrap, Wishaw, 60013/14/15-60017/18 Doncaster Works

Gresley 'A4' class Pacific 60014 SILVER LINK was the first of the 'A4' class engines to enter service. The loco is pictured as it arrives at Darlington with a down East Coast Main Line service; note the reversed headboard (from a previous journey) as this was presumably not a named train, August 1961. *Rail Photoprints Collection*

Gresley 'A4' class Pacific No 60015 QUICKSILVER gets smartly away from London Kings Cross with an Anglo Scottish express on 29 April 1956. *M.J. Reade/Colour Rail*

Gresley 'A4' class Pacific No 60016 SILVER KING backs down to its train at Newcastle station in 1958. Note the DMUs in the adjacent platform. *Mike Bentley Collection*

Gresley 'A4' class Pacific No 60016 SILVER KING seen as No 16; the location is uncertain but the year is certainly 1947. Note that the locomotive's valances have been removed. *Mike Bentley Collection*

Gresley 'A4' class Pacific No 60016 SILVER KING in this 30 September 1951 image is in BR livery; the loco is on shed at its then home Gateshead depot (52A). *Mike Bentley Collection*

Gateshead-allocated Gresley 'A4' No 60016 SILVER KING was looking a lot smarter than in the previous image, in the later applied BR garter blue livery; the loco awaits departure from Newcastle Central station. *Mike Morant Collection*

Gresley 'A4' Pacific No 60019 BITTERN at Manchester Piccadilly with the Williams Deacon's Bank Club special to Derby, 6 March 1966. The author (very much an LMS man at that time, and not known for his love of 'A4' Pacifics) did try to turn out for this special run, but to the great amusement of his LNER mates he failed to get there on time. His Ford Anglia gave up the ghost in Altrincham; arriving late all he saw was a wisp of smoke as the train headed away, therefore on that occasion it was a case of Doncaster 1–0 Crewe! The late Colin Whitfield did not suffer that fate, as his wonderfully atmospheric image confirms. *Rail Photoprints Collection*

'A4' class nameplate seen displayed alongside 4468 MALLARD at the then erstwhile Clapham Transport Museum. *Mike Morant Collection*

Talking of steamy dreams, how about this super image of Gresley 'A4' Pacific No 20 GUILLEMOT (became BR 60020) pictured under the roof at Newcastle station in 1947; the 'A4' was resplendent in garter blue livery. You can almost smell the heady steam and smoke mix! *Mike Morant Collection*

In this super image the low setting sun lights up No 60020 as the loco gets smartly away from York with an up express in March 1957. *W. Oliver/Colour Rail*

Gresley 'A4' Pacific No 60021 WILD SWAN waits to depart from London Kings Cross station with the down 'Norseman' in this August 1958 image; note the double chimney. The 'Norseman' was originaly a boat train service between London Kings Cross and Newcastle Tyne Commision Quay which was introduced in 1931 and withdrawn in 1939. In June 1950 'The Norseman' boat train (which operated over the same route) was introduced and that train last ran 3 September 1966. *J.M. Chamney/Colour Rail*

Numbers	Names	Built	Completed	Double Chimney	Withdrawn
LNER 4467 and 21, BR 60021	WILD SWAN	Doncaster 1869	02/1938	04/1958	10/1963
LNER 4468 and 22, BR 60022	MALLARD*	Doncaster 1870	03/1938	03/1938*	04/1963 Preserved
LNER 4482 and 23, BR 60023	GOLDEN EAGLE	Doncaster 1847	12/1936	09/1958	10/1964
LNER 4483 and 24, BR 60024	KINGFISHER	Doncaster 1848	12/1936	08/1958	09/1966
LNER 4484 and 25, BR 60025	FALCON	Doncaster 1849	02/1937	09/1958	10/1963
LNER 4485 and 26, BR 60026#	KESTREL pre 11/1947 MILES BEEVOR	Doncaster 1850	02/1937	08/1957	12/1965
LNER 4486 and 27, BR 60027	MERLIN	Doncaster 1851	03/1937	02/1958	09/1965
LNER 4487 and 28, BR 60028	SEA EAGLE pre 10/1947 WALTER K. WHIGHAM	Doncaster 1852	04/1937	01/1958	12/1962
LNER 4497 and 29, BR 60029	WOODCOCK pre 06/1937 DOMINION OF CANADA	Doncaster 1858	07/1937	10/1958	10/1963
LNER 4495 and 30, BR 60030	GREAT SNIPE pre 09/1937 GOLDEN FLEECE	Doncaster 1860	08/1937	05/1958	12/1962

* Built with Kylchap blast pipe and double chimney, also No 60022 carries plaques on both sides of the boiler casing acknowledging the loco as World Speed Steam Traction record holder.
Disposal: 60021–60025–60028/29/30 Doncaster Works, 60023 Motherwell Machinery & Scrap, Wishaw, 60044–60026 Hughes Bolckows, North Blyth#, 60027 Campbells, Sheildhall
No 60026 was first withdrawn to Crewe Works where the driving wheels were swopped with those of preserved engine No 60007

In this, Gresley 'A4' Pacific No 60021 WILD SWAN is pictured whilst about to take over the up 'Flying Scotsman' service at Grantham in May 1957; note the single chimney. Perhaps the most famous named train in the world 'The Flying Scotsman' was introduced in July 1927 and ran between London Kings Cross and Edinburgh Waverley with a portion for Aberdeen. The service continued to run as a titled express during the war years and was still running via the East Coast Main Line in 2010. *E.V. Fry/Colour Rail*

This is a classic 'A4' shot in a much loved location, Gresley 'A4' Pacific No 60022 MALLARD pictured leaving Edinburgh Waverley station with that day's up 'The Elizabethan' in September 1961. 'The Elizabethan' service between London Kings Cross and Edinburgh Waverley was introduced on 29 June 1953 and last ran on 7 September 1962. *J.T. Inglis/Colour Rail*

Gresley 'A4' Pacific No 60022 MALLARD, ready for the 'off' at Kings Cross with the Aberdeen Flyer Railtour which took place on 2 and 3 June 1962. The mainline sections of this comprehensive tour ran London Kings Cross via York and Newcastle to Edinburgh Waverley with 'A4' loco 60022 MALLARD, Edinburgh Waverley via Dundee Tay Bridge to Aberdeen with loco 'A4' No 60004 WILLIAM WHITELAW and returned south hauled Aberdeen to Carlisle by 'Princess Royal' No 46201 PRINCESS ELIZABETH and Carlisle–Crewe–London Euston by 'Princess Royal' No 46200 THE PRINCESS ROYAL. *David Anderson*

Gresley 'A4' Pacific No 60022 MALLARD (holder of the World steam locomotive speed record), attracts the attention of a camera crew who were on hand to record the Aberdeen Flyer Railtour departure from London Kings Cross station on 2 June 1962. *David Anderson*

Two for the price of one! Gresley 'A4' Pacifics No 60023 GOLDEN EAGLE and 60004 WILLIAM WHITELAW pictured at Carlisle station. Loco No 60023 prepares to take over from No 60004 during the 'Three Summits Railtour' on 30 June 1963. The 'Three Summits Railtour' utilised three locos for the mainline section; the 'A4s' were joined by Stanier Pacific 46255 CITY OF HEREFORD. Route Leeds–Carlisle via S&C No 60023, Carlisle–Beattock–Carstairs (WCML) No 46255, Auchinleck–Carlisle via Dumfries No 60004 and Carlisle–Leeds City No 60023. Highland Railway 4-6-0 'Jones Goods' No 103 and ex Caledonian Railway '812' class 0-6-0 No 57581 operated the out and back Carstairs Junction–Auchinleck section. *Rail Photoprints Collection*

On foreign territory! Gresley 'A4' Pacific No 60024 KINGFISHER is seen being coaled at BR Southern Region depot Nine Elms (70A), whilst on railtour duty, 29 March 1966. *Keith Langston*

Gresley 'A4' Pacific No 60024 KINGFISHER on familiar territory; the loco is pictured taking water at Forfar whilst in charge of an Aberdeen–Glasgow service in July 1965. *Brian Robbins/Rail Photoprints Collection*

Gresley 'A4' Pacific No 60024 KINGFISHER. One of the last 'A4s' in service, the loco is depicted here inside the smoky confines of St Rollox shed (65B), Glasgow, in August 1966; it was then almost the end of the steam era in Scotland. *Mike Morant Collection*

Gresley 'A4' Pacific No 60025 FALCON is pictured taking water just outside the main area of Doncaster station in August 1957. That was an uncommon event because as can be seen the loco is hauling 'The Elizabethan', which was a non-stop service. *Mike Stokes Archive*

Gresley 'A4' Pacific No 60025 FALCON pictured near Great Ponton on the ECML with the up 'White Rose' in June 1963. 'The White Rose' express service was introduced in May 1949 and ran from London Kings Cross–Leeds Central–Bradford Exchange until 13 June 1964. *Paul Riley/Colour Rail*

Gresley 'A4' Pacific No 60026 MILES BEEVOR seen outside the coaling plant at Kings Cross shed (34A) in April 1956. *M.J. Reade/Colour Rail*

Gresley 'A4' Pacific No 60026 MILES BEEVOR pictured in July 1961 with the down 'Tees-Tyne Pullman' near New Southgate. 'The Tees-Tyne Pullman' as the name implies ran between London Kings Cross and Newcastle being introduced at the end of Serptember 1948 and last running on 30 April 1976. *A.C. Sterndale/Colour Rail*

A visitor from Doncaster! Gresley 'A4' Pacific No 60026 MILES BEEVOR (minus nameplates and smokebox casing) is pictured at Crewe Works on 21 May 1967. Loco No 60026 was first withdrawn to Crewe Works where the driving wheels were swopped with those of preserved engine No 60007; thereafter the loco was moved for cutting up at Hughes Bolckows of North Blyth. *John Chalcraft/Rail Photoprints Collection*

Gresley 'A4' Pacific No 60027 MERLIN pictured entering York station 'on the up' with 'The Elizabethan' in 1959. *Mike Bentley Collection*

Gresley 'A4' Pacific No 60027 MERLIN at full speed on the ECML near Pilmoor Junction, in 1957 again with 'The Elizabethan'. *Mike Bentley Collection*

Gresley 'A4' Pacific No 60027 MERLIN pictured again with 'The Elizabethan' this time whilst entering London Kings Cross station on 31 July 1959; the enthusiasts look delighted to see the Gresley Pacific at work. *Mike Morant Collection*

Peppercorn meets Gresley! 'A4' Pacific No 60028 WALTER K. WHIGHAM climbs out of Grantham with the 'Tees-Tyne Pullman' as the then unnamed 'A1' Pacific No 60139 (later named SEA EAGLE) drops down from Stoke Tunnel, circa 1949. *Rail Photoprints Collection*

Gresley 'A4' Pacific No 60030 GOLDEN FLEECE is seen when newly arrived at a rainy London Kings Cross station on 11 August 1954. *Mike Stokes Archive*

Numbers	Names	Built	Completed	Double Chimney	Withdrawn
LNER 4497 and 31, BR 60031	GOLDEN PLOVER	Doncaster 1862	10/1937	03/1958	11/1965
LNER 4900 and 32, BR 60032	GANNET	Doncaster 1874	05/1938	11/1958	10/1963
LNER 4902 and 33, BR 60033	SEAGULL	Doncaster 1876	06/1938	06/1938*	12/1962
LNER 4903 and 34, BR 60034	PEREGRINE pre 03/1948 LORD FARINGDON	Doncaster 1877	07/1938	07/1938*	08/1966

* Built with Kylchap blastpipe and double chimney
Disposal: 60031 Campbells, Sheildhall, 60032/33 Doncaster Works, 60034 Hughes Bolckows, North Blyth

Gresley 'A4' Pacific 60033 SEAGULL eases out of the GWR's London terminus, Paddington station, during the 1948 loco exchanges. *Mike Morant Collection*

This is the classic spotters' vantage point at Kings Cross station but wasn't necessarily the best spot for photography in view of the huge number of onlookers that would gather there. Here we see an occasion during the 1956 summer holiday period when the coast was clear for the photographer and Gresley 'A4' 60033 SEAGULL awaits departure whilst another 'Top Shed' stalwart, 60008 DWIGHT D. EISENHOWER, lurks expectantly in the background. *Mike Morant Collection*

Despite seeming to be in good condition externally Gresley 'A4' Pacific No 60034 LORD FARINGDON had reached the end of the road at Perth motive power depot in the last week of August 1966. Reportedly the tender was required for use with another member of the class in better mechanical condition. *Mike Morant Collection*

Gresley 'A4' Pacific No 60034 LORD FARINGDON seen in happier times than in the previous image; the loco is entering Bridge of Dun station, with the 13.30 Aberdeen–Glasgow Buchanan Street, in July 1965. *Brian Robbins/Rail Photoprints Collection*

Again with an Aberdeen–Glasgow service Gresley 'A4' Pacific No 60034 LORD FARINGDON pictured whilst taking water at Forfar, with the 13.30 Aberdeen–Glasgow Buchanan Street in July 1965. *Brian Robbins/Rail Photoprints Collection*

Gresley 'A4' Pacific No 60034 LORD FARINGDON took part in the 1948 locomotive trials; the 'A4' Pacific is seen on LMS territory travelling south on the West Coast Mainline approaching Weaver Junction with the 09.00 Perth to Euston service. Note the trailing load of sixteen coaches, 28 May 1948. Charmingly the photographer has included his then three-year-old son in the picture. *Roy Whitfield/Rail Photoprints Collection*

Gresley 'A4' Pacific No 60034 with Stanier 4-6-0 Black Five No 44720 on shed at Perth (63A) in 1966. *Brian Robbins/Rail Photoprints Collection*

Chapter 19

1937–1948

London Midland & Scottish Railway 'Princess Coronation/Duchess' Class 4-6-2, designed by Stanier

Introduced in 1937 the streamlined four-cylinder 'Princess Coronation/Duchess' class Pacific locomotives and matching 'Coronation Scot' train sets were a 'total concept' designed and built by the LMS (London Midland & Scottish Railway) in order to achieve fast travel between London Euston and Glasgow Central. The specially designed locomotives were built at Crewe Works and the carriage sets at the LMS works Wolverton. Perchance a little unkindly, some railway observers of that time described Stanier's streamlined casing as being representative of an upturned bathtub! The casings did of course add over 2 tons in weight to the engines; meaning that the effect of that weight on performance characteristics would need to first be overcome, before any actual benefit could be gained!

Begging the question: did aerodynamic streamlining greatly improve the performance/economy of the Stanier Pacifics in particular and furthermore of steam locomotives in general? With the

Streamlined LMS 'Princess Coronation/Duchess' class Pacific LMS No 6226 (BR 46226) DUCHESS OF NORFOLK seen passing South Kenton with the down 'Mid-Day Scot', in this superb 1938 image. The 'Mid-Day Scot' ran between London Euston and Glasgow Central from 26 September 1927 until 13 June 1965, with an enforced break in service during the war years. *D. Cobbe Collection/C.R.L. Coles/Rail Photoprints Collection*

benefit of hindsight perhaps not greatly so would seem to be the general consensus of opinion. Was the real value of streamlining therefore the effect of the attendant publicity in attracting the public to travel by rail?

At that time on the lucrative and prestige routes from the capital to the north the rival LNER (London & North Eastern Railway) had effectively stolen a march on the LMS by introducing their Gresley-built streamlined A4 locomotives on Silver Jubilee trains over the East Coast Main Line.

In July 1937 the LMS staged an attempted record run; no doubt in order to counter the publicity gained by the LNER. In short the trial was a success, as streamlined loco No 6220 CORONATION did attain a maximum speed of 114mph, with a down train just south of Crewe station, and that effort took the steam locomotive speed record from the LNER, albeit only temporarily!

In a 1937 article for the railway press the LMS gave the following summation of the new 'Coronation Scot' concept. *'New 4-6-2 locomotives and nine-coach trains for working the LMSR accelerated 6½ hour express service between Euston and Glasgow'*, which they announced would commence on July 5th of that year. *'The engines are streamlined, and, like the trains are finished throughout in blue and silver. The name 'Coronation Scot' was chosen in order to commemorate the Coronation of King George VI'* (12th May 1937).

The stylised named train ran from July 1937 until the start of the Second World War in 1939. Initially five of the new Stanier Pacific locomotives were built specifically for use on 'Coronation Scot' services and the striking livery was described as being a match to the Prussian blue of the former Caledonian Railway with silver used for the stripes and numerals. The 'Coronation Scot' colour was commonly referred to as Caledonian blue. Thereafter a further thirty-three engines were built between 1938 and 1949, for more general express passenger use.

In January 1939 streamlined engine No 6229 DUCHESS OF HAMILTON changed identities with sister engine No 6220 CORONATION in order to appear as that loco (together with a matching train) during a tour of the USA, and an appearance at the 'New York World's Fair'. Because of the intervention of the Second World War the loco remained in the USA until 1943.

Single chimneys were originally fitted to the first five engines of the class and they were replaced in 1938 with Kylchap blastpipes and double chimneys; thereafter all the members of the class were so fitted/built with that genuine performance-enhancing feature. The non-streamlined examples (6230–6234, 6249–6256 and 46257) were fitted with smoke deflectors. The streamlined locomotives (6220–6229, 6235–6248) all had their casings removed between 1946 and 1948, and were then also fitted with smoke deflectors.

Other obvious physical differences included the fact that the ex-streamlined engines together with the last two built, No 6256 and No 46257, did not have a steel plate joining the front end of the running plate with the buffer beam (colloquially referred to as 'Utility front

Stanier Pacific streamlined loco LMS No 6220 CORONATION attained a maximum speed of 114mph in July 1937; the loco is seen outside Crewe Works in this LMS publicity picture. *Crewe Archive*

end') whilst the non-streamlined class members did. Until smokebox changes were made (as required) the ex-streamlined engines were easily identified by the sloping front aspect of those units, a feature which led to the use of the nickname 'Semi', i.e. semi-streamlined.

The locomotives trailing axles (6220–6255) were incorporated into a trailing truck assembly usually called a 'Bissel Truck' which in traffic occasionally gave problems; furthermore, as the locomotives aged reported incidences of fatigue cracking increased. To counteract that the designers made a major change to the design of the trailing truck used on the last two engines (6256 and 46257); those units were called 'Delta Trucks' and the change in construction (appearance) was easily discernable even to the unpractised eye.

Other design modifications for the two Ivatt 1947–1948 built engines included the use of roller bearings throughout and a visually evident alteration in cab style. Also the last two engines had their reversing shaft/tube located outside of the locos nearside; that component was located under the cab floor in the original design. The tubes could be seen running in a sloping manner downwards from the cab front to a point on the running plate just behind the rear driving wheels, where the shaft connected with the actual reversing screw located within the frames. Examining photographs (drawings) of the nearside of the aforementioned two engines the AWS conduit can be seen running along the bottom edge of the running plate; the point where the conduit 'doglegs' inward marks the approximate location of the reversing screw.

In order to more easily de-clinker the fire grate after burning poor-quality coal these engines were also fitted with rocking grate mechanisms, the success of which led to five other members of the class being so fitted. The 'Princess Coronation/Duchess' class Pacific locomotives' tenders were fitted with a steam operated coal pusher which greatly helped the fireman bring coal forward to the firing plate, especially during the 299-mile long-distance non-stop runs between London and Carlisle, whilst operating the Anglo Scottish express services.

LMS 4-6-2 'Princess Coronation/Duchess' class, BR numbers 46220–46257

Introduced: 1937–48

Power Classification: 7P (reclassified 8P in 1951), thirty-eight locomotives

Built: Crewe Works

Designer: William Stanier

Modified: Nos 46256 and 46257 built 1947–48 as modified by Ivatt

Company: London Midland & Scottish Railway

Driving Wheel: 6ft 9ins

Boiler Pressure: 250psi superheated

Cylinders: 4 – 16½ins diameter x 28ins stroke

Tractive Effort @ 85%: 40,000lbf

Valve Gear: Outside Walschaerts with rocking shafts (piston valves)

Water Capacity: 4000 gallons

Coal Capacity: 10 tons

Locos 6220–6224 LMS Crewe Works, Lot No 138

Numbers	Names	Built	Completed	Streamlining removed	Withdrawn
LMS 6220, BR 46220	CORONATION	Crewe	06/1937 S	09/1946	04/1963
LMS 6221, BR 46221	QUEEN ELIZABETH	Crewe	06/1937 S	05/1946	05/1963
LMS 6222, BR 46222	QUEEN MARY	Crewe	06/1937 S	05/1946	10/1963
LMS 6223, BR 46223	PRINCESS ALICE	Crewe	07/1937 S	08/1946	10/1963
LMS 6224, BR 46224	PRINCESS ALEXANDRA	Crewe	07/1937 S	05/1946	10/1963

S – Streamlined
Locos: 46220–46224 Running plate and buffer beam not joined at the front end
Disposal: 46220–46224 Crewe Works

The 'Princess Coronation/Duchess' class Pacific locos were generally accepted to have been magnificent engines; they hauled the heaviest trains at high speeds over the West Coast Mainline, and other routes, on a daily basis for over twenty-five years. British Railways took into stock thirty-six of the class and thereafter built two more bringing the total 'in class' to thirty-eight engines.

Withdrawal of the class started in 1962 with thirty-five locos remaining in service at the end of that year; a further thirteen engines were withdrawn in 1963, leaving twenty-two engines in service during 1964. However, no member of the class remained in service beyond the end of that year. As withdrawn a great number of the class were in full working order, having only recently been outshopped following routine maintenance.

Liveries used included Caledonian blue and silver ('Coronation Scot' locos), crimson lake and gold, crimson lake, plain black, experimental blue/grey (No 6234), BR blue and BR green.

The first streamlined LMS 'Princess Coronation/Duchess' class Pacific No 6220 CORONATION is pictured in this official LMS publicity picture taken at Crewe in June 1937. *Richard Metcalfe Collection*

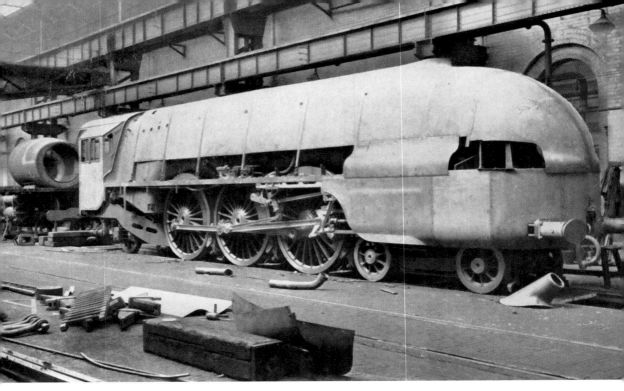

The first streamlined LMS 'Princess Coronation/Duchess' class Pacific No 6220 CORONATION is pictured whilst under construction at Crewe Works in this May 1937 image. *Crewe Archive*

Streamlined Stanier Pacific LMS No 6220 CORONATION caused quite a stir when it first emerged from Crewe Works. It was one of five engines given blue livery with silver bands, which was intended to match the coaching stock of the then newly introduced Anglo Scottish 'Coronation Scot' express service. *Crewe Archive*

The leader of the class, 'Princess Coronation/Duchess' Pacific No 46220 CORONATION, seen at Edinburgh Princess Street station whilst waiting to depart with a train for Glasgow Central station. Note that this loco was streamlined but at this time had been fitted with a new (non-sloping) smokebox. Importantly this loco is part of an ex-streamlined batch, up to and including No 46229, which had front ends with a gap between the running plate and the buffer beam. *David Anderson*

'Princess Coronation/Duchess' Pacific No 46220 CORONATION is again pictured on the Edinburgh–Glasgow route passing Balerno Junction with an all-stations passenger train for Glasgow. Note that the locomotive's firebox at that time still had the sloping profile which was formed to accommodate the streamlined casing. The retention of that shape led to enthusiasts using the term 'Semis' in respect of that style of loco (i.e. semi-streamlined). *David Anderson*

The second of the class to emerge from Crewe Works, streamlined LMS 'Princess Coronation/Duchess' class Pacific LMS No 6221 QUEEN ELIZABETH (then of course named for HRH Queen Elizabeth I), is pictured at the North shed, Crewe, on 10 October 1937; the loco had then been in service for four months. *Dr Ian C. Allen/Transport Treasury*

This image of 'Princess Coronation/Duchess' class Pacific No 46221 QUEEN ELIZABETH, again employed on the Edinburgh–Glasgow service, clearly shows the use of an ex-Caledonian Railway semaphore route indicator; on this occasion the device is located in the centre of the buffer beam but they were often alternatively carried on the top lamp bracket. *David Anderson*

'Princess Coronation/Duchess' class Pacific No 46223 PRINCESS ALICE gets the southbound 'Royal Scot' smartly away from Glasgow Central station. The 'Royal Scot' ran daily, between London Euston and Glasgow Central from 11 July 1927 until 1 June 2002, with an enforced break during the war years. *Mike Morant Collection*

Busy scene outside Carlisle Upperby (12B) as 'Royal Scot' 46140 THE KING'S ROYAL RIFLE CORPS takes over the 'Royal Scot' from Stanier Pacific 46222 QUEEN MARY, circa 1956. *Dave Cobbe Collection/Rail Photoprints Collection*

'Princess Coronation/Duchess' class Pacific LMS No 6224 PRINCESS ALEXANDRA, streamlined, blue and silver stripes, takes water at Shrewsbury station whilst on a running-in turn, in 1938. *P.B. Whitehouse/Ron White Collection*

Locos 6225–6234 LMS Crewe Works, Lot No 145

Numbers	Names	Built	Completed	Streamlining removed	Withdrawn
LMS 6225, BR 46225	DUCHESS OF GLOUCESTER	Crewe	05/1935 S	02/1947	10/1964
LMS 6226, BR 46226	DUCHESS OF NORFOLK	Crewe	05/1938 S	06/1947	10/1964
LMS 6227, BR 46227	DUCHESS OF DEVONSHIRE	Crewe	06/1938 S	02/1947	12/1962
LMS 6228, BR 46228	DUCHESS OF RUTLAND	Crewe	06/1938 S	07/1947	10/1964
LMS 6229, BR 46229	DUCHESS OF HAMILTON	Crewe	09/1938 S	06/1947	02/1964 Preserved*

S: Streamlined * Streamlining re-applied in preservation (2010)
Locos 46225–46229 Running plate and buffer beam not joined at front end

'Princess Coronation/Duchess' class Pacific No 46225 DUCHESS OF GLOUCESTER pictured at Carstairs Junction with an up 'Mid-Day Scot' working, the loco was at that time in BR blue livery. *David Anderson*

'Princess Coronation/Duchess' class Pacific No 46225 DUCHESS OF GLOUCESTER is again on the WCML but this time with only a local service, pictured at Norton near Runcorn in August 1963. *R.A. Whitfield/Rail Photoprints Collection*

'Princess Coronation/Duchess' class Pacific No 46226 DUCHESS OF NORFOLK has a full load in tow as pictured passing Bourne End Signal Box with the down 'Lakes Express' in this July 1960 image. 'The Lakes Express' was a summer-timetable-only service that ran from London Euston–Windermere and Workington (the Windermere portion being detached at Oxenholme, for the branch line). The train ran from 11 July 1927 until 28 August 1964 with a break from September 1939 until June 1950. *P. Pescod/Transport Treasury*

Brand new! 'Princess Coronation/Duchess' class Pacific LMS No 6227 DUCHESS OF DEVONSHIRE is pictured having just been passed as fit for traffic in the erecting shop at Crewe Works; this was the third of the Crimson Lake- and Gold-liveried engines to be completed, May 1938. *Mike Bentley Collection*

'Princess Coronation/Duchess' class Pacific No 46227 DUCHESS OF DEVONSHIRE in BR blue is pictured hard at work with the 'Royal Scot' at Shap Wells; note that the loco at that time still had a sloping smokebox top, August 1951. *Pursey C. Short/Colour Rail*

'Princess Coronation/Duchess' class Pacific No 46227 DUCHESS OF DEVONSHIRE, seen at Crewe Works when fresh from its last overhaul. Note that one of the Crewe batch of 'new order' Peaks (awaiting painting) stands alongside the Stanier Pacific, May 1961. *Jim Carter/Rail Photoprints*

'Princess Coronation/Duchess' class Pacific No 46228 DUCHESS OF RUTLAND pictured at work on the Cumberland Fells 1956. *Rail Photoprints Collection*

Numbers	Names	Built	Completed	Streamlining removed	Withdrawn
LMS 6230, BR 46230	DUCHESS OF BUCCLEUCH	Crewe	07/1938	N/A	11/1963
LMS 6231, BR 46231	DUCHESS OF ATHOLL	Crewe	07/1938	N/A	12/1962
LMS 6232, BR 46232	DUCHESS OF MONTROSE	Crewe	07/1938	N/A	11/1963
LMS 6233, BR 46233	DUCHESS OF SUTHERLAND	Crewe	07/1938	N/A	02/1964 Preserved
LMS 6234, BR 46234	DUCHESS OF ABERCORN	Crewe	08/1938	N/A	01/1963

Locos 46230–46234: Running plate and buffer beam joined at front end
Disposal: 46225/26 Arnott Young, Troon, 46227–46230/32–46234 Crewe Works, 46228 Cashmores, Great Bridge

'Princess Coronation/Duchess' class Pacific No 46230 DUCHESS OF BUCCLEUCH was the first of a batch of five non-streamlined members of the class to be completed in July/August 1938. The driver gives the photographer a wave as the loco thunders up Camden Bank with a down 'Royal Scot' working (no headboard carried) in this 1948 image. *D.Cobbe collection/C.R.L. Coles/Rail Photoprints/Collection*

A very clean 'Princess Coronation/Duchess' class Pacific No 46232 DUCHESS OF MONTROSE waits at Carlisle to take over the down 'Royal Scot' in May 1958. *M.D. Marston/Ron White Collection*

DUCHESS OF MONTROSE is again seen again whilst waiting to take over a down 'Royal Scot' working at Carlisle Kingmoor depot (12A) in this detail-filled 1955 image. Pacific No 46232 was at that time allocated to Glasgow Polmadie depot (66A). Note the fireman 'on top' attending to 'the bag'; also seen is Stanier Black Five No 44931. *Rail Photoprints Collection*

'Princess Coronation/Duchess' class Pacific No 46234 DUCHESS OF ABERCORN is pictured at Camden in September 1959. The loco has dropped off the 'Royal Scot's' empty stock having banked it out of Euston station. It's unusual to see clearly both the end board of the stock and the headboard on the loco. *Mike Morant Collection*

Locos 6235–6239 LMS Crewe Works, Lot No 150

Numbers	Names	Built	Completed	Streamlining removed	Withdrawn
LMS 6235, BR 46235	CITY OF BIRMINGHAM	Crewe	07/1939 S	04/1946	10/1964 Preserved
LMS 6236, BR 46236	CITY OF BRADFORD	Crewe	07/1939 S	12/1947	03/1964
LMS 6237, BR 46237	CITY OF BRISTOL	Crewe	08/1939 S	01/1947	10/1964
LMS 6238, BR 46238	CITY OF CARLISLE	Crewe	09/1939 S	11/1946	10/1964
LMS 6239, BR 46239	CITY OF CHESTER	Crewe	09/1939 S	06/1947	10/1964

S – Streamlined
Locos 46235–46239: Running plate and buffer beam not joined at front end
Disposal: 46236 Crewe Works, 46237/38 Arnott Young, Troon, 46239 Cashmores, Great Bridge

'Princess Coronation/Duchess' class Pacific No 46235 CITY OF BIRMINGHAM pictured passing Rugby No 4 Signal Box. Importantly this loco is part of an ex-streamlined batch up to and including No 46248 which had front ends with a gap between the running plate and the buffer beam. *N.E. Stead/Author's Collection*

'Princess Coronation/Duchess' class Pacific No 46236 CITY OF BRADFORD approaching Weaver Junction on the WCML with the down 'Caledonian',1960. 'The Caledonian' between London Euston and Glasgow Central was introduced on 17 June 1957 and ran until 4 September 1964. *Colin Whitfield/Rail Photoprints Collection*

'Princess Coronation/Duchess' class Pacific No 46237 CITY OF BRISTOL (at that time carrying BR blue livery) pictured at Carstairs Junction with an up 'Mid-Day Scot' working in July 1953. *David Anderson*

'Princess Coronation/Duchess' class Pacific No 46238 CITY OF CARLISLE is pictured in BR red livery, with an up train passing Beattock summit on 29 July 1961. *Keith Langston Collection*

'Princess Coronation/Duchess' class Pacific No 46239 CITY OF CHESTER pictured near Weaver Junction on the WCML with the down 'Caledonian', 24 July 1958. *R.A. Whitfield/Rail Photoprints Collection*

Locos 6240–6244 LMS Crewe Works, Lot No 150

Numbers	Names	Built	Completed	Streamlining removed	Withdrawn
LMS 6240, BR 46240	CITY OF COVENTRY	Crewe	03/1940 S	06/1947	10/1964
LMS 6241, BR 46241	CITY OF EDINBURGH	Crewe	04/1940 S	01/1947	09/1964
LMS 6242, BR 46242	CITY OF GLASGOW	Crewe	05/1940 S	03/1947	10/1963
LMS 6243, BR 46243	CITY OF LANCASTER	Crewe	06/1940 S	05/1949*	10/1964
LMS 6244, BR 46244	CITY OF LEEDS renamed KING GEORGE VI in 1941	Crewe	07/1940 S	08/1947	10/1964

S – Streamlined * No 46243 was the only member of the class to carry streamlining and a number in the BR series

Locos 46240–46244: Running plate and buffer beam not joined at front end

Disposal: 46240/41 Cashmores, Great Bridge, 46242 Crewe Works, 46243 Central Wagon, Ince, 46244 Arnott Young, Troon

A Stanier 'Princess Coronation/Duchess' class Pacific is again seen in charge of the 'The Caledonian'; this time No 46241 CITY OF EDINBURGH is pictured passing Hartford with the northbound train on 2 May 1958. *R.A. Whitfield/Rail Photoprints Collection*

The ill-fated 'Princess Coronation/Duchess' class Pacific LMS No 6242 CITY OF GLASGOW ('Semi' form) is pictured in happier times thrashing southward on the descent from Shap summit. This locomotive was the engine which ploughed into a stationary train at Harrow & Wealdstone station on 8 October 1952; in the resulting disaster (which involved 3 trains and 4 locomotives) 112 persons tragically perished, and over 200 were injured. *Mike Morant Collection*

BR Pacific No 46242 CITY OF GLASGOW is seen in the station goods yard at Harrow & Wealdstone station after the crash and prior to being removed to Crewe Works. Note that the motion, cylinders and almost all boiler fittings including the smokebox are missing. Despite the severe damage No 46242 was rebuilt and put back into service. *BR Midland Region/Crewe Archive*

This side profile shot of the rebuilt No 46242 CITY OF GLASGOW at speed on the WCML, near to Elvanfoot, with a down 'Royal Scot' working, shows clearly the difference in running plate front end design from the loco's original form. *David Anderson*

The last Stanier 'Princess Coronation/Duchess' class Pacific to have the streamlined casing removed was No 46243 CITY OF LANCASTER (thus the only member of the class to carry a BR series number whilst streamlined); the loco is pictured passing Weaver Junction (WCML) with a down Liverpool service, circa 1948. Upturned bathtub or no? *R.A. Whitfield/Rail Photoprints Collection*

'Princess Coronation/Duchess' class Pacific No 46243 CITY OF LANCASTER in un-streamlined form and BR red livery storms past Camden motive power depot in September 1959. *A.E. Durant/Mike Morant Collection*

Camden-allocated 'Princess Coronation/Duchess' class Pacific No 46244 KING GEORGE VI in de-streamlined 'Semi' form rattles through Tebay with the northbound 'Mid-Day Scot', no headboard carried. *Rail Photoprints Collection*

Locos 6244–6248 LMS Crewe, Lot No 150

Numbers	Names	Built	Completed	Streamlining removed	Withdrawn
LMS 6245, BR 46245	CITY OF LONDON	Crewe	06/1943 S	08/1947	10/1964
LMS 6246, BR 46246	CITY OF MANCHESTER	Crewe	08/1943 S	09/1946	01/1963
LMS 6247, BR 46247	CITY OF LIVERPOOL	Crewe	09/1943 S	05/1947	06/1963
LMS 6248, BR 46248	CITY OF LEEDS	Crewe	10/1943 S	12/1946	09/1964

S – Streamlined
Locos 46235–46239: Running plate and buffer beam not joined at front end
Disposal: 46245–46247 Cashmores, Great Bridge, 46246/47 Crewe Works

'Princess Coronation/Duchess' class Pacific No 46245 CITY OF LONDON is seen at Crewe station in this fine portrait study, taken during August 1963. Note that the 'Bissel' style trailing truck design, incorporated on all of class except locomotives No 46256 and No 46257, can be clearly identified. *R.A. Whitfield/Rail Photoprints Collection*

Waiting for their respective turns of duty at Glasgow Polmadie depot (66A) are two ex-LMS Stanier Pacifics. 'Princess Coronation/Duchess' class Pacific No 46246 CITY OF MANCHESTER and 'Princess Royal' class No 46203 PRINCESS MARGARET ROSE, 22 April 1956. *David Anderson*

On familiar territory, 'Princess Coronation/Duchess' class Pacific No 46246 (still in 'Semi' form) tops Beattock Summit with the southbound 'Mid-Day Scot'. The engine was in BR blue livery but in need of a clean, when pictured on 4 July 1959. *David Anderson*

'Princess Coronation/Duchess' class Pacific No 46247 CITY OF LIVERPOOL stands 'centre road' on the down at Carlisle station in 1963. *Mike Stokes Archive*

'Princess Coronation/Duchess' class Pacific No 46248 CITY OF LEEDS still in 'Semi' form awaits departure from London Euston, in the summer of 1956. All steam traction enthusiasts will note the presence of 'the enemy' in the form of Ivatt Co-Co diesel No 10001 to the right of the Stanier Pacific. *Mike Morant*

'Princess Coronation/Duchess' class Pacific No 46248 CITY OF LEEDS (then in BR red livery and with a new smokebox) pictured near Wem whilst heading for Crewe with a train from the Welsh Marshes. *Mike Morant Collection*

'Princess Coronation/Duchess' class Pacific No 46248 CITY OF LEEDS prepares to head south from Crewe, circa 1960. Note that the attachment of the coaches is still being completed. *Alan H. Bryant ARPS/Rail Photoprints Collection*

Locos 6249-6252 LMS Crewe, Lot No 150

Numbers	Names	Built	Completed	Withdrawn
LMS 6249, BR 46249	CITY OF SHEFFIELD	Crewe	04/1944	11/1963
LMS 6250, BR 46250	CITY OF LICHFIELD	Crewe	04/1944	10/1964
LMS 6251, BR 46251	CITY OF NOTTINGHAM	Crewe	06/1944	12/1964
LMS 6252, BR 46252	CITY OF LEICESTER	Crewe	06/1944	06/1963

Locos 46249–46252: Running plate and buffer beam joined at front end
These four engines although un-streamlined were originally coupled with streamlined tenders

'Princess Coronation/Duchess' class Pacific No 46249 CITY OF SHEFFIELD takes water on Moore Troughs whilst heading south on the WCML, circa 1949. *R.A. Whitfield/Rail Photoprints Collection*

'Princess Coronation/Duchess' class Pacific No 46250 CITY OF LICHFIELD was in danger of choking prospective passengers when pictured under the roof at Carlisle Citadel station in August 1957. *Rail Photoprints Collection*

'Princess Coronation/Duchess' class Pacific No 46251 CITY OF NOTTINGHAM, in BR red livery, was seen 'on shed' at Crewe North (5A) whilst awaiting its next turn of duty, in this 1963 image. *Keith Langston*

'Princess Coronation/Duchess' class Pacific No 46251 CITY OF NOTTINGHAM is pictured in foreign territory! The loco is seen whilst reducing speed rounding the West Curve between Foxhall Junction and Didcot North Signal Box with The Railway Correspondence and Travel Society 'East Midlander' special train, which is returning via Oxford from a visit to Swindon Works on 8 May 1964. *David Anderson*

Locos 6253–6255 LMS Crewe, Lot No 184

Numbers	Names	Built	Completed	Withdrawn
LMS 6253, BR 46253	CITY OF ST ALBANS	Crewe	09/1946	01/1963
LMS 6254, BR 46254	CITY OF STOKE-ON-TRENT	Crewe	09/1946	10/1964
LMS 6255, BR 46255	CITY OF HEREFORD	Crewe	10/1946	10/1964

Locos 46249–46252: Running plate and buffer beam not joined at front end
Disposal: 46249–46252–46253 Crewe Works, 46250–46255 Arnott Young, Troon, 46251–46254 Cashmores, Great Bridge

'Princess Coronation/Duchess' class Pacific No 46253 CITY OF ST ALBANS passes over Christelton Troughs and does not appear to be taking water, as it leaves Chester with a Bowater Group special from Chester returning to Euston, on 3 June 1959. The author recalls seeing several such special trains at Rhyl station during that period. *R.A. Whitfield/Rail Photoprints Collection*

'Princess Coronation/Duchess' class Pacific No 46253 CITY OF ST ALBANS in tandem with a 'Semi' passing Crewe station and heading towards the north shed. Note the old facade of Crewe station and the Crosville Bus Services double deckers. *Mike Morant Collection*

The late Roy Whitfield photographed the WCML steam action extensively and on many occasions his young son accompanied him, as can be seen in this image. 'Princess Coronation/Duchess' class Pacific No 6254 CITY OF STOKE-ON-TRENT picks up water from Moore Troughs as it heads south with an up express. Note that the loco, although in BR black livery, is still proudly displaying LMS on the tender, 1949. *R.A. Whitfield/Rail Photoprints Collection*

'Princess Coronation/Duchess' class Pacific No 6254 CITY OF STOKE-ON-TRENT is again seen on the WCML, this time passing Weaver Junction with an up Anglo Scottish express, 1948. *R.A. Whitfield/Rail Photoprints Collection*

Locos 6256 and 46257 LMS/BR Crewe, Lot No 184

Numbers	Names	Built	Completed	Withdrawn
LMS 6256, BR 46256	SIR WILLIAM A. STANIER, FRS	Crewe	12/1947	10/1964
BR 46257	CITY OF SALFORD	Crewe	05/1948	10/1964
Locos 46256–46257: Running plate and buffer beam not joined at front end Disposal: 46256 Cashmores, Great Bridge, 46257 Arnott Young, Troon				

Named after the designer, 'Princess Coronation/Duchess' class Pacific No 46256 SIR WILLIAM A. STANIER, FRS, seen in immaculate condition whilst waiting to head an up WCML express at Carlisle in June 1959. Note the shallower cab side panels and redesigned pattern of trailing truck, both as fitted to this loco and No 46257; the new trailing axle carrier was called a 'Delta Truck' and replaced the previously used 'Bissell Truck'. *G.L. Wilson/Colour Rail*

Relegated to freight work under the wires, 'Princess Coronation/Duchess' class Pacific No 46256 SIR WILLIAM A. STANIER FRS (the lack of a cabside yellow stripe indicates that the overhead power cables were not at that time energised). The loco was pictured travelling northbound on the WCML at Weaver Junction during May 1963. Note that the last two engines in the class had their reversing shaft located outside of the loco's nearside; that component was located under the cab floor in the original design. The tubes could be seen running in a sloping manner downwards from the cab front to a point on the running plate just behind the rear driving wheels. *R.A. Whitfield/Rail Photoprints Collection*

'Princess Coronation/Duchess' class Pacific No 46257 CITY OF SALFORD was the last of the class to be built complete with detail differences which included electric lights which can clearly be seen. Loco No 46257 was pictured passing Weaver Junction with an up express when new to traffic in 1949. *R.A. Whitfield/Rail Photoprints Collection*

'Princess Coronation/Duchess' class Pacific No 46257 CITY OF SALFORD, the last of the class to be built, is seen at Penrith with a down express. *David Anderson*

Chapter 20

1941–1949

Southern Railway/British Railways 'Merchant Navy' Class 4-6-2, designed by Bulleid

Oliver Bulleid began his railway career in 1912 and in the course of it he clocked up a total of twenty-two years working with the man whose name became synonymous with the successful streamlining of steam locomotives, one Nigel Gresley. Bulleid was renowned for his flare and innovation and put both facets to good use at the LNER during the design and building of the streamlined 'Silver Jubilee' concept train. Encouraged by the then Chairman of the LNER he became a firm advocate for streamlining and he is said to have had much more than a watching brief in the design and construction of the 'A4' class Pacifics.

Bulleid 'Merchant Navy' class Pacific No 21C2 UNION CASTLE (BR 35002) was pictured whilst storming westwards up Honiton Bank in Devon. The un-rebuilt loco is hauling a rake of stock that was of Maunsell origin; this 'entirely Southern' image was taken circa 1947. Note the raised numerals used for the loco's number plates. *Mike Morant Collection*

In September 1937 Bulleid joined the Southern Railway and began working alongside his predecessor, R.E.L. Maunsell. His first few years in post were spent working on design improvements with locomotives of the existing SR fleet. When, in 1939, the Southern Railway board identified their urgent need for a new fast heavy passenger locomotive they turned to their new Chief Mechanical Engineer.

His original proposals were for locomotives in the 4-8-0, 4-8-2 and 2-6-2 configurations, ideas which did not find favour with the board in general, and the railway's civil engineer in particular. Bulleid therefore turned his attention to designing a three-cylinder 4-6-2 Pacific with a lighter than at first proposed axle loading that project did receive the blessing of his directors.

The later to be named 'Merchant Navy' class engines were the first Pacific tender engines built for and operated on the Southern Railway. It should perhaps be remembered that Marsh had in 1910 and 1912 respectively introduced a pair 4-6-2T locomotives for the LBSCR, which of course later became part of the Southern system.

Bulleid's final design and building programme for the 'Merchant Navy' Pacifics was slowed down by the onset of the Second World War, however he did gain permission to commence building the first ten of his unique '8P' Pacifics. The first example of his revolutionary design was rolled out of Eastleigh Works in February 1941, and the streamlined (or 'air-smoothed' casing design, as Bulleid preferred to call it) caused quite a stir.

Worthy of mention is the point that Bullied and the Southern Railway were rebuked by the Ministry of Labour, who accused them of building streamlined express passenger locomotives and thus wasting valuable wartime resources. Undaunted, the locomotive designer managed to convince the powers that be otherwise, stating that his new class of engines was in fact a mixed traffic type and drawing their attention to the 6-foot-2-inch-diameter driving wheels!

Innovation was very much the Bulleid way and much has been written about the originality of his design which in addition to 'that casing' included an almost revolutionary system of chain-driven valve gear. The modified Walschaerts gear was located between the engine's frames and completely encased in an oil bath.

The earliest-built 'Merchant Navy' class locomotives did not have smoke deflectors cut into the air-smoothed casing as Bulleid's original intention was to create smooth, easy to clean surfaces. However, the lack of them caused problems with drifting smoke obscuring the driver's forward vision. This historically important image shows No 21C3 ROYAL MAIL in original form at Salisbury at the end of September 1941. *Mike Morant Collection*

In an attempt to overcome smoke drift problems the casings were altered by first extending the roof over the top of the smokebox and incorporating a slot. Later, and after several trials, smoke deflectors were also incorporated, but reportedly those modifications never completely solved the drifting smoke problem. In this front-end view of 'Merchant Navy' class Pacific No 35015 ROTTERDAM LLOYD the addition of smoke deflectors and a cowl, formed by extending the casing roof, can clearly be seen. *Colour Rail*

In theory the 'oil bath' should have been a maintenance fitter's dream but in fact it caused a great many more problems than it solved. Corrosion problems were exacerbated by water seeping into the oil bath, and leaking oil falling on to the track caused instances of wheel slip. Additionally on many occasions fires were started in the boiler cladding as a result of the ignition of leaked oil.

The design also included a steam/hydraulic reverser, American style 'Boxpok' cast steel wheels with holes and recesses on their discs, and an all welded construction steel (not copper) firebox incorporating two thermic siphons*.

* Simply put the 'Thermic Syphon' is generally a funnel-shaped fabrication which connects the throat plate (front wall of the firebox) with the crown sheet (roof of the firebox). Feed water flows upwards through the syphons and is therefore exposed directly to the radiant heat of the firebox. The flow therefore increases thermal efficiency and additionally improves water circulation in the boiler.

Electric lighting was also a feature of the class not just to the locomotive headcode and tail lights but it was also used to illuminate the injectors, driving wheels, front bogie, trailing truck and mechanical lubricators.

The locomotive's boiler pressure was originally set at 280psi but was later reduced to 250psi, a multiple-jet blastpipe was incorporated and the air-smoothed casing in addition to totally enclosing the firebox and boiler also covered the outside cylinders.

The steel fireboxes had a less than satisfactory service life with the first ten all being replaced after only seven years in service. On the credit side the class were a whole lot better performers than any other SR express passenger locomotives of the time and importantly the 'Merchant Navy's' greatly reduced 'hammer blow' considerably. The type was very popular with locomotive crews but not universally so with maintenance departments.

The engines of the new class were all named for famous shipping lines of the era, hence the collective term 'Merchant Navy' class. The unusual Bulleid air-smoothed casing led to the locos being called after the acronym for the containers of that wartime 'wonder food', 'Special Processed American Meat', SPAM; they are irreverently known to the present day as 'Spam Cans'.

Bulleid originally used a continental-style numbering system for all of his 'air-smoothed casing' Pacific locomotives. The system was an adaption of the International Union of Railways (UIC) system where '2' and '1' refer to the number of un-powered leading and trailing axles respectively, and 'C' refers to three driving axles. As an example, the first 'Merchant Navy' class locomotive was numbered 21C1. British Railways discontinued the system and took the numerals after the letter 'C' and incorporated them as the last numerals of a 35000 series of numbers (in the case of the 'Merchant Navy' class) e.g. UIC number 21C20 became BR 35020. The BR-built 'MN' class engines (35021–35030) never carried UIC-system numbers.

Rebuilt Bulleid 'Merchant Navy' class Pacific No 35014 NEDERLAND LINE was pictured passing Weybridge on 4 July 1966. Under Bulleid's original numbering this loco was No 21C14. This loco was part of a batch of six engines rebuilt in 1956. *Keith Langston Collection*

After only a relatively short time in service the Bulleid 'Merchant Navy' class Pacific locomotives were extensively rebuilt by British Railways. The whole thirty engines were put through the works between 1956 and 1959. Essentially the rebuilding centered on the removal of the 'air-smoothed casing' and the replacement of the chain-driven valve gear with three sets of normal-style valve gear. The excellent boilers were retained and square-type smoke deflectors with grab rails were added; consequently many observers commented upon the similarity in looks between the rebuilt Bulleid locomotives and the BR Standard Pacifics, with of course the obvious exception of the 'Boxpok' wheels which were retained. The trailing truck arrangement incorporated in the 'MN' class rebuilds was adopted for use in the design of the BR Standard Pacific classes.

The general consensus was that the rebuilt 'Merchant Navy' class Pacifics were/are a class of good-looking reliable engines which served British Railways well.

Scrapping of the class did not start until 1964 and the first two locos of the class to be withdrawn (in February of that year) were No 35002 and No 35015. By the end of 1965 only sixteen of the class remained in service and only ten locos saw service past the end of 1966, with none lasting beyond the end of 1967. The last eight engines of the class were withdrawn in July 1967.

Several colour schemes and livery styles were used with the class and they included matt malachite green, wartime black, SR malachite green, BR blue and BR green.

SR 4-6-2 'Merchant Navy' class, BR numbers 35001–35030

Introduced: 1941–49

ReBuilt: 1956 onwards (BR) all 30 locomotives

Power Classification: 7P (reclassified 8P in 1951)

Built: Eastleigh Works

Designer: Oliver Bulleid

Company: Southern Railway/British Railways

Driving Wheel: 6ft 2ins 'Boxpok' pattern

Boiler Pressure: 280psi superheated, later reduced as re-built to 250psi superheated

Cylinders: 3 – 18ins diameter x 24ins stroke

Tractive Effort @ 85%: 37,515lbf, later reduced to 33,495lbf

Valve Gear: Bulleid (piston valves) as rebuilt Walschaert (piston valves)

Valve Gear: Outside Walschaerts with derived motion (piston valves)

Water Capacity: 5000–5100 gallons–6000 gallons as rebuilt

Coal Capacity: 5 tons

Numbers	Names	Built	Completed	Re-built	Withdrawn
SR 21C1, BR 35001	CHANNEL PACKET	Eastleigh	02/1941	08/1959	11/1964
SR 21C2, BR 35002	UNION CASTLE	Eastleigh	06/1941	05/1958	02/1964
SR 21C3, BR 35003	ROYAL MAIL	Eastleigh	09/1941	09/1959	07/1967
SR 21C4, BR 35004	CUNARD WHITE STAR	Eastleigh	12/1941	07/1958	10/1965

Disposal: 35001 Birds, Swansea, 35002 Slag Reduction Co Ltd, Yorkshire, 35003 John Cashmore, Newport, 35004 Cohens at Eastleigh depot

Bulleid 'Merchant Navy' class Pacific No 35001 CHANNEL PACKET (the first of the class to enter service) was pictured in re-built condition near Basingstoke with an up express in the summer of 1964. *David Anderson*

Bulleid 'Merchant Navy' class Pacific No 35001 CHANNEL PACKET was pictured on shed at Nine Elms (70A) in 1963. *Mike Stokes Archive*

CHANNEL PACKET 'Merchant Navy' class style nameplate. *David Anderson*

'Merchant Navy' class Pacific No 21C2 UNION CASTLE (BR 35002) in original form, but with the addition of smoke deflectors and smokebox top cowl, shuffles away from Semley with an up express, circa 1949. *Rail Photoprints Collection*

'Merchant Navy' class Pacific No 21C3 ROYAL MAIL (BR 35003) in Southern malachite livery, was pictured with the southbound train named 'The Devon Belle' on the down slow line near to Clapham Junction. The 'Devon Belle' was an all Pullman summer's only train which ran between London Waterloo and Ilfracombe (also Plymouth until 1949). The first service ran on 20 June 1947 and the last on 19 September 1954; various styles of headboard were used (note also the smoke deflector wingplate nameboards). The headboard/wingplate styles seen date this image as circa 1947. *Mike Morant Collection*

'Merchant Navy' class Pacific No 35003 ROYAL MAIL in re-built form was the object of the photographer's attention for this typical Waterloo station scene; the other Bulleid locomotive is thought to be No 35028. *Mike Stokes Archive*

'Merchant Navy' class Pacific No 35003 ROYAL MAIL was captured again by the same photographer; this time the loco was seen on shed at Nine Elms (70A) on 5 March 1966. *Mike Stokes Archive*

Rebuilt 'Merchant Navy' class Pacific No 35003 ROYAL MAIL was seen leaving Sidmouth Junction with the up 'Atlantic Coast Express' (no headboard carried on this occasion) having just attached the Sidmouth and Exmouth coaches on 4 September 1962. The 'Atlantic Coast Express' was often referred to by enthusiasts simply as the 'ACE'; that service ran between Waterloo–Padstow/Ilfracombe/Bude and other similar destinations. The train first ran in July 1926 and after a break during the war years last ran 5 September 1964. Several styles of headboard were carried over the years. *Dave Cobbe/Rail Photoprints Collection*

Rebuilt 'Merchant Navy' class Pacific No 35004 CUNARD WHITE STAR was photographed at Seaton Junction with an up express in June 1961. *David Anderson*

Numbers	Names	Built	Completed	Re-built	Withdrawn
SR 21C5, BR 35005	CANADIAN PACIFIC	Eastleigh	01/1942	06/1959	08/1964 Preserved
SR 21C6, BR 35006	PENINSULAR & ORIENTAL S. N. CO.	Eastleigh	01/1942	10/1959	08/1964 Preserved
SR 21C7, BR 35007	ABERDEEN COMMONWEALTH	Eastleigh	06/1942	05/1958	07/1967
SR 21C8, BR 35008	ORIENT LINE	Eastleigh	06/1942	06/1957	07/1967
SR 21C9, BR 35009	SHAW SAVILL	Eastleigh	06/1942	03/1957	09/1964 Preserved
SR 21C10, BR 35010	BLUE STAR	Eastleigh	07/1942	01/1957	09/1966 Preserved

Disposal: 35007–8 J Buttigieg, Newport

Rebuilt 'Merchant Navy' class Pacific No 35007 ABERDEEN COMMONWEALTH was pictured whilst receiving attention at its home depot Weymouth (then 70G), during March 1966. The oblong box situated below the step on the buffer beam contains the battery for the Automatic Warning System (AWS) equipment, note also the electric lights. *Brian Robbins Rail/Photoprints Collection*

'Merchant Navy' class Pacific No 35008 ORIENT LINE is seen with the 'ACE' headboard. The loco was pictured lurking in the carriage sidings at Clapham Junction and would have brought the Atlantic Coast Express into Waterloo from Salisbury and then hauled another rake of empty stock to Clapham Junction via the washing plant, hence the appearance of a newly cleaned engine. Note that the tender is almost devoid of coal and No 35008 would thereafter move forwards to Nine Elms depot for servicing. *Mike Morant*

Rebuilt 'Merchant Navy' class Pacific No 35008 ORIENT LINE was caught by the camera whilst 'brewing up' at Waterloo before leaving with the 'Bournemouth Belle' Pullman service (no headboard carried on this occasion). The 'Bournemouth Belle' ran between London Waterloo and Bournemouth from July 1961 until July 1967, with a break during the war years. *Ian Turnbull/Rail Photoprints Collection*

Rebuilt 'Merchant Navy' class Pacific No 35008 ORIENT LINE seen in partial silhouette with Didcot depot (81E) to the right and whilst travelling at speed heading north on the 'East Avoiding Line' with the 'Pines Express' on a frosty 2 January 1965. The 'Pines Express' famously ran between Manchester and Bournemouth from May 1928 until 8 September 1962 via the Somerset & Dorset Joint Railway route. After the S&DJ was closed the train ran via Oxford and Southampton until 4 October 1965, and thereafter the service was extended to Poole, last running on 4 March 1967. *David Anderson*

'Merchant Navy' class Pacific No 35010 BLUE STAR in Southern malachite livery is pictured climbing westwards on Honiton bank. Note that the BR numbers had been applied but the tender is still lettered SOUTHERN, in this 1949 image. *Mike Morant Collection*

Rebuilt 'Merchant Navy' class Pacific No 35010 BLUE STAR bursts from under the road bridge when leaving Axminster with a stopping train from Exeter, in this 1964 image. *David Anderson*

Numbers	Names	Built	Completed	Re-built	Withdrawn
SR 21C11, BR 35011	GENERAL STEAM NAVIGATION	Eastleigh	12/1944	07/1959	02/1966 Preserved

Rebuilt 'Merchant Navy' class Pacific No 35012 UNITED STATES LINE (which was rebuilt by BR in March 1957) waits for the 'off' at London Waterloo station in April 1967.The Bullied Pacific designs specified cast steel BFB 'Boxpok' wheels with holes and recesses on their disks; they can clearly be seen in this image. *Keith Langston Collection*

Numbers	Names	Built	Completed	Re-built	Withdrawn
SR 21C12, BR 35012	UNITED STATES LINE	Eastleigh	01/1945	03/1957	04/1967
SR 21C13, BR 35013	BLUE FUNNEL* CERTUM PETE FINEM	Eastleigh	02/1945	06/1956	07/1967
SR 21C14, BR 35014	NEDERLAND LINE	Eastleigh	02/1945	07/1956	03/1967
SR 21C15, BR 35015	ROTTERDAM LLOYD	Eastleigh	03/1945	06/1958	02/1964
SR 21C16, BR 35016	ELDERS FYFFES	Eastleigh	03/1945	04/1957	08/1965
SR 21C17, BR 35017	BELGIAN MARINE	Eastleigh	04/1945	04/1957	07/1966
SR 21C18, BR 35018	BRITISH INDIA LINE	Eastleigh	05/1945	02/1956	08/1964 Preserved
SR 21C19, BR 35019	French Line CGT	Eastleigh	06/1945	05/1959	09/1965
SR 21C20, BR 35020	BIBBY LINE	Eastleigh	06/1945	04/1956	02/1965

* Loco 35013 formerly named Blue Funnel Line. Loco 35019 was the only BR steam locomotive which carried a name in both upper and lower case; the nameplate was made in the 'house style' of the shipping company

Disposal: 35012–35014–35019 John Cashmore, Newport, 35013–35017 J Buttigieg, Newport, 35015 Slag Reduction Co Ltd, Yorkshire, 35016 Birds (Swansea) Ltd, 35020 Eastleigh Works

Rebuilt 'Merchant Navy' class Pacific No 35012 UNITED STATES LINE was pictured whilst on Pullman duty at Vauxhall in June 1966. *Keith Langston Collection*

'Merchant Navy' class Pacific 21C13 BLUE FUNNEL LINE (later BLUE FUNNEL) making loads of black smoke; the loco was pictured heading the westbound 'Bournemouth Belle' circa 1947; the plume of smoke has all but obliterated the view of Clapham Junction signal box which was being passed. The 'Bournemouth Belle' carried three different styles of headboard and the one seen was the first, introduced at the beginning of October 1946; note also the extra-full tender. *Rail Photoprints Collection*

Rebuilt 'Merchant Navy' class Pacific 35013 BLUE FUNNEL was pictured at Waterloo station whilst waiting to depart with a train for Southampton and Bournemouth on 11 August 1959. *Keith Langston Collection*

'Merchant Navy' class Pacific No 35015 ROTTERDAM LLOYD in BR blue and complete with an old-style headboard pictured on the turntable at sub-shed Branksome (ex-S&DJ 71G located on the then Bournemouth triangle). 'The Bournemouth Belle' headboard is already in place prior to the pending up journey, August 1952. *Pursey C. Short/Colour Rail*

There is a little motion blur in this pre-BR image but nevertheless 'Merchant Navy' class Pacific No 21C16 ELDERS FYFFES makes a fine sight with the up 'Bournemouth Belle' service and was pictured passing Bournemouth (71B) shed on the way into the town's Central station. Note the square-style headboard. *Mike Morant Collection*

Rebuilt 'Merchant Navy' class Pacific No 35016 ELDERS FYFFES, in re-built form, was pictured at Exeter Central having just worked with an 'Atlantic Coast Express' working in 1959. The headboard style carried was introduced in 1953. *Mike Stokes Archive*

'Merchant Navy' class Pacific No 21C17 BELGIAN MARINE is pictured passing Esher with a down 'Bournemouth Belle' service; note the square headboard in this 1947 image. *Dave Cobbe Collection/C.R.L. Coles/Rail Photoprints Collection*

Bulleid Pacific BELGIAN MARINE is pictured as BR No 35017 and with a Stanier tender lettered BRITISH RAILWAYS. This picture was taken near to Acton Bridge on the WCML during the 1948 locomotive trials on 14 May; the Bulleid Pacific had charge of the sixteen-coach Perth–London Euston service. The reason for the tender change was to allow water to be picked up from troughs, as the SR engine tenders were not fitted with that facility. *Roy Whitfield/Rail Photoprints Collection*

Rebuilt 'Merchant Navy' class Pacific No 35017 BELGIAN MARINE is set to depart from London Waterloo station with a service for Portsmouth on 10 May 1966. *Keith Langston Collection*

Rebuilt 'Merchant Navy' class Pacific No 35018 BRITISH INDIA LINE was almost fresh from the works after rebuilding when pictured descending Honiton Bank in May 1956. *David Anderson*

Rebuilt 'Merchant Navy' class Pacific No 35018 BRITISH INDIA LINE was still in pristine condition when pictured at Exmouth Junction shed after arrival with the down 'ACE' working on 25 July 1956. Note that the loco is fitted with electric lights, but no AWS at that time. *David Anderson*

'Merchant Navy' class Pacific No 35019 French Line C.G.T. was the only BR steam locomotive which carried a name in both upper and lower case; the nameplate was made in the 'house style' of the shipping company. The loco was putting down quite a smoke screen when pictured at Harringay during the 1948 Locomotive Exchanges, on 17 May 1948. *Mike Morant Collection*

'Merchant Navy' class Pacific No 35019 French Line C.G.T. was making a little less smoke when pictured on Honiton Bank with an up 'ACE' working (headboard not carried on this occasion) in June 1955. *David Anderson*

Numbers	Names	Built	Completed	Re-built	Withdrawn
BR 35021	NEW ZEALAND LINE	Eastleigh	09/1948	06/1959	08/1965
BR 35022	HOLLAND AMERICA LINE	Eastleigh	10/1948	06/1956	05/1966 Preserved
BR 35023	HOLLAND AFRIKA LINE	Eastleigh	11/1948	02/1957	07/1967
BR 35024	EAST ASIATIC COMPANY	Eastleigh	11/1948	05/1959	01/1965
BR 35025	BROCKLEBANK LINE	Eastleigh	11/1948	12/1956	09/1964 Preserved
BR 35026	LAMPORT & HOLT LINE	Eastleigh	12/1948	01/1957	03/1967
BR 35027	PORT LINE	Eastleigh	12/1948	05/1957	07/1967 Preserved
BR 35028	CLAN LINE	Eastleigh	12/1948	11/1959	07/1967 Preserved

Disposal: 35021 Birds (Swansea) Ltd, 35023 J Buttigieg, Newport, 35024 C. Woodfield & Sons Newport, 35026 John Cashmore, Newport

Rebuilt 'Merchant Navy' class Pacific No 35022 HOLLAND AMERICA LINE pictured on shed at Nine Elms and in a very clean condition, on 6 March 1965. *Dave Cobbe/Rail Photoprints Collection*

The neat lines of rebuilt 'Merchant Navy' class Pacific No 35023 HOLLAND-AFRIKA LINE are clearly defined in this picture taken on the Didcot East Avoiding Line as the loco worked a Midlands–South West express in 1964. *David Anderson*

Rebuilt 'Merchant Navy' class Pacific No 35024 EAST ASIATIC COMPANY was pictured near to Basingstoke with a down 'Bournemouth Belle' express (headboard not carried on this occasion) in 1964. *David Anderson*

'Merchant Navy' class Pacific No 35025 BROCKLEBANK LINE attracts the attention of the footplate crew on Ivatt 2-6-2T No 41314 whilst leaving Exeter Central with the up 'Atlantic Coast Express', circa 1952. Note that the headboard carried is one of an original 1947 style. *Rail Photoprints Collection*

Rebuilt 'Merchant Navy' class Pacific No 35025 BROCKLEBANK LINE, in rebuilt form, was seen when passing a 1950s-style signal box at Wimbledon on 26 June 1964. *Keith Langston Collection*

Rebuilt 'Merchant Navy' class Pacific No 35026 LAMPORT & HOLT LINE pictured passing Vauxhall on 24 April 1966. *Keith Langston Collection*

'The Royal Wessex' train (Waterloo–Weymouth–Swanage–Bournemouth West) was named especially for the Festival of Britain in 1951 and comprised of brand new BR Mk1 coaching stock in Carmen and cream livery (last ran 8 July 1967). Rebuilt 'Merchant Navy' class loco No 35027 PORT LINE was pictured 'on shed' at Nine Elms on 14 August 1959, complete with headboard. *Keith Langston Collection*

Rebuilt 'Merchant Navy' class Pacific No 35027 PORT LINE had lost its front number plate (number chalked on smokebox door) when pictured west of Woking with a Waterloo–Bournemouth service, in April 1967. *Brian Robbins/Rail Photoprints Collection*

Ready for the off! Rebuilt 'Merchant Navy' class Pacific No 35028 CLAN LINE pictured at Waterloo with a Portsmouth service in May 1966. *Keith Langston Collection*

Rebuilt 'Merchant Navy' class Pacific No 35028 CLAN LINE again pictured departing Waterloo on the occasion of the last weekend of scheduled running over the Somerset & Dorset route, on 5 May 1966. The Locomotive Club of Great Britain, Somerset & Dorset Railtour utilised six locomotives on that memorable occasion. No 35028 Waterloo–Templecombe; thereafter locos No 41307 and No 41249 Templecombe–Highbridge–Glastonbury–Evercreech Junction; then for the next leg locos No 34006 and No 34057 Evercreech Junction–Bath Green Park–Bournemouth Central; and finally No 35028 Bournemouth Central–London Waterloo. *Keith Langston Collection*

Rebuilt 'Merchant Navy' class Pacific No 35029 ELLERMAN LINES was waiting for the off at Salisbury with a down 'ACE' working, when pictured in June 1963. *David Anderson*

Numbers	Names	Built	Completed	Re-built	Withdrawn
BR 35029	ELLERMAN LINES	Eastleigh	02/1949	09/1959	09/1966 Preserved
BR 35030	ELDER-DEMPSTER LINES	Eastleigh	04/1949	04/1958	07/1967
Disposal: 35030 J Buttigieg, Newport					

'Merchant Navy' class Pacific No 35030 ELDER-DEMPSTER LINES pictured at work on Honiton Bank with an up 'ACE' working in June 1955. *David Anderson*

Chapter 21

1943

London & North Eastern Railway 'A2/2' Class 4-6-2, designed by Thompson

Edward Thompson's Pacific locomotives were designed quite differently to those of Gresley and the collective 'A2' class comprised of forty engines divided into four very different sub-classes of 'Mixed Traffic' category locomotives. Thompson has credit for all four of those designs; however, his final fifteen engines were redesigned by his successor Peppercorn who, although retaining many of Thompson's original features made several notable changes.

Thompson 'A2/2' class Pacific No 60501 COCK O' THE NORTH climbs effortlessly past Little Ponton with an up express, circa 1950. Note the un-lipped chimney and small wing-type smoke deflectors. *Rail Photoprints Collection*

In common the sub-classes all had three cylinders with divided drive, the inside cylinder driving on the leading coupled axle whilst the outside cylinders drove on the second axle. The separate sets of Walschaerts gear replaced the previously troublesome Gresley 'Conjugated Gear'. The 'A2s' had a coupled wheelbase approximately one foot longer than the other Gresley Pacifics. When first introduced the locomotives had double chimneys without a lip, but later lipped chimneys were fitted.

To assist with eliminating any problems created by smoke drift the 'A2/2' class engines were also fitted with small wing-type smoke deflectors, positioned high up on the smokebox on either side of the chimney.

The first of Thompson's new Pacific design loco No 2005 THANE OF FIFE (BR 60505), appeared in February 1943, the other five followed in 1944; all were built at Doncaster Works.

Effectively those engines were rebuilds of Gresley's not overly successful 'P2' class three-cylinder 2-8-2 locomotives, which were built in streamlined form between 1934 and 1936 and intended for use on routes in the north of Scotland. Those engines had a rigid coupled wheelbase of 19-foot-6-inch-length, which in traffic had proved too long for the routes the 2-8-2 type were allocated to; accordingly, frame cracking became a problem.

In the rebuilt form the 'A2/2' class retained the original 'P2' boilers which were shortened in length by some 2 feet. The locomotives were at first allocated to Scotland to work services on the Edinburgh–Aberdeen route. At the end of 1949 the engines moved south of the border and were divided between York and New England motive power depots. History records that the 'A2/2' class engines were in the main disliked by engine crews due to their propensity to slip badly. The type was generally regarded as having been Thompson's least successful Pacifics, but it must be remembered that he built them from the flawed 'P2' class.

The withdrawal of the type started in 1959 when locos No 60503 and No 60505 ended their service lives, in the November of that year, with No 60501 following in February 1960. The three remaining members of the class were also withdrawn in 1961 and the last in service was No 60502, which was withdrawn in the July of that year.

LNER 4-6-2 'A2/2' class, BR numbers 60501–60506

Introduced: 1943

Rebuilt: From Gresley 'P2' class 2-8-2 locos

Power Classification: 7MT

Built: Doncaster Works, 6 locomotives

Designer: Edward Thompson

Company: London & North Eastern Railway

Driving Wheel: 6ft 2ins

Boiler Pressure: 225psi superheated

Cylinders: 3 – 20ins diameter x 26ins stroke

Tractive Effort @ 85%: 40,318lbf

Valve Gear: Walschaerts (piston valves)

Water Capacity: 5000 gallons

Coal Capacity: 9 tons

Numbers	Names	Built Lot/Wks Number	Completed	Withdrawn
LNER 2001, 990 and 501, BR 60501	COCK O' THE NORTH	Doncaster 1789	09/1944	02/1960
LNER 2002, 991 and 502, BR 60502	EARL MARISCHAL	Doncaster 1796	06/1944	07/1961
LNER 2003, 992 and 503, BR 60503	LORD PRESIDENT	Doncaster 1863	12/1944	11/1959
LNER 2004, 993 and 504, BR 60504	MONS MEG	Doncaster 1839	11/1944	01/1961
LNER 2005, 994 and 505, BR 60505	THANE OF FIFE	Doncaster 1840	01/1943	11/1959
LNER 2006, 995 and 506, BR 60506	WOLF OF BADENOCH	Doncaster 1842	05/1944	04/1961

Disposal: 60501/506 Doncaster Works

The Thompson 'A2/2' class engines were rebuilds of Gresley's 'P2' 2-8-2 locomotives which were at one time streamlined after the style of the LNER 'A4' class. 'P2' No 2002 EARL MARISCHAL is seen with the 'Night Scotsman' sleeping car train to Aberdeen at Stonehaven station. *Bill Rhind Brown*

Chapter 22

1944–1945

London & North Eastern Railway 'A2/1' Class 4-6-2, designed by Thompson

Four Thompson Pacifics appeared in 1946; they were also three-cylinder engines with divided drive (see also 'A2/2' chapter). The locos were built at Darlington Works during the period May 1944 to January 1945. These engine were originally ordered as 'V2' class 2-6-0 engines but were then redesigned as Pacifics, but incorporating a 'B1' pattern bogie, 19-inch cylinders and additionally were fitted with steam reversers. However the originally intended 'V2' boilers were retained.

As built they were coupled to 4200-gallon capacity six-wheel tenders, the first of which was replaced on loco No 3696 (BR No 60507) with the repaired eight-wheel tender which

Thompson 'A2/1' class Pacific No 60507 is pictured waiting to depart with a train for the north from London Kings Cross station, on 18 April 1949. *M.J. Reade/Colour Rail*

LNER 4-6-2 'A2/1' class, BR numbers 60507–60510

Introduced: 1946

Power Classification: 6MT

Built: Darlington Works, 4 locomotives

Designer: Edward Thompson

Company: London & North Eastern Railway

Driving Wheel: 6ft 2ins

Boiler Pressure: 225psi superheated

Cylinders: 3 – 19ins diameter x 26ins stroke

Tractive Effort @ 85%: 36,387lbf

Valve Gear: Walschaerts (piston valves)

Water Capacity: 5000 gallons

Coal Capacity: 9 tons

had been attached to the 'A4' No 4469 that was destroyed by wartime bombing. The other three engines all received similar tenders between that date and 1950.

The 'A2/1' firebox design incorporated a rocking grate and hopper-type ashpan, both features which markedly improved the disposal procedure.

Thompson introduced electric lighting on the 'A2/1' class by fitting a new design of axle-driven alternator, a system he also used on later locomotive designs.

As built the locos were fitted with wing-type smoke deflectors and also un-lipped double chimneys. However, after the 'A2/3' variant was introduced (1946) the 'A2/1' locos were fitted with similar large smoke deflectors on which their names were carried.

In traffic, allocation of the class was split between England and Scotland and the 'A2/1s' were generally rostered for working only express passenger and express goods trains.

British Railways withdrew all four of the class between August 1960 and February 1961; the last to be withdrawn was loco No 60507.

Liveries carried included wartime unlined black, LNER green and Brunswick green with orange and black lining.

Numbers	Names	Built Lot/Wks Number	Completed	Withdrawn
LNER 3696, 884 and 507, BR 60507	HIGHLAND CHIEFTAIN	Darlington 1930	05/1944	12/1960
LNER 3697,885 and 508, BR 60508	DUKE OF ROTHESAY	Darlington 1933	06/1944	02/1961
LNER 3698, 886 and 509, BR 60509	WAVERLEY	Darlington 1944	11/1944	08/1960
LNER 3699, 887 and 510, BR 60510	ROBERT THE BRUCE	Darlington 1950	01/1945	11/1960

Disposal: 60507/10 Doncaster Works

Thompson 'A2/1' class Pacific No 60509 WAVERLEY obviously impresses the father and his young family as the loco gets smartly away from Perth with a train for Edinburgh, in this 1958 image. Note that the loco has full smoke deflectors and lipped double chimney. *Keith Langston Collection*

Thompson 'A2/1' class Pacific No 60509 WAVERLEY pictured earlier in the loco's working life on shed at Gateshead (52A) in 1955; note the un-lipped chimney. The loco is carrying a headboard lettered 'The Queen of Scots'; that train was first introduced in May 1928 to run between London Kings Cross and Glasgow Queen Street via Leeds and Harrogate as a Pullman car service; the name was withdrawn on 1 September 1939. It was then reintroduced on 5 July 1948 and ran between Kings Cross and Edinburgh Waverley via Leeds, again as a Pullman service which last ran on 13 June 1964. *Rail Photoprints Collection*

Chapter 23

1945–1951

Southern Railway/British Railways 'Battle of Britain' and 'West Country' Class 4-6-2, designed by Bulleid

Following the introduction of the 'Merchant Navy' (MN) class, the Southern Railway decided to add to their stock of Pacific-type locomotives and accordingly instructed Bulleid to design a lighter version of the 'airsmoothed casing' 4-6-2s with a much wider route availability than the restricted 'MN' class locos.

Oliver Bulleid originally used a continental-style numbering system for all of his 'air-smoothed casing' Pacific locomotives. The system was an adaption of the International Union of Railways (UIC) system where '2' and '1' refer to the number of un-powered leading and trailing axles respectively, and 'C' refers to three driving axles. As an example, the first 'West Country' class locomotive was numbered 21C101 (BR 34001). British Railway discontinued the system and took the last two numerals after the 'C1' prefix and incorporated them as the

The first Bulleid Light Pacific No 21C101 (BR 34001) leaves Semley with an up London & South Western Railway route service, circa 1948. *Rail Photoprints Collection*

last numerals of a 34000 series of numbers (e.g. UIC number 21C120 became BR 34020). The BR Bulleid light Pacific engines (34071–34110) never carried UIC system numbers. Immediately after railway nationalisation in 1948 the Bulleid numbering system was for a short period retained on the first seventy (ex SR) light Pacifics, but with the addition of a smaller font size 's' prefix, e.g. s21C101.

The weight in original form of the MN engines (loco only) was 94 tons 15cwts whilst the new 'WC' and 'BB' engines weighed only 86 tons (rebuilt 'MN' 97 ton 18cwt, rebuilt 'WC & BB' 90 ton 1cwt).

The new type became known by two class names, which were, respectively, 'West Country' (WC) and 'Battle of Britain' (BB). However the new 'WC' and 'BB' locomotives, which incorporated most of the features of the 'MN' class engines, were in all respects identical to each other.

In common with the 'MN' class the light Pacifics had problems with the enclosed valve gear and associated oil baths, which on occasions leaked and caused fires; oil seepages also proliferated instances of driving wheels slipping as trains were accelerated away from stops.

In 1957 British Railways commenced a rebuilding programmed during which, as with the 'MN' class, the oil baths were removed, conventional valve gear was fitted and the air-smoothed casings were discarded; however, rebuilding was only carried out on sixty of the light Pacific engines. In the rebuilt form the light Pacifics were hailed as good-looking reliable engines which were equally appreciated by management and footplate crews.

Southern Railway-built locomotives No 21C101 (34001) to 21C170 (34070) were constructed with 8-foot-6-inch-wide driving cabs, whilst BR-built locomotives No 34071 to 34110 were constructed with 9-foot-wide driving cabs.

This charming image taken at Winchester station on 1 June 1967 shows re-built Bulleid Light Pacific No 34008 PADSTOW just a couple of weeks before the engine was withdrawn; note that the nameplate had already been removed. The 'Boxpok/Firth-Brown' cast driving wheels are attracting the attention of the youthful photographer whilst the two youngsters talking to the footplate crew is reminiscent of an age when the 'celebrity cult' did not rule supreme. In that era boy's heroes were likely to be well-known sportsmen or indeed engine drivers! *Mike Stokes Archive*

The first batch of locomotives to be outshopped from Brighton Works were named after West Country holiday resorts, hence the name 'West Country' class. 'WC' class loco numbers allocated were 21C101 (34001) to 21C148 (34048) and 34091 to 34108, with numbers 21C149 (34049) to 34090 and 34109–34110 being allocated to 'BB' class engines.

The names with a reference to the Battle of Britain, as applied to later built locomotives of the same type, are significantly important in that they commemorate a dark time in Britain's history, when against enormous odds the country fought for her very existence. Indeed if the heroic acts of 'The Few' had failed during the summer of 1940 you would certainly be reading a very different history of those events. No doubt Winston Churchill (loco No 21C151/34051 carried his name) would have been branded a war criminal, and furthermore this book may well have been written in a different language! It is no exaggeration to say that in September 1940 the British nation hovered on the very brink of extinction! The origins of the names selected for the 'Battle of Britain' class engines help to tell the story of that historically important time.

Sadly one un-rebuilt member of the 'BB' class, loco No 34066 SPITFIRE, was involved in the disastrous 'Lewisham Rail Crash' which occurred on 4 December 1957 (just outside St. Johns station); 90 people lost their lives and 173 were injured. The train hauled by No 34066 reportedly passed two yellow caution signals in foggy conditions, and as a result crashed into the back of a stationary train. Restricted visibility from the footplate of the un-rebuilt members of the class was judged to be a factor and thereafter all of the light Pacifics were over time fitted with Automatic Warning System (AWS) equipment. No 34066 was later repaired and put back into service.

Withdrawal of the Bulleid light Pacific classes started in 1963 and by the end of 1964 only seventy examples were listed as serviceable. That total was reduced to fifty-four by the end of 1965 and further reduced to thirty-six engines by the end of 1966. None of the class survived in service beyond July 1967.

Livery styles varied greatly over the life of the class and the colours used included Southern Railway malachite green with sunshine yellow horizontal lining, BR malachite green, and BR Brunswick green with orange and black lining.

SR/BR 4-6-2 'Battle of Britain' & 'West Country' class, BR numbers 34001–34110

Introduced: 1945–51

Rebuilt: 1957 onwards 60 locos

Power Classification: 7MT (reclassified 7P5F in 1953 and 7P6F in 1961)

Built: Brighton Works, 110 locomotives (BR 40 1948/51)

Designer: Oliver Bulleid

Company: Southern Railway/British Railways

Driving Wheel: 6ft 2ins 'Boxpok' pattern

Boiler Pressure: 280psi superheated, later reduced to 250psi superheated

Cylinders: 3 – 16⅜ins diameter x 24ins stroke

Tractive Effort @ 85%: 31,050lbf, later reduced to 27,715lbf

Valve Gear: Bulleid (piston valves) as rebuilt Walschaerts (piston valves)

Water Capacity: 4500/5000//5250/5500 gallons according to size of tender

Coal Capacity: 5 tons

Numbers		Names	Built	Completed	Re-built	Withdrawn
SR 21C101, BR 34001	WC	EXETER	Brighton	06/1945	11/1957	07/1967
SR 21C102, BR 34002	WC	SALISBURY	Brighton	06/1945		04/1967
SR 21C103, BR 34003	WC	PLYMOUTH	Brighton	06/1945	09/1957	09/1964
SR 21C104, BR 34004	WC	YEOVIL	Brighton	06/1945	02/1958	07/1967
SR 21C105, BR 34005	WC	BARNSTAPLE	Brighton	07/1945	06/1957	10/1966
SR 21C106, BR 34006	WC	BUDE	Brighton	08/1945		03/1967
SR 21C107, BR 34007	WC	WADEBRIDGE	Brighton	09/1945		10/1965 Preserved
SR 21C108, BR 34008	WC	PADSTOW	Brighton	09/1945	06/1960	06/1967
SR 21C109, BR 34009	WC	LYME REGIS	Brighton	09/1945	01/1961	10/1966
SR 21C110, BR 34010	WC	SIDMOUTH	Brighton	09/1945	02/1959	03/1965 Preserved
SR 21C111, BR 34011	WC	TAVISTOCK	Brighton	10/1945		11/1963
SR 21C112, BR 34012	WC	LAUNCESTON	Brighton	10/1945	01/1958	12/1966
SR 21C113, BR 34013	WC	OKEHAMPTON	Brighton	10/1945	10/1957	07/1967
SR 21C114, BR 34014	WC	BUDLEIGH SALTERTON	Brighton	11/1945	03/1958	03/1965
SR 21C115, BR 34015	WC	EXMOUTH	Brighton	11/1945		04/1967
SR 21C116, BR 34016	WC	BODMIN	Brighton	11/1945	04/1958	06/1964 Preserved
SR 21C117, BR 34017	WC	ILFRACOMBE	Brighton	12/1945	11/1957	10/1966
SR 21C118, BR 34018	WC	AXMINSTER	Brighton	12/1945	09/1958	07/1967
SR 21C119, BR 34019	WC	BIDEFORD	Brighton	12/1945*		03/1967
SR 21C120, BR 34020	WC	SEATON	Brighton	12/1945		09/1964

* Loco No 21C119 was temporarily converted to 'oil burning' in 1947
Disposal: 34001/2–34006–34012/13–34015–34018/19 John Cashmore, Newport, 34003 Woods Queenborough, Kent, 34005–34008/9–34017 J Buttigieg, Newport, 34011 Eastleigh Works, 34014 Birds, Bridgend, 34020 Birds, Morriston

Bulleid 'West Country' class light Pacific No 34002 SALISBURY was pictured with an up train at Southampton Central in October 1965. *Keith Langston Collection*

Bulleid 'West Country' class light Pacific No 34005 BARNSTAPLE took part in the 1948 Locomotive Exchange Trials; the engine was pictured arriving into London St Pancras station. Note the LMS tender attached to the SR 4-6-2 during the trials. The SR routes did not have water troughs; therefore a change of tender was necessary whilst working on other regions and on routes that required water to be taken whilst on the move. *Colour Rail*

Bulleid 'West Country' class light Pacific No 34006 BUDE waits to get away from London Waterloo station with a train for Dorset. Note the battery for the AWS equipment mounted under the smokebox step on the buffer beam. The future in the shape of 'Warship' class diesel hydraulic loco No D817 FOXHOUND stands at the adjacent platform. The 'Spam Can' had already lost its nameplate, February 1967. *Keith Langston Collection*

Bulleid Light Pacific SR BR No 34007 WADEBRIDGE is seen at Raynes Park with a down Bournemouth West working on 12 April 1963. *Mike Morant Collection*

Rebuilt Bulleid 'West Country' class light Pacific No 34013 OKEHAMPTON was pictured with an up train at Southampton Central in November 1965. *Keith Langston Collection*

Bulleid 'West Country' class light Pacific No 34015 EXMOUTH pictured in the carriage sidings between Exeter (St David) and Exeter (Central) in July 1956. *David Anderson*

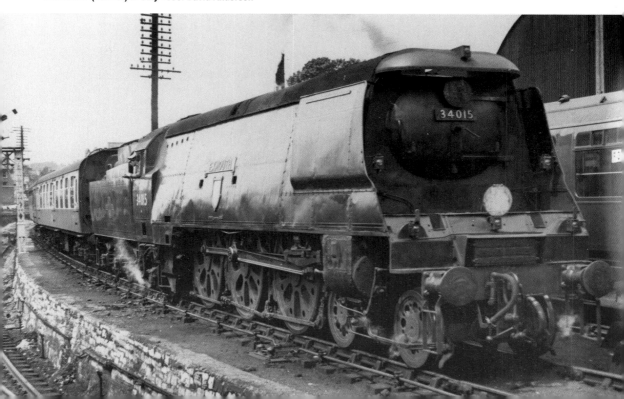

Bulleid 'West Country' class light Pacific No 34019 BIDEFORD was pictured on the depot at Bournemouth (then 71B) in 1957. *Colour Rail*

Bulleid 'West Country' class light Pacific No 34019 BIDEFORD was a light engine on a through road at Bournemouth station in September 1963. Note the attractive town crest under the nameplate and despite the extensive fitting of electric loco lighting the station still had a large stock of traditional lamps a selection of which can be seen beside the telephone kiosk. *Colour Rail*

Bulleid Light Pacific SR No 21C19 BIDEFORD in Southern livery, pictured at Exmouth Junction (72A), became BR No 34019. This loco together with class mate No 34036 was temporarily converted to oil burning in 1947 and then reconverted to coal burning. *Mike Stokes Archive*

Bulleid 'West Country' class light Pacific No 34020 SEATON was pictured sporting 'Malachite' livery and the full BRITISH RAILWAYS legend on the tender as the loco skirted the River Teign with a rake of Great Western Railway (GWR) stock, circa 1948. Of interest is the fact that this period image was painstakingly lifted from a glass negative which had been broken into several pieces, remarkable! *Mike Morant Collection*

Numbers		Names	Built	Completed	Re-built	Withdrawn
SR 21C121, BR 34021	WC	DARTMOOR	Brighton	01/1946	12/1957	07/1967
SR 21C122, BR 34022	WC	EXMOOR	Brighton	02/1946	12/1957	04/1965
SR 21C123, BR 34023	WC	BLACKMOOR VALE BLACKMORE VALE	Brighton	02/1946		07/1967 Preserved
SR 21C124, BR 34024	WC	TAMAR VALLEY	Brighton	02/1946	02/1961	07/1967
SR 21C125, BR 34025	WC	WHIMPLE*	Brighton	03/1946	10/1957	07/1967
SR 21C126, BR 34026	WC	YES TOR	Brighton	04/1946	03/1958	09/1966
SR 21C127, BR 34027	WC	TAW VALLEY	Brighton	04/1946	09/1957	08/1964 Preserved
SR 21C128, BR 34028	WC	EDDYSTONE	Brighton	05/1946	08/1958	05/1964 Preserved
SR 21C129, BR 34029	WC	LUNDY	Brighton	05/1946	12/1958	09/1964
SR 21C130, BR 34030	WC	WATERSMEET	Brighton	05/1946		09/1964
SR 21C131, BR 34031	WC	TORRINGTON	Brighton	06/1946	12/1958	02/1965
SR 21C132, BR 34032	WC	CAMELFORD	Brighton	06/1946	10/1960	10/1966
SR 21C133, BR 34033	WC	CHARD	Brighton	07/1946		12/1965
SR 21C134, BR 34034	WC	HONITON	Brighton	07/1946	08/1960	07/1967
SR 21C135, BR 34035	WC	SHAFTESBURY	Brighton	07/1946		06/1963
SR 21C136, BR 34036	WC	WESTWARD HO	Brighton	07/1946*	08/1960	07/1967
SR 21C137, BR 34037	WC	CLOVELLY	Brighton	08/1946	03/1958	07/1967
SR 21C138, BR 34038	WC	LYNTON	Brighton	09/1946		06/1966
SR 21C139, BR 34039	WC	BOSCASTLE	Brighton	09/1946	01/1959	05/1965 Preserved
SR 21C140, BR 34040	WC	CREWKERNE	Brighton	09/1946	10/1960	07/1967

* Loco No 21C136 was temporarily converted to 'oil burning' in 1947. Loco No 34025 also carried the name ROUGH TOR for a few days in 1948.
Disposal: 34021–34024/25–34031–34036/38–34040 John Cashmore, Newport, 34022 Woodfields, Newport, 34026–34032/34 J Buttigieg, Newport, 34029 Woods Queenborough, Kent, 34030 Birds, Morriston, 34035 Eastleigh Works

Re-built Bulleid 'West Country' class light Pacific No 34021 DARTMOOR was pictured hurrying through Ashford station (now the haunt of Eurostars) with an up 'Man of Kent' working (although no headboard was carried on this occasion) in May 1958. First run on 8 June 1953 'The Man of Kent' express operated between London Charing Cross and Margate. The last titled running of the service was on 10 June 1961. *D.C. Ovenden/Colour Rail*

During the weekend of 3 and 4 June 1967 the 'A4 Locomotive Society' chartered two rail tours utilising their Gresley 'A4' class Pacific No 4498 SIR NIGEL GRESLEY. Both tours started and ended at London Waterloo with the first on Saturday in fine weather, journeying to Bournemouth via Salisbury. The Sunday tour, in inclement weather, went directly to Weymouth entirely with No 4498 in charge. The Saturday outing wasn't entirely with No 4498 as part of the trip was hauled by Bulleid light Pacific class No 34023 BLACKMORE VALE. Here we have the opportunity to see these two dissimilar variations on air-smoothed casing in the same shot taken at Bournemouth depot (then 70F). *Mike Morant Collection*

Bulleid 'West Country' class light Pacific No 34023 BLACKMORE VALE was pictured whilst making a spirited departure from Winchfield in Hampshire with an up semi-fast train in this undated image. This locomotive carried its name in two different spellings; from 1946 until 1948 it was lettered as BLACKMOOR VALE and thereafter as detailed above. Note that, post SR, Southern smokebox door roundels were removed. The permanent way work in this view is evidence of early-stage electrification work taking place. *Mike Morant Collection*

Re-built Bulleid 'West Country' class light Pacific No 34025 WHIMPLE was pictured passing Micheldever with a Waterloo–Bournemouth service on 2 July 1967, just weeks before the loco was withdrawn. This view lends a whole new meaning to the phrase 'please mind the gap between the train and platform'! *David Rostance/Rail Photoprints Collection*

Re-built Bulleid 'West Country' class light Pacific No 34028 EDDYSTONE was observed by a young enthusiast and his senior companion whilst pictured running light engine southbound through Midford station (on the long lamented Somerset & Dorset Joint Railway route) in July 1971. Note the BR poster announcing new increased fares, seems it was forever thus! *Malcolm Thompson/Colour Rail*

Re-built Bulleid 'West Country' class light Pacific No 34030 WATERSMEET (minus nameplate) was pictured drifting through Vauxhall in this August 1964 image, just a month before being withdrawn. *Keith Langston Collection*

Once again we see a re-built Bulleid light Pacific departing London Waterloo station, again with a view of the immediate future alongside! No 34034 HONITON was pictured with 'Warship' class No D831 MONARCH. *Keith Langston Collection*

Re-built Bulleid 'West Country' class light Pacific No 34037 CLOVELLY was pictured on shed at Eastleigh (then 71A) in July 1967. *Rail Photoprints Collection*

Bulleid 'West Country' class light Pacific No 34038 LYNTON illustrates well the Bulleid 'oil bath' Pacific propensity to driving wheel slip (often due to oil seepage) as the loco gets into a dramatic wheel spin whilst departing from Waterloo station. *Keith Langston Collection*

Numbers			Names	Built	Completed	Re-built	Withdrawn
SR 21C141, BR 34041	WC		WILTON	Brighton	09/1946		01/1966
SR 21C142, BR 34042	WC		DORCHESTER	Brighton	10/1946	01/1959	10/1965
SR 21C143, BR 34043	WC		COMBE MARTIN	Brighton	10/1946		06/1963
SR 21C144, BR 34044	WC		WOOLACOMBE	Brighton	10/1946	05/1960	05/1967
SR 21C145, BR 34045	WC		OTTERY ST MARY	Brighton	10/1946	10/1958	06/1964
SR 21C146, BR 34046	WC		BRAUNTON	Brighton	11/1946	02/1959	10/1965 Preserved
SR 21C147, BR 34047	WC		CALLINGTON	Brighton	11/1946	11/1958	06/1967
SR 21C148, BR 34048	WC		CREDITON	Brighton	11/1946	03/1959	03/1966

Disposal: 34041–34044–34048 John Cashmore, Newport, 34042–34047 J Buttigieg, Newport, 34043 Eastleigh Works, 34045 Woodham Bros, Barry

Bulleid 'West Country' class light Pacific No 34044 WOOLACOMBE sporting malachite livery and the full BRITISH RAILWAYS legend on the tender pounds up the south side of Honiton bank in July 1949. *Mike Morant Collection*

Bulleid 'West Country' class light Pacific No 34048 CREDITON was pictured in ex-works condition, at Salisbury depot (72B) circa 1949. *John Day Collection/Rail Photoprints Collection*

Numbers		Names	Built	Completed	Re-built	Withdrawn
SR 21C149, BR 34049	BB	ANTI-AIRCRAFT COMMAND	Brighton	12/1946		11/1963
SR 21C150, BR 34050	BB	ROYAL OBSERVER CORPS	Brighton	12/1946	08/1958	08/1965
SR 21C151, BR 34051	BB	WINSTON CHURCHILL	Brighton	12/1946		09/1965 Preserved
SR 21C152, BR 34052	BB	LORD DOWDING	Brighton	12/1946	09/1958	07/1967
SR 21C153, BR 34053	BB	SIR KEITH PARK	Brighton	01/1947	11/1958	10/1965 Preserved
SR 21C154, BR 34054	BB	LORD BEAVERBROOK	Brighton	01/1947		09/1964
SR 21C155, BR 34055	BB	FIGHTER PILOT	Brighton	02/1947		06/1963
SR 21C156, BR 34056	BB	CROYDON	Brighton	02/1947	12/1960	05/1967
SR 21C157, BR 34057	BB	BIGGIN HILL	Brighton	03/1947		05/1967
SR 21C158, BR 34058	BB	SIR FREDERICK PILE	Brighton	04/1947	11/1960	10/1964 Preserved
SR 21C159, BR 34059	BB	SIR ARCHIBALD SINCLAIR	Brighton	04/1947	03/1960	05/1966 Preserved
SR 21C160, BR 34060	BB	25 SQUADRON	Brighton	04/1947	11/1960	07/1967
SR 21C161, BR 34061	BB	73 SQUADRON	Brighton	04/1947		08/1964
SR 21C162, BR 34062	BB	17 SQUADRON	Brighton	05/1947	04/1959	06/1964
SR 21C163, BR 34063	BB	229 SQUADRON	Brighton	05/1947		08/1965
SR 21C164, BR 34064	BB	FIGHTER COMMAND	Brighton	07/1947*		05/1966
SR 21C165, BR 34065	BB	HURRICANE	Brighton	07/1947		04/1964
SR 21C166, BR 34066	BB	SPITFIRE	Brighton	09/1947		09/1966
SR 21C167, BR 34067	BB	TANGMERE	Brighton	09/1947		11/1963 Preserved
SR 21C168 BR 34068	BB	KENLEY	Brighton	10/1947		12/1963

* Loco No 34064 was fitted with a 'Giesl' ejector and chimney in 1962
Disposal: 34049–34055–34068 Eastleigh Works, 34050–34065 Birds, Morriston, 34052–34056/57–34060 John Cashmore, Newport, 34054 Birds, Bynea, 34061 Woods Queenborough, Kent, 34062/64 Birds, Bridgend, 34066 J Buttigieg, Newport

Bulleid 'Battle of Britain' class light Pacific No s21C149 (34049) ANTI-AIRCRAFT COMMAND was pictured at Exmouth Junction depot (72A). Note that the cabside number has the additional s prefix and that the tender is lettered BRITISH RAILWAYS but the loco still carries the SR smokebox door roundel, all factors which combine to make this a rare image, and date it as being taken between 13 March 1948 and 18 February 1949. Immediately after railway nationalisation in 1948 the Bulleid numbering system was for a short period retained on the first 70 (ex-SR) light Pacifics, but with the addition of a smaller font size 's' prefix e.g. s21C149. *Mike Morant Collection*

Re-built Bulleid 'Battle of Britain' class light Pacific No 34050 ROYAL OBSERVER CORPS was pictured departing Basingstoke in this May 1963 image. Note additional plaques were presented and fitted below the cabside number. *David Anderson*

Bulleid 'Battle of Britain' class light Pacific No 34051 WINSTON CHURCHILL completes an idyllic railway scene whilst starting a semi-fast service from Axminster station; note the water column beside the signal box and the handcart on the opposite platform, circa 1955. *David Anderson*

London Waterloo station is again the setting for this 1955 image of Bulleid 'Battle of Britain' class light Pacific No 34054 LORD BEAVERBROOK. *David Anderson*

Re-built Bulleid 'Battle of Britain' class light Pacific No 34058 SIR FREDERICK PILE was pictured passing Vauxhall with a down train in this summer 1964 image; note that the nameplate has been removed but its backing plate remained in place. *Mike Stokes Archive*

Bulleid 'Battle of Britain' class light Pacific No 34060 25 SQUADRON seen on shed at Bournemouth (then 71B). *Colour Rail*

Two 'Battle of Britain' light Pacifics were pictured on shed at Exmouth Junction (72A) in June 1955. They are No 34061 73 SQUADRON and No 34060 25 SQUADRON. *David Anderson*

'Battle of Britain' light Pacific No 34067 TANGMERE was pictured at Woodham Bros scrap yard, Barry, prior to being rescued. *Keith Langston Collection*

Numbers		Names	Built	Completed	Re-built	Withdrawn
SR 21C169, BR 34069	BB	HAWKINGE	Brighton	10/1947	05/1964	11/1963
SR 21C170, BR 34070	BB	MANSTON	Brighton	10/1947		08/1964 Preserved
BR 34071	BB	601 SQUADRON*	Brighton	04/1948	05/1960	09/1967
BR 34072	BB	257 SQUADRON	Brighton	04/1948		10/1964 Preserved
BR 34073	BB	249 SQUADRON	Brighton	05/1948		06/1964 Preserved
BR 34074	BB	46 SQUADRON	Brighton	05/1948		06/1964
BR 34075	BB	264 SQUADRON	Brighton	06/1948		06/1966
BR 34076	BB	41 SQUADRON	Brighton	07/1948		01/1966
BR 34077	BB	603 SQUADRON	Brighton	07/1948	07/1960	03/1967
BR 34078	BB	222 SQUADRON	Brighton	071948		09/1964
BR 34079	BB	141 SQUADRON	Brighton	08/1948		02/1966
BR 34080	BB	74 SQUADRON	Brighton	08/1948		09/1964
BR 34081	BB	92 SQUADRON	Brighton	09/1948		08/1964 Preserved
BR 34082	BB	615 SQUADRON	Brighton	09/1948	04/1960	04/1966
BR 34083	BB	605 SQUADRON	Brighton	10/1948		07/1964
BR 34084	BB	253 SQADRON	Brighton	11/1948		10/1965
BR 34085	BB	501 SQUADRON	Brighton	11/1948	06/1960	09/1965
BR 34086	BB	219 SQUADRON	Brighton	12/1948		06/1966
BR 34087	BB	145 SQUADRON	Brighton	12/1948	12/1960	07/1967
BR 34088	BB	213 SQUADRON	Brighton	12/1948	04/1960	03/1967
BR 34089	BB	602 SQUADRON	Brighton	12/1948	11/1960	07/1967
BR 34090	BB	SIR EUSTACE MISSENDEN SOUTHERN RAILWAY	Brighton	01/1949	08/1960	07/1967

* Loco No 34071 also carried the name 615 SQUADRON for a short while in 1948.
Disposal: 34069–34074 Eastleigh Works, 34071–34076/77–34079–34082–34087/90 John Cashmore, Newport, 34075–34083 Birds, Bridgend, 34078–34080 Birds, Morriston, 34084/86 J Buttigieg, Newport#

London Victoria station was the location for this September 1964 picture of 'Battle of Britain' light Pacific No 34074 46 SQUADRON. *L. Rowe/Colour Rail*

'Battle of Britain' light Pacific No 34076 41 SQUADRON was pictured coming off shed at Bournemouth (71B) in this 1958 image. *Keith Langston Collection*

One of the Southern Railway's most important London depots was Nine Elms (70A). Re-built 'Battle of Britain' light Pacific No 34077 603 SQUADRON was pictured on the turntable there in June 1966. *Keith Langston Collection*

Bulleid 'Battle of Britain' class light Pacific No 34078 222 SQUADRON was pictured at Padstow after arriving with the 11.00 am 'Atlantic Coast Express' from Waterloo, on 2 July 1964. *Dave Cobbe/Rail Photoprints Collection*

Bulleid 'Battle of Britain' class light Pacific No 34080 74 SQUADRON was pictured when about to enter Honiton Tunnel with an up fitted freight train during July 1963. Note that the engine had recently caught fire due to oil bath leakage, the tell tale sign being the lighter in colour central casing panel, which had been recently fitted but not yet painted in the correct colour. *David Anderson*

Re-built Bulleid 'Battle of Britain' class light Pacific No 34085 501 SQUADRON was pictured whilst departing from Oxford station with a southbound 'Pines Express' working, in the summer of 1965. *David Anderson*

Bulleid 'Battle of Britain' class light Pacific No 34086 219 SQUADRON was pictured whilst exiting the western portal of Honiton Tunnel with a London Waterloo–Exeter–Plymouth express service on 26 July 1956, which the photographer recorded was a very hot summers day, with the midday temperature reaching 85 degrees Fahrenheit in the shade! *David Anderson*

The glorious New Forest region of Hampshire was the setting for this image of re-built Bulleid 'Battle of Britain' class light Pacific No 34089 602 SQUADRON. The location is recorded as being between Beaulieu Road and Lyndhurst Road, the train was the 13.30 Waterloo–Weymouth, on 28 March 1967. *David Rostance/Rail Photoprints Collection*

This atmospheric image is a real blast from the past, in more ways than one. Rebuilt 'Battle of Britain' class light Pacific No 34090 SIR EUSTACE MISSENDEN SOUTHERN RAILWAY waits at Eastleigh in 1967; note that the loco's nameplate had by that time been removed. Of great interest, given the events concerning High Street store chains etc. during the first decade of this century, is the fact that the 'wooden boats' of fruit which have been unloaded onto the platform truck carry the message 'More top grade Dutch tomatoes for FW Woolworth & Co'. Perchance the tomatoes were destined for 'Woolies' Eastleigh shop. Note the floral buttonhole worn by the train guard and the very 60s hairstyle favoured by the young loader! *Keith Langston Collection*

The so-called 'Iron Curtain' had been lifted a little at the time when this picture was taken. The special Pullman train hauled by Bulleid 'West Country' class light Pacific No 34092 CITY OF WELLS was pictured passing Fratton with Messrs Bulganin and Krushchev on board; the date was April 1956. After his state visit the Russian Premier reportedly remarked 'You don't like Communism. We do not like capitalism. There is only one way out – peaceful co-existence.' *Pursey C. Short/Colour Rail*

Numbers		Names	Built	Completed	Re-built	Withdrawn
BR 34091	WC	WEYMOUTH	Brighton	09/1949		09/1964
BR 34092	WC	WELLS CITY OF WELLS from March 1950	Brighton	09/1949		11/1964 Preserved
BR 34093	WC	SAUNTON	Brighton	10/1949		07/1967
BR 34094	WC	MORTEHOE	Brighton	10/1949		08/1964
BR 34095	WC	BRENTOR	Brighton	10/1949	01/1961	07/1967
BR 34096	WC	TREVONE	Brighton	11/1949	04/1961	09/1964
BR 34097	WC	HOLSWORTHY	Brighton	11/1949	03/1961	04/1966
BR 34098	WC	TEMPLECOMBE	Brighton	12/1949	02/1961	06/1967
BR 34099	WC	LYNMOUTH	Brighton	12/1949		11/1964
BR 34100	WC	APPLEDORE	Brighton	12/1949	09/1960	07/1967
BR 34101	WC	HARTLAND	Brighton	02/1950	09/1960	07/1966 Preserved
BR 34102	WC	LAPFORD	Brighton	03/1950		07/1967
BR 34103	WC	CALSTOCK	Brighton	02/1950		09/1965
BR 34104	WC	BERE ALSTON	Brighton	04/1950	05/1961	06/1967
BR 34105	WC	SWANAGE	Brighton	03/1950		10/1964 Preserved
BR 34106	WC	LYDFORD	Brighton	03/1950		09/1964
BR 34107	WC	BLANDFORD became BLANDFORD FORUM 10/1952	Brighton	04/1950		09/1964
BR 34108	WC	WINCANTON	Brighton	04/1950	04/1961	06/1967

Disposal: 34091 Woods Queenborough, Kent, 34093–34095–34097–34100 John Cashmore, Newport, 34094 Woodham Bros, Barry, 34096 Birds, Bynea, 34098–34102/104–34108 J Buttigieg Newport, 34099–34106/107–Birds Morriston

Bulleid 'West Country' class light Pacific No 34092 CITY OF WELLS is seen again, this time with a 'Motorail' train and the 'Spam can', was piloting a BR Standard 'Class 5' when pictured passing Seaton Junction in 1958. British Railways operated Motorail services from 1955 and some of those services continued into the post privatisation era. Passengers in Scotland, the North of England and the Midlands would drive their cars onto the custom-built carriers, travel in the coaches at the front of the train and on arrival would then de-train their vehicles, for use during their holidays. *David Anderson*

Re-built Bulleid 'West Country' class light Pacific No 34100 APPLEDORE departs from Dover Marine station with the final steam-hauled 'Golden Arrow', on 11 June 1961. The 'Golden Arrow' Pullman train first ran between London Victoria station and Dover Marine (for Calais Maritime and Paris Nord) on 15 May 1929 and after a break during wartime was re-introduced as a public service on 15 April 1946. The last run of this famous boat train took place 30 September 1972 (modern traction 'Class 71' electric loco hauled). *Mike Morant Collection*

Bulleid 'West Country' class light Pacific No 34102 LAPFORD has just been 'coaled' for the last time at Nine Elms motive power depot (70A) and would later that afternoon make her final journey from Waterloo. *Mike Morant Collection*

The nameplate of re-built 'West Country' light Pacific No 34104. *Keith Langston Collection*

Bulleid 'West Country' light Pacific No 34105 SWANAGE was pictured on shed at Oxford (81F) having worked in with a 'Pines Express' train, July 1961. *David Anderson*

Bulleid 'West Country' light Pacific No 34107 BLANDFORD FORUM (carried the name BLANFORD until October 1952) in ex-works condition simply gleamed in the bright sunshine when this picture was taken at Weymouth depot (then still 71G) in July 1963. *C.L. Caddy/Colour Rail*

Numbers		Names	Built	Completed	Re-built	Withdrawn
BR 34109	BB	SIR TRAFFORD LEIGH-MALLORY	Brighton	05/1950	03/1961	09/1964
BR 34110	BB	66 SQUADRON	Brighton	01/1951		11/1963
Disposal: 34109 Birds, Morriston, 34110 Eastleigh Works						

Re-built Bullied 'Battle of Britain' class light Pacific No 34109 SIR TRAFFORD LEIGH-MALLORY was pictured whilst calling at Seaton Junction station in 1963. *David Anderson*

Re-built Bulled 'Battle of Britain' class light Pacific No 34077 603 SQUADRON waits to get away from London Waterloo station, note the way that the nameplates were mounted on the rebuilt members of the class. This image dates from the loco's last few months in service, January 1967. *Keith Langston Collection*

Bullied 'Battle of Britain' class light Pacific No 34057 BIGGIN HILL had virtually come to the end of its working life when this picture was taken of the loco at Nine Elms depot (70A) in April 1967. Note that the smokebox number plate had been removed and replaced by a stencilled version and also the nameplate had been removed. *Keith Langston Collection*

Chapter 24

1945

London & North Eastern Railway 'A1/1' Class 4-6-2, modified by Thompson from the Original Gresley design

Edward Thompson introduced a prototype locomotive in September 1945 which was later classified 'A1/1' class and ran with BR number 60113; it was named GREAT NORTHERN. The Thompson prototype was a rebuild of Gresley's Doncaster-built prototype pacific 4470, also named GREAT NORTHERN, and first introduced in 1922.

The rebuilt three-cylinder locomotive was given an 'A4' class boiler, double blastpipe and chimney and had the wheelbase extended to 38 feet 5 inches. The cylinders were driven by three sets of Walschaerts gear (piston valves).

'A1' class Pacific 60113 GREAT NORTHERN, with a crested nameplate, is seen near Potters Bar with a Kings Cross–Leeds express passenger service during October 1959. *Hugh Ballantyne/Rail Photoprints Collection*

Numbers	Names	Built/Re-built	Completed	Withdrawn
LNER 113, BR 60113	GREAT NORTHERN	Doncaster	09/1945	12/1962
Disposal: 60113 Doncaster Works				

Originally the loco was fitted with wing-type smoke deflectors (similar to those incorporated in the 'A2/2' class design). However, they proved to be less than effective and were replaced in December 1945 with large (plate) smoke deflectors.

There were plans to convert all the remaining 'A10' class locos in this manner but they were never acted upon, similarly streamlining plans were also abandoned.

In the first few years of service, the Thompson-rebuilt Pacific suffered a number of teething problems. These were all rectified, but even so the prototype loco never played a prominent role on East Coast Main Line trains. Although No 60113 was occasionally allocated to Kings Cross depot, it spent much of its working life based at Doncaster or Grantham. GREAT NORTHERN was even ignominiously diagrammed to Grantham pilot duty for a while during the mid-1950s.

The locomotive was withdrawn on 19 November 1962 with a badly worn middle cylinder and cut up by British Railways at Doncaster Works in May 1963.

LNER 4-6-2 'A1/1' class, BR number 60113

Introduced: 1922 Gresley

Power Classification: 7P (reclassified 8P in 1951)

Built: Doncaster Works, 1 locomotive

ReBuilt: 1945 by Edward Thompson as a prototype

Company: London & North Eastern Railway

Driving Wheel: 6ft 8ins

Boiler Pressure: 250psi superheated

Cylinders: 3 – 19ins diameter x 26ins stroke

Tractive Effort @ 85%: 37,397lbf

Valve Gear: Walschaerts (piston valves)

Water Capacity: 5000 gallons

Coal Capacity: 8 tons

Chapter 25

1946–1947

London & North Eastern Railway 'A2/3' Class 4-6-2, designed by Thompson

The 'A2/3' class was Thompson's own new design of Pacific; the fifteen engines (from an initial order for thirty) were built at Doncaster and introduced between April 1946 and September 1947. They were intended to be his standard 4-6-2 design and were based on his 'A2/2' class design ('P2' rebuilds). The new-design loco's boiler pressure was increased to 250psi, whilst the cylinder diameter was reduced to 19 inches. The fifteen engines that were built came into service with the London & North Eastern Railway just after Thompson had retired, the balance of the order were built by his predecessor Peppercorn.

This was the first new Pacific design built at Doncaster for a little over eight years and they were built with the inclusion of several innovations. Those changes included steam brakes, a hopper ashpan, electric lighting and a self-cleaning smokebox (SC). However, Thompson did not included rocking fire grates or his trademark V-shaped cab. The original design called for small wing-type smoke deflectors, but that specification was changed to large plate smoke deflectors prior to the commencement of the actual build.

Thompson 'A2/3' class Pacific No 60514 CHAMOSSAIRE was certainly receiving plenty of attention from the motive power depot staff when pictured on shed at New England (34E) in the late summer of 1958. Note the un-lipped chimney. *Ron White Collection*

LNER 4-6-2 'A2/3' class, BR numbers 60500, 60511–60524

Introduced: 1946–47

Power Classification: 7MT

Built: Doncaster Works, 15 locomotives

Designer: Edward Thompson

Company: London & North Eastern Railway

Driving Wheel: 6ft 2ins

Boiler Pressure: 250psi superheated

Cylinders: 3 – 19ins diameter x 26ins stroke

Tractive Effort @ 85%: 40,430lbf

Valve Gear: Walschaerts (piston valves)

Water Capacity: 9000 gallons

Coal Capacity: 9 tons

Numbers	Names	Built	Lot/Wks Number	Completed	Withdrawn
LNER 500, BR 60500	EDWARD THOMPSON	Doncaster	2000	04/1946	06/1963
LNER 511, BR 60511	AIRBORNE	Doncaster	2002	07/1946	10/1962
LNER 512, BR 60512	STEADY AIM	Doncaster	2003	08/1946	06/1965
LNER 513, BR 60513	DANTE	Doncaster	2004	08/1946	06/1963
LNER 514, BR 60514	CHAMOSSAIRE	Doncaster	2005	09/1946	12/1962
LNER 515, BR 60515	SUN STREAM	Doncaster	2006	10/1946	10/1962
LNER 516, BR 60516	HYCILLA	Doncaster	2007	11/1946	10/1962
LNER 517, BR 60517	OCEAN SWELL	Doncaster	2008	11/1946	10/1962
LNER 518, BR 60518	TEHRAN	Doncaster	2009	12/1946	10/1962
LNER 519, BR 60519	HONEYWAY	Doncaster	2010	02/1947	12/1962
LNER 520, BR 60520	OWEN TUDOR	Doncaster	2011	03/1947	06/1963
LNER 521, BR 60521	WATLING STREET	Doncaster	2012	05/1947	10/1962
LNER 522, BR 60522	STRAIGHT DEAL	Doncaster	2013	06/1947	06/1965
LNER 523, BR 60523	SUN CASTLE	Doncaster	2014	09/1947	06/1963
LNER 524, BR 60524	HERRINGBONE	Doncaster	2015	09/1947	02/1965

Disposal: 60500–60511–60513/521–60523 Doncaster Works, 60512–60522–60524 Motherwell Machinery & Scrap, Wishaw

During running in, it was discovered that the shorter-style boiler used on the class, in combination with the highly efficient steam operated brakes, caused boiler water to slosh forward following a sharp brake application, and in doing so enter the steam pipe. That could cause the injectors to shut off if they were in use. Following instances of boiler water ingress to the steam pipe the ejector, when next used, could then force water out of the chimney, drenching anyone in the vicinity.

The fault was cured by lengthening the steam pipe and locating it high enough to allow the unwanted water to drain back into the boiler. Additionally a drain valve was added to the ejector exhaust pipe; all later-built engines of the class were given the modifications from new.

When newly introduced into traffic, five of the class were allocated to the LNER Southern area, one to Scotland and the balance to the North East area. They were found to be wasteful on coal during light runs and so it was decided that they would be best employed on heavier duties.

Withdrawal of the class started in 1962 with eight members of the class being retired in the autumn of that year. Only three locos remained in traffic at the start of 1965 but they did not survive beyond the end of the year.

Liveries carried included LNER lined green, and Brunswick green with orange and black lining.

Thompson 'A2/3' class Pacific No 60513 DANTE was certainly not being overworked when photographed at Walton with a two-coach train, which we can probably assume was an ex-maintenance 'running in' turn, June 1956. *D.C. Ovenden/Colour Rail*

Thompson 'A2/3' class Pacific No 60513 DANTE was pictured in ex-works condition on shed at Doncaster (36A) in 1955. Note the lipped chimney. *Rail Photoprints Collection*

Thompson 'A2/3' class Pacific No 60520 OWEN TUDOR was pictured hard at work near Retford in 1960. *Mike Morant Collection*

Chapter 26

1947–1948

London & North Eastern Railway/British Railways 'A2' Class 4-6-2 re-designed by Peppercorn (from Thompson 'A2/3' class)

Thompson was originally given the go-ahead to produce thirty engines to his own three-cylinder Pacific design and the first fifteen appeared in 1946 and 1947 and were designated 'A2/3' class. The final fifteen engines of the order were not produced until after Thompson's retirement as CME of the LNER; they were redesigned by his successor Peppercorn, who was credited with the design which became designated as the 'A2' class. All but loco No 60525 A.H. PEPPERCORN were built by the then newly created network operator British Railways during the first six months of 1948.

Peppercorn 'A2' class Pacific No E531 BAHRAM (BR 60531), which was by just three months a BR-built locomotive and at the time of this picture carried LNER apple green livery and was allocated to Gateshead (52A), is seen storming southwards through Durham station on 25 November 1948. *Mike Morant Collection*

LNER 4-6-2 'A2' class, BR numbers 60525–60539

Introduced: 1947–48

Power Classification: 7MT

Built: Doncaster Works, 15 locomotives

Designer: Edward Thompson – redesigned and built by Peppercorn

Company: London & North Eastern Railway

Driving Wheel: 6ft 2ins

Boiler Pressure: 250psi superheated

Cylinders: 3 – 19ins diameter x 26ins stroke

Tractive Effort @ 85%: 40,430lbf

Valve Gear: Walschaerts (piston valves)

Water Capacity: 9000 gallons

Coal Capacity: 9 tons

The Peppercorn re-design kept Thompson's original cylinder and valve arrangement but by incorporating a modified bogie position the engines had a shorter wheelbase than the 'A2/3' class.

Other changes saw the retention of the self-cleaning smokebox, the addition of a rocking fire grate but the exclusion of a Kylchap exhaust, as that component would have been difficult to fit in the 'A2s' shortened 'SC' smokebox.

Numbers	Names	Built	Lot/Wks Number	Completed	Withdrawn
LNER 525, BR 60525	A.H. PEPPERCORN	Doncaster	2016	12/1947	03/1963
LNER 526, BR 60526	SUGAR PALM	Doncaster	2017	01/1948	10/1962
LNER E527, BR 60527	SUN CHARIOT	Doncaster	2018	01/1948	04/1965
LNER E528, BR 60528	TUDOR MINSTREL	Doncaster	2019	02/1948	06/1966
LNER E529, BR 60529	PEARL DIVER	Doncaster	2020	02/1948	12/1962
LNER E530, BR 60530	SAYAJIRAO	Doncaster	2021	03/1948	11/1966
LNER E531, BR 60531	BAHRAM	Doncaster	2022	03/1948	12/1962
LNER 532, BR 60532	BLUE PETER	Doncaster	2023	03/1948	12/1966 Preserved
BR 60533	HAPPY KNIGHT	Doncaster	2024	04/1948	06/1963
BR 60534	IRISH ELEGANCE	Doncaster	2025	04/1948	12/1962
BR 60535	HORNETS BEAUTY	Doncaster	2026	05/1948	06/1965
BR 60536	TRIMBUSH	Doncaster	2027	05/1948	12/1962
BR 60537	BACHELORS BUTTON	Doncaster	2028	06/1948	12/1962
BR 60538	VELOCITY	Doncaster	2029	06/1948	10/1962
BR 60539	BRONZINO	Doncaster	2030	08/1948	10/1962

As the production run got underway the order was at first increased from fifteen to thirty-five engines but in May 1948 the additional order was cancelled, reportedly pending the results of the 1948 'Locomotive Interchange Trials'.

The last 'A2' class 4-6-2 to be built, loco No 60539 BRONZINO, was fitted with a Kylchap exhaust system and in order to accommodate that component the 'Self Cleaning' gear was discarded. That design variation was by all accounts successful as five more of the class were similarly modified during 1949. Electric lighting was included as a standard feature.

Initially the 'A2' locomotives were all allocated to English sheds but five of the class were sent to Scotland in 1949, to make up for the deficiencies in the 'A2/2' class engines. The 'A2' Pacifics were extensively used on passenger services between Aberdeen and Edinburgh.

Of the English-allocated 'A2s', York-allocated loco No 60526 SUGAR PALM set a speed record for the class in 1961 by attaining a speed of 101mph whilst descending Stoke Bank.

BR started a planned withdrawal of the class in 1962 when eight locos were retired, with the last three serviceable engines being withdrawn in 1966.

Liveries applied included LNER apple green and BR Brunswick green.

Peppercorn 'A2' class Pacific No 60525 A.H. PEPERCORN on familiar territory; the loco which was named after the locomotive designer was pictured at Edinburgh Waverley station on 2 June 1963. *Mike Stokes Archive*

Peppercorn 'A2' class Pacific No 60527 SUN CHARIOT was pictured heading through Hookhills Cutting towards North Queensferry with an Aberdeen–Dundee Tay Bridge–Edinburgh Waverley express on 20 June 1959. *David Anderson*

Peppercorn 'A2' class Pacific No 60528 TUDOR MINSTREL was pictured with an Aberdeen–Edinburgh Waverley service at Dalmeny Junction in this 1959 image; note that the loco then at that time carried BR green livery. *David Anderson*

The preserved Peppercorn 'A2' class Pacific No 60532 BLUE PETER was pictured whilst on shed at Aberdeen Ferryhill depot (61B). Note the double chimney (Kylchap exhaust). *Rail Photoprints Collection*

Peppercorn 'A2' class Pacific No 60533 HAPPY KNIGHT simmers at the platform whilst waiting to exit back down onto a northbound train at London Kings Cross on 17 September 1956. *M.J. Reade/Colour Rail*

Peppercorn 'A2' class Pacific No 60535 HORNETS BEAUTY was unusually at work on the West Coast Main Line (WCML) at Kirtlebridge when pictured there in April 1964. For a while that loco, together with No 60527, No 60522 and No 60530, was allocated to Glasgow Polmadie depot and occasionally diagrammed for the ex-Caledonian Railway route Glasgow–Carlisle services, but rarely, as this one was, for the local stopping train! Reportedly the 'A2' class engines were never popular with Polmadie engine crews and in fact saw little service from that depot; presumably they replaced retired ex-LMS Pacifics. *A.E. Durrant/Rail Photoprints Collection*

Peppercorn 'A2' class Pacific No 60537 BACHELORS BUTTON was pictured heading westwards near Haymarket West Junction with the midday Edinburgh Waverley to Glasgow Queen Street express on 29 May 1955. *David Anderson*

Peppercorn 'A2' class Pacific No 60534 IRISH ELEGANCE was pictured powering the Leeds City–Edinburgh Waverley–Glasgow Queen Street 'North Briton' (minus headboard) past Haymarket Central Junction on 21 April 1956. The 'North Briton' titled train ran between Leeds City and Glasgow Queen Street (via York) from 26 September 1949 until 4 May 1968. This was the only ER titled train to use Leeds City station and the trains concerned were the 8.48 a.m. ex Leeds and the 4 p.m. ex Glasgow. The service enjoyed several incarnations not least of which lapsing for four years and then being reinstated in 1972 when it became a Leeds–Dundee service which actually carried no headboard. *David Anderson*

Chapter 27

1948–1949

London & North Eastern Railway 'A1' Class 4-6-2, built by British Railways, designed by Peppercorn

The LNER 'A1' class Pacifics were designed by Arthur H. Peppercorn, the last Chief Mechanical Engineer of the London & North Eastern Railway. They were the last in a line of famous express passenger steam locomotives for the East Coast Main Line, an auspicious list which included the Stirling Singles, the Ivatt Atlantics and the Gresley Pacifics.

Peppercorn 'A1' class Pacific No 60114 W.P. ALLEN was pictured adjacent to the coaling plant at the loco's home shed of Doncaster (36A) in 1963. Note the turbo-generator for the electric lighting power supply is in this instance mounted alongside the smokebox, inside the loco's off-side smoke deflector plate. Other Peppercorn engines were alternatively fitted with axle mounted alternators. *Mike Stokes Archive*

The original forty-nine Peppercorn Class A1s were ordered by the LNER and built at Doncaster (twenty-six locos) and Darlington (twenty-three locos) for British Railways (BR) between 1948 and 1949, during the first two years of railway nationalisation. As designed they were 6-foot-8-inch-diameter wheeled versions of the 'A2' class Pacific types and as such they were ideally suited for the post-war railway world of poor maintenance and heavy trains. Equipped with a huge 50sq ft grate, the locos were able to use lower grade coal than their predecessors. The locos at first ran without names, but eventually they all carried names on the side of their smoke deflectors.

The Peppercorn engines were originally fitted with plain topped (un-lipped) double chimney castings which were eventually changed for lipped chimneys, a move that many thought greatly improved the look of the class.

The 'A1' class 4-6-2 engines were heralded as being excellent performers by engine crews; they ran and steamed well even on relatively poor quality coal. They fulfilled the designer's intentions with regard to low maintenance requirements, in fact reportedly needing less routine maintenance than any of the other express locomotives running on BR at the time of their introduction.

Five of the 'A1s' (Nos 60153–60157) were fitted with Timken roller bearings on all of their axles. These had already been tried successfully on some of the 'A4' loco tenders. The bearings were trialled with the intention of further increasing the period between heavy repairs. Although the roller bearing experiment was judged a success, the fitting of them was never expanded to include other members of the class.

An undesirable side effect with the 'A1' class Kylchap exhaust arrangement was the loud operating sound of the associated ejectors when used whilst standing in the station, as the

---

LNER 4-6-2 'A1' class, BR numbers 60114–60162

Introduced: 1948–49

Power Classification: 7P (reclassified 8P in 1951)

Built: Doncaster Works 60114–60129 (1948), 60153–60162 (1949)

    Darlington Works 60130–60152 (1948–49)

    Total 49 locomotives

Designer: Arthur Peppercorn

Company: British Railways

Driving Wheel: 6ft 8ins

Boiler Pressure: 250psi superheated

Cylinders: 3 – 19ins diameter x 26ins stroke

Tractive Effort @ 85%: 37,397lbf

Valve Gear: Walschaerts (piston valves)

Water Capacity: 5000 gallons

Coal Capacity: 9 tons

noise was reportedly loud enough to drown out tannoy announcements to passengers. Silencers were fitted experimentally, and were found to work. Similar units were then recommended for the remaining Peppercorn 'A1s' and additionally the Kylchap-fitted Peppercorn 'A2s'. Because of the smaller size smokebox used it was not possible to include both Kylchap gear and self-cleaning equipment and as a result the latter was removed.

Withdrawal started with No 60123 H.A. IVATT in October 1962 after an accident; by the end of 1964 only twenty-six of the class remained in service. The last two Peppercorn 'A1' class engines were withdrawn in 1966.

Livery styles used included LNER apple green, BR Brunswick green (pre 1957 shade), BR Brunswick green (post 1957 shade) and BR blue.

Numbers	Names	Built	Lot/Wks Number	Completed	Withdrawn
BR 60114	W.P. ALLEN	Doncaster	2031	08/1948	12/1964
BR 60115	MEG MERRILIES	Doncaster	2032	09/1948	10/1962
BR 60116	HAL O' THE WYND	Doncaster	2033	10/1948	06/1965
BR 60117	BOIS ROUSSEL	Doncaster	2034	10/1948	06/1965
BR 60118	ARCHIBALD STURROCK	Doncaster	2035	11/1948	10/1965
BR 60119	PATRICK STIRLING	Doncaster	2036	11/1948	05/1964
BR 60120	KITTIWAKE	Doncaster	2037	12/1948	01/1964
BR 60121	SILURIAN	Doncaster	2038	12/1948	10/1965
BR 60122	CURLEW	Doncaster	2039	12/1948	11/1962
BR 60123	H.A. IVATT	Doncaster	2040	02/1949	10/1962
BR 60124	KENILWORTH	Doncaster	2041	03/1949	03/1966
BR 60125	SCOTTISH UNION	Doncaster	2043	04/1949	07/1964
BR 60126	SIR VINCENT RAVEN	Doncaster	2042	04/1949	01/1965
BR 60127	WILSON WORSDELL	Doncaster	2044	05/1949	06/1965
BR 60128	BONGRACE	Doncaster	2045	05/1949	01/1965
BR 60129	GUY MANNERING	Doncaster	2046	06/1949	10/1965
BR 60130	KESTREL	Darlington	2049	09/1948	10/1965
BR 60131	OSPREY	Darlington	2050	10/1948	10/1965
BR 60132	MARMION	Darlington	2051	10/1948	06/1965
BR 60133	POMMERN	Darlington	2052	10/1948	07/1965

Disposal: 60115–60122/23 Doncaster Works, 60114–60116–60127–60132 Hughes Bolckows, North Blyth, 60117–60132 Clayton & Davie, Dunston-on-Tyne, 60118 Wards, Beighton, 60119–670125 Cox & Danks, Wadsley Bridge, 60120–60124 Darlington Works, 60121–60131 Wards, Killamarsh, 60126–60128 Drapers, Hull, 60129 Kings Norwich, 60130 Cashmores, Great Bridge

Peppercorn 'A1' class Pacific No 60115 MEG MERRILIES was pictured whilst passing through York's impressive station in this delightful period image. Loco No 60115 was in LNER apple green livery with BRITISH RAILWAYS in full on the tender at that time, and the Peppercorn 4-6-2 had not yet received its name; note also the un-lipped double chimney. The vehicle behind the tender is a 'Coronation' beaver tail observation car of 1929 vintage. Close examination of the original image more than suggests that the 'Coronation' car was then virtually straight out of the 'York Carriage Works' paint shop. *Mike Morant Collection*

Peppercorn 'A1' class Pacific No 60125 SCOTTISH UNION was pictured at New England (then 35A) prior to being named. *K.C.H. Fairey/Colour Rail*

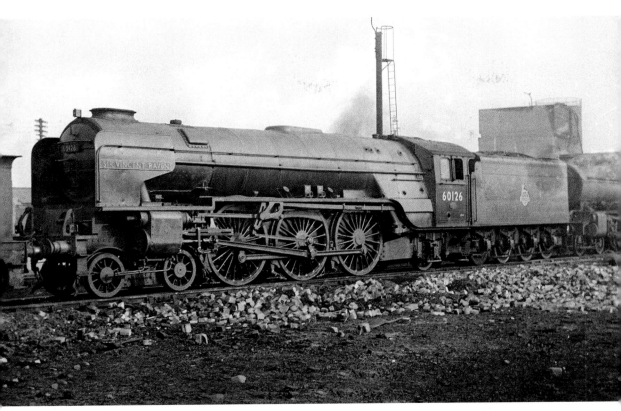

Peppercorn 'A1' class Pacific No 60126 was named after the steam locomotive engineer SIR VINCENT RAVEN; the loco was seen on shed at Retford GC (36E) on 18 March 1956. *Rail Photoprints Collection*

Peppercorn 'A1' class Pacific No 60127 was also named after a locomotive engineer, in this instance WILSON WORSDELL, although the loco was still un-named when this image was taken. The Peppercorn 4-6-2 looked to be in ex-works condition when pictured at York station in April 1950; note the fireman on the tender with the 'bag'. *Colour Rail*

The front-end detail of Peppercorn 'A1' class Pacific No 60129 GUY MANNERING, then a Gateshead-allocated loco, was pictured in this image taken at Darlington station in June 1960. Note the LNER-style fitted electric lighting; however the engine also carries traditional lamps in this instance. *Mike Stokes Archive*

Numbers	Names	Built	Lot/Wks Number	Completed	Withdrawn
BR 60134	FOXHUNTER	Darlington	2053	11/1948	10/1965
BR 60135	MADGE WILDFIRE	Darlington	2054	11/1948	10/1962
BR 60136	ALCAZAR	Darlington	2055	11/1948	05/1963
BR 60137	REDGAUNTLET	Darlington	2056	12/1948	10/1962
BR 60138	BOSWELL	Darlington	2057	12/1948	10/1965
BR 60139	SEA EAGLE	Darlington	2058	12/1948	06/1964
BR 60140	BALMORAL	Darlington	2059	12/1948	01/1965
BR 60141	ABBOTSFORD	Darlington	2060	12/1948	10/1964
BR 60142	EDWARD FLETCHER	Darlington	2061	02/1949	06/1965
BR 60143	SIR WALTER SCOTT	Darlington	2062	02/1949	05/1964
BR 60144	KING'S COURIER	Darlington	2063	03/1949	04/1963
BR 60145	SAINT MUNGO	Darlington	2064	03/1949	06/1966
BR 60146	PEREGRINE	Darlington	2065	04/1949	10/1965
BR 60147	NORTH EASTERN	Darlington	2066	05/1949	08/1964
BR 60148	ABOYEUR	Darlington	2067	05/1949	06/1965
BR 60149	AMADIS	Darlington	2068	05/1949	06/1964
BR 60150	WILLBROOK	Darlington	2069	06/1948	10/1964
BR 60151	MIDLOTHIAN	Darlington	2070	06/1948	11/1965
BR 60152	HOLYROOD	Darlington	2071	07/1948	06/1965

Disposal: 60134 Wards Beighton, 60135/37–60144 Doncaster Works, 60138–60146 Wards, Killamarsh, 60139–60149 Cox & Danks, Wadsley Bridge, 60140/41–60143–60145–60147–60150 Drapers, Hull, 60142 Hughes Bolckows, North Blyth, 60148 Arnott Young, Dinsdale, 60151 George W. Station Steel, Wath, 60152 Cashmores Great Bridge

Peppercorn 'A1' class Pacific No 60138 BOSWELL was pictured on shed at York (50A) in this 1961 image; note the lipped double chimney and electric lights. *Mike Stokes Archive*

Steam in abundance! Peppercorn 'A1' class Pacific No 60138 BOSWELL prepares to depart with a down train from York in this atmospheric October 1951 image. *Mike Stokes Archive*

Peppercorn 'A1' class Pacific No 60140 BALMORAL stands at York with a southbound East Coast Main Line service, circa 1960. *Roy Whitfield/Rail Photoprints Collection*

Peppercorn 'A1' class Pacific No 60141 ABBOTSFORD effortlessly hauls 'up' express 'The West Riding' through Wymondly. 'The West Riding Limited' between London Kings Cross–Leeds Central–Bradford Exchange was introduced in 1937 and withdrawn in August 1939; however in May 1949 'The West Riding' was introduced over the same route and that service last ran on 4 March 1967. Just to confuse matters there was also a 'West Riding Pullman' train which ran from July 1927 until 28 September 1935. *A.E. Durrant/Mike Morant Collection*

March 23 1951 sees Peppercorn 'A1' class Pacific No 60142 EDWARD FLETCHER at Platform 8 under the magnificent awning at Newcastle station. Note that again traditional lamps are carried above the electric lights. *W.J. Wyse/Mike Morant Collection*

Peppercorn 'A1' class Pacific No 60145 SAINT MUNGO, with lipped double chimney, was pictured on shed at York (50A) in this 1963 image. *Mike Stokes Archive*

Peppercorn 'A1' class Pacific No 60148 ABOYEUR effortlessly hauls the heavy down 'Queen of Scots' Pullman train through Wymondly in March 1961. The original 'Queen of Scots' was introduced in 1928 and ran between London Kings Cross and Glasgow Queen Street (via Leeds and Harrogate) and that Pullman service was discontinued on 2 September 1939. In July 1948 the train was re-introduced running via Leeds and Edinburgh and that train last ran on 13th June 1964. *A.E. Durrant/Mike Morant Collection*

On a clear, cold morning Peppercorn 'A1' class Pacific No 60152 HOLYROOD was pictured taking water at St Boswells whilst heading a Waverley route service during January 1962. Note the impressive lattice signal on the platform and the rear of a BR Standard 'Class 2' engine in the bay platform. *Dave Cobbe Collection/Rail Photoprints Collection*

Numbers	Names	Built	Lot/Wks Number	Completed	Withdrawn
BR 60153*	FLAMBOYANT	Doncaster	2047	08/1948	10/1962
BR 60154*	BON ACCORD	Doncaster	2048	09/1949	10/1965
BR 60155*	BORDERER	Doncaster	2049	09/1949	10/1965
BR 60156*	GREAT CENTRAL	Doncaster	2050	10/1949	04/1965
BR 60157*	GREAT EASTERN	Doncaster	2051	10/1949	01/1965
BR 60158	ABERDONIAN	Doncaster	2052	11/1949	12/1964
BR 60159	BONNIE DUNDEE	Doncaster	2053	11/1949	10/1963
BR 60160	AULD REEKIE	Doncaster	2054	12/1949	12/1963
BR 60161	NORTH BRITISH	Doncaster	2055	12/1949	10/1963
BR 60162	SAINT JOHNSTOUN	Doncaster	2056	12/1949	10/1963

* Locomotives fitted with roller bearings
Disposal: 60153 Doncaster Works, 60154 Wards, Beighton, 60155 Wards, Killamarsh, 60156 Clayton & Davie, Dunston-on-Tyne, 60157 Drapers, Hull, 60158 Hughes Bolckows, North Blyth, 60159–60161/62 Inverurie Works, 60160 Darlington Works

Peppercorn 'A1' class Pacific No 60154 BON ACCORD, then a Neville Hill (55H) allocated loco, was pictured at Leeds City station in 1963 whilst standing at the platform alongside 'the future' in the shape of No D86 (which became a preserved BR 'Class 45' loco, No 45105). *Mike Stokes Archive*

Peppercorn 'A1' class Pacific No 60157 GREAT EASTERN was pictured whilst heading an up Newcastle express past Brookmans Park in February 1959. *T.B. Owen/Colour Rail*

Peppercorn 'A1' class Pacific No 60161 NORTH BRITISH storms off shed at Haymarket (64B) and heads light engine down to Edinburgh Waverley station in this evocative 1956 image; note the crested nameplate. *David Anderson*

Peppercorn 'A1' class Pacific No 60161 NORTH BRITISH had certainly enjoyed the attentions of the cleaning staff at Haymarket depot when this image was taken in 1958. Note the non-standard red backing used on the crested nameplate. *J. Robertson/Colour Rail*

Peppercorn 'A1' class Pacific No 60162 ST JOHNSTOUN was pictured at speed passing Haymarket Junction with an Edinburgh Waverley–Dundee–Aberdeen express service in this 1959 image. *David Anderson*

Chapter 28

1951–1954

British Railways 'Britannia' Class 4-6-2, designed by Riddles

Bitish Railways Standard 'Britannia Class' was the first of the Riddles-designed Standard types to enter service with BR. The first loco of the class to be completed was No 70000 BRITANNIA which rolled out of Crewe Locomotives Works to great acclaim, in January 1951. The new class of fifty-five engines was considered at the time to be a striking design of Mixed Traffic locomotives; they were intended to have wide route availability. The 'Britannia' class were roughly equal in power to the WR 'Castle', the LMR 'Royal Scot', the SR 'West Country' and 'Battle of Britain' and the Eastern Region 'V2'.

BR Standard 'Britannia' class Pacific locomotives No 70004 WILLIAM SHAKESPEARE and No 70014 IRON DUKE were pictured together getting spruced up at their then home shed, Stewarts Lane (73A), on 6 September 1953. It can be seen that No 70004 was being prepared for the next 'Golden Arrow' working. *Dave Cobbe Collection – C. R. L. Coles/Rail Photoprints Collection*

The 4-6-2 locomotives were designed in the Derby drawing office of BR and all were built at Crewe. They were given the number series 70000 to 70054 with 70000 to 70024 entering service in 1951, 70025 to 70044 entering service in 1952/53 and 70045 to 70054 following in 1954.

The class was at first distributed around the network with fifteen engines going to the Eastern Region, five to the Western Region, fifteen to the London Midland Region and five to the Scottish Region. Thereafter some changes in allocation were made which meant that three engines went to the Southern Region and additional engines from the LMR allocation transferred to the Eastern Region.

The Britannia design was generally considered to be a complete success and when first in service the type put in some memorable performances on the former Great Eastern Railway main line into East Anglia, as a result of which timings were appreciably improved.

As dieselisation (and later electrification) became more advanced all of the Britannias were transferred to the London & Midland Region. The first to be scrapped was 70007 COEUR-DE-LION which was cut up at Crewe in July 1965, having worked in BR service for only fourteen years. By 1966 just forty-two of the class were still in use.

Originally BR intended to preserve 70000 BRITANNIA as part of the national collection but then dropped that plan following vandalism of the class leader whilst it was stored in their care. The British Railways Board alternatively chose 70013 OLIVER CROMWELL for the collection, as a result of which the loco was overhauled and repainted at Crewe Works in January 1967, prior to preservation. The engine was then returned to traffic, hauling special trains right up to the end of steam on BR, including the final leg of a 'Farewell to Steam' special from Manchester to Carlisle on 11th August 1968.

No 70000 was initially turned out in BR unlined black livery; however, later all of the class were essentially painted in BR Brunswick green lined with orange and black. Nos 70000 and 70004 received added embellishments in their early service lives which included bright metal

---

BR 4-6-2 'Britannia' class, BR numbers 70000–70054

Introduced: 1951–54

Power Classification: 7MT (7P6F)

Built: Crewe Works, 55 locomotives

Designer: Robert Riddles

Company: British Railways

Driving Wheel: 6ft 2ins

Boiler Pressure: 250psi superheated

Cylinders: Outside – 20ins diameter x 28ins stroke

Tractive Effort @ 85%: 32,160lbf

Valve Gear: Walschaerts (piston valves)

Water Capacity: 4250, 4725 and 5000 gallons depending on tender type

Coal Capacity: 7 tons and 9 tons depending on tender type

wheel trims, handrails, buffers and draw gear; they also were given red-backed nameplates. Some of the engines later received a Crewe Works BR so-called economy green unlined livery. For additional detailed information about the Riddles-designed BR Standard Pacific locomotives please refer to the Pen & Sword Books publication ***British Steam – BR Standard Locomotives*** written by the same author. Please visit www.pen-and-sword.co.uk/British-Steam-BR-Standard-Locomotives

Number	Name	Built	Date	Withdrawn
BR 70000	BRITANNIA	BR Crewe	01/1951	06/1966 Preserved
BR 70001	LORD HURCOMB	BR Crewe	02/1951	08/1966
BR 70002	GEOFFREY CHAUCER	BR Crewe	03/1951	01/1967
BR 70003	JOHN BUNYAN	BR Crewe	03/1951	03/1967
BR 70004	WILLIAM SHAKESPEARE	BR Crewe	03/1951	12/1967
BR 70005	JOHN MILTON	BR Crewe	04/1951	07/1967
BR 70006	ROBERT BURNS	BR Crewe	04/1951	05/1967
BR 70007	COEUR-DE-LION	BR Crewe	04/1951	06/1965
BR 70008	BLACK PRINCE	BR Crewe	04/1951	01/1967
BR 70009	ALFRED THE GREAT	BR Crewe	05/1951	01/1967
BR 70010	OWEN GLENDOWER	BR Crewe	05/1951	09/1967
BR 70011	HOTSPUR	BR Crewe	05/1951	12/1967
BR 70012	JOHN OF GAUNT	BR Crewe	05/1951	12/1967
BR 70013	OLIVER CROMWELL	BR Crewe	06/1951	08/1968 Preserved
BR 70014	IRON DUKE	BR Crewe	06/1951	12/1967
BR 70015	APOLLO	BR Crewe	06/1951	08/1967
BR 70016	ARIEL	BR Crewe	06/1951	08/1967
BR 70017	ARROW	BR Crewe	06/1951	09/1966
BR 70018	FLYING DUTCHMAN	BR Crewe	06/1951	12/1966
BR 70019	LIGHTNING	BR Crewe	06/1951	03/1966

Disposal: 70001–70018 Motherwell Machinery & Scrap, Wishaw, 70002/3–70005–70008 Campbells, Airdrie, 70004–70012–70014 Wards, Inverkeithing, 70006–70009/11–70015/16 McWilliams, Shettleston, 70007 Crewe Works, 70017 John Cashmore Newport, 70019 Arnott Young, Troon

BR Standard 'Britannia' class Pacific No 70005 ROBERT BURNS was pictured when brand new in grey primer and yet to re-visit the paint shop at Crewe Works, on 1 April 1951. *Mike Morant Collection*

This picture of the Crewe Works erecting shop taken on 16 January 1966 and it shows BR Standard 'Britannia' class Pacific No 70011 HOTSPUR undergoing its last major overhaul. Note that No 70011 was withdrawn only eleven months later! *Brian Robbins/Rail Photoprints Collection*

BR Standard 'Britannia' class Pacific No 70016 ARIEL was selected as the locomotive that would be presented to the public as the bearer of the then newly to be unveiled British Railways crest at Marylebone station in London. Here we see her resplendent in exhibition finish prior to that ceremony at Neasden depot (14D) on June 21st, 1956. *Mike Morant Collection*

BR Standard 'Britannia' class Pacific No 70035 RUDYARD KIPLING pictured with a northbound freight climbing Grayrigg, on 26 August 1967. *David Rostance/Rail Photoprints Collection*

Number	Name	Built	Date	Withdrawn
BR 70020	MERCURY	BR Crewe	07/1951	01/1967
BR 70021	MORNING STAR	BR Crewe	08/1951	12/1967
BR 70022	TORNADO	BR Crewe	08/1951	12/1967
BR 70023	VENUS	BR Crewe	08/1951	12/1967
BR 70024	VULCAN	BR Crewe	08/1951	12/1967
BR 70025	WESTERN STAR	BR Crewe	09/1952	12/1967
BR 70026	POLAR STAR	BR Crewe	10/1952	01/1967
BR 70027	RISING STAR	BR Crewe	10/1952	06/1967
BR 70028	ROYAL STAR	BR Crewe	10/1952	09/1967
BR 70029	SHOOTING STAR	BR Crewe	11/1952	10/1967
BR 70030	WILLIAM WORDSWORTH	BR Crewe	11/1952	06/1967
BR 70031	BYRON	BR Crewe	11/1952	11/1967
BR 70032	TENNYSON	BR Crewe	11/1952	09/1967
BR 70033	CHARLES DICKENS	BR Crewe	12/1952	07/1967
BR 70034	THOMAS HARDY	BR Crewe	12/1952	05/1967
BR 70035	RUDYARD KIPLING	BR Crewe	12/1952	12/1967
BR 70036	BOADICEA	BR Crewe	12/1952	10/1966
BR 70037	HEREWARD THE WAKE	BR Crewe	12/1952	10/1966
BR 70038	ROBIN HOOD	BR Crewe	01/1953	08/1967
BR 70039	SIR CHRISTOPHER WREN	BR Crewe	02/1953	09/1967

Disposal: 70020–70028/29–70034–70037/39 McWilliams, Shettleston, 70021/22-70035 Wards, Inverkeithing, 70023/24 Wards, Killamarsh, 70025–70033 Campbells, Airdrie, 70026 John Cashmore, Newport, 70027–70031/32–70036 Motherwell, Machinery & Scrap, Wishaw, 70030 Wards, Beighton

BR Standard 'Britannia' class Pacific No 70037 HEREWARD THE WAKE was pictured when spotlessly turned out by Stratford depot. No 70037 prepares to head out of London Liverpool Street station with the Railway Correspondent & Travel Society (RCTS London Branch) 'Fensman' special train, 24 July 1955. The charter ran from London Liverpool Street–Cambridge–London Liverpool Street hauled by the 'Britannia Pacific' and trips to several local lines were made during the stop over using loco No 65562, an ex-GER Holden 'S56' class 0-6-0T (BR class J69/1). *Hugh Ballantyne/Rail Photoprints Collection*

Number	Name	Built	Date	Withdrawn
BR 70040	CLIVE OF INDIA	BR Crewe	03/1953	04/1967
BR 70041	SIR JOHN MOORE	BR Crewe	03/1953	04/1967
BR 70042	LORD ROBERTS	BR Crewe	04/1953	05/1967
BR 70043	LORD KITCHENER	BR Crewe	06/1953	08/1965
BR 70044	EARL HAIG	BR Crewe	06/1953	12/1956
BR 70045	LORD ROWALLAN	BR Crewe	06/1954	12/1967
BR 70046	ANZAC	BR Crewe	06/1954	07/1967
BR 70047	Not named	BR Crewe	06/1954	07/1967
BR 70048	THE TERRITORIAL ARMY, 1908–1958	BR Crewe	07/1954	05/1967
BR 70049	SOLWAY FIRTH	BR Crewe	07/1954	12/1967
BR 70050	FIRTH OF CLYDE	BR Crewe	08/1954	08/1966
BR 70051	FIRTH OF FORTH	BR Crewe	08/1954	12/1967
BR 70052	FIRTH OF TAY	BR Crewe	08/1954	04/1967
BR 70053	MORAY FIRTH	BR Crewe	09/1954	04/1967
BR 70054	DORNOCH FIRTH	BR Crewe	09/1954	11/1966

Disposal: 70040/42–70048/49–70051–70053 McWilliams, Shettleston, 70043/45 Wards, Beighton, 70046/47–70050–70052 Campbells, Airdrie, 70054 Motherwell Machinery & Scrap, Wishaw

BR Standard 'Britannia' class Pacific No 70043 was pictured when brand new and fresh from the paintshop at Crewe Works, on 10 May 1953. This was one of the two 'Britannia' class engines to be fitted experimentally with Westinghouse brake gear, the other being No 70044. Once the experiment was deemed to be finished those two locos had the gear removed and the standard smoke deflectors were set in place. Loco No 70043 subsequently received the name LORD KITCHENER and No 70044 was named EARL HAIG. *Mike Morant Collection*

BR Standard 'Britannia' class Pacific No 70045 LORD ROWALLAN was depicted at Holyhead station with the up 'Irish Mail' on 14 August 1954; note that the then two months in traffic engine still awaited the fitting of its nameplates. The 'Irish Mail' was by reputation the oldest title ever given to a named train. After earlier uses of the title on trains with mail bound for Ireland via Irish Sea ferryboats the title was first carried on the Euston–Holyhead mail train service on 26 September 1927, and after a break during the war years ran on beyond the steam era with the last modern traction-hauled run being on 12 May 1985. *Mike Morant Collection*

BR Standard 'Britannia' class Pacific No 70046 ANZAC was pictured at Willesden (1A) depot whilst in light steam on 11 August 1963. Note that the engine, which was still to remain in service for almost another five years, was on this occasion minus its nameplates! *Rail Photoprints Collection*

BR Standard 'Britannia' class Pacific No 70048 then unnamed, but which in 1958 became THE TERRITORIAL ARMY 1908–1958, was depicted awaiting departure from Holyhead station with the up 'Irish Mail' on 17 September 1954. *Mike Morant Collection*

Chapter 29

1951–1952

British Railways 'Clan' Class 4-6-2, designed by Riddles

Between 1951 and 1952 ten lighter versions of the 'Britannia' class were constructed; they were the Standard 'Class 6' 6MT 4-6-2 'Clans' and accordingly were named after ten Scottish Clans.

The new class had higher running plates, smaller diameter boilers and taller steam domes and chimneys than their '7MT' cousins. However the Crewe built 'small' Pacifics were not as successful as their bigger cousins and in fact were generally considered to be poor machines lacking anything like the punch of the Britannias.

The thinking behind the Standard 'Class 6' design centered on the need to provide a Pacific type locomotive for use on the routes which prohibited the use of the larger 'Class 7' 4-6-2 engines, because of axle loading restrictions.

The smaller Clan boiler was carried on the same chassis as the 'Britannia' class engines and the achieved lower axle loading was as a consequence only 19 tons in full working order, i.e. 1½ tons per axle lighter than the 'Class 7s'.

BR Standard 'Clan' class Pacific No 72000 CLAN BUCHANAN pictured when in full cry on the West Coast Main Line (WCML) between Crawford and Elvanfoot, with a Glasgow Central to Blackpool holiday relief on 11 April 1960. *David Anderson*

BR 4-6-2 'Clan' class, BR numbers 72000–70009

Introduced: 1951–52

Power Classification: 6MT (6P5F)

Built: Crewe Works, 10 locomotives

Designer: Robert Riddles

Company: British Railways

Driving Wheel: 6ft 2ins

Boiler Pressure: 225psi superheated

Cylinders: Outside – 19½ins diameter x 28ins stroke

Tractive Effort @ 85%: 27,520lbf

Valve Gear: Walschaerts (piston valves)

Water Capacity: 4250 gallons

Coal Capacity: 7 tons

The tenders used were the same as those supplied to the first batch of Britannias; designated BR1 they had a water capacity of 4250 gallons and a 7-ton capacity coal space.

All of the Crewe-built class were allocated to the Scottish Region but did not, as anticipated, work regularly over the testing Highland Line due to a lack of adhesive power, but instead worked mainly on Glasgow–Manchester/Liverpool express services. Examples of the class were briefly trialled on the Midland Main Line and also on the Great Eastern routes to Ipswich and Norwich.

Number	Name	Built	Date	Withdrawn
BR 72000	CLAN BUCHANAN	BR Crewe	12/1951	12/1962
BR 72001	CLAN CAMERON	BR Crewe	12/1951	12/1962
BR 72002	CLAN CAMPBELL	BR Crewe	01/1952	12/1962
BR 72003	CLAN FRASER	BR Crewe	01/1952	12/1962
BR 72004	CLAN MACDONALD	BR Crewe	02/1952	12/1962
BR 72005	CLAN MACGREGOR	BR Crewe	02/1952	05/1965
BR 72006	CLAN MACKENZIE	BR Crewe	02/1952	05/1966
BR 72007	CLAN MACKINTOSH	BR Crewe	03/1952	12/1965
BR 72008	CLAN MACLEOD	BR Crewe	03/1952	04/1966
BR 72009	CLAN STEWART	BR Crewe	04/1952	08/1965

Disposal: 72000/04 Darlington Works, 72005 Arnott Young, Troon, 72006–72008 McWilliams, Shettleston, 72007 Campbells, Airdrie, 72009 Motherwell Machinery & Scrap, Wishaw

The 6P5F's below par performances in traffic coupled with the quickening pace of dieselisation caused a planned order for a further fifteen of the class to be cancelled and those locomotives, if built, would have been numbers 72010–72014 allocated to BR Southern Region and 72015–72024 for the BR Scottish Region.

Locomotives numbered 72000–72004 were taken out of service in 1962, numbers 72005, 72007 and 72009 in 1965, whilst 72006 and 72008 lasted until 1966. None were preserved but a long-standing project to build a new 'Clan' 4-6-2 was reportedly still in its initial stages during 2012.

Livery applied was BR Brunswick green lined in orange and black.

BR Standard 'Clan' class Pacific No 72003 CLAN FRASER was pictured whilst having been serviced at Glasgow Polmadie depot (66A) in April 1956. *David Anderson*

BR Standard 'Clan' class Pacific No 72004 CLAN MACDONALD looked to be making heavy weather of the four-coach Carlisle–Glasgow Central stopping train when pictured on the WCML north of Harthope, on the famous Beattock Bank, 18 April 1959. *David Anderson*

BR Standard 'Clan' class Pacific No 72005 CLAN MACGREGOR was pictured after being serviced at Corkerhill depot (67A) on 27 April 1955. *David Anderson*

Chapter 30

1954

British Railways 'Duke of Gloucester' Class 4-6-2, designed by Riddles

That the Riddles-designed 8P BR Standard Pacific was ever built at all is an interesting railway story in its own right, as it was a direct result of the fatal Harrow & Wealdstone crash, which happened on 8th October 1952. That horrific crash, which claimed 112 lives and injured approximately 350 persons, involved three steam-hauled trains.

There were two locomotives double heading a down Liverpool express train and they were both damaged beyond repair; they were 'Jubilee' class 4-6-0 No 45637 WINDWARD ISLANDS and Stanier 8P Pacific No 46202 PRINCESS ANNE. Loco No 46202 had only some weeks earlier returned to service as a conventional locomotive, having been rebuilt as a 'Princess Royal' class engine from the experimental steam turbine referred to as the 'Turbomotive'.

BR 'Duke of Gloucester' class Pacific No 71000 DUKE OF GLOUCESTER was pictured at Holyhead depot (6J) in 1961. Note the Caprotti valve gear and also the filthy condition of the engine. *Keith Langston Collection*

The decision to scrap the 'Princess Royal' class loco left a serious gap in the number of 8P locomotives available to British Railways and afforded BR Standard Locomotive Group team leader R.A. Riddles the opportunity to introduce the prototype of his 8P Pacific Standard design. In the event only one member of that class was built. No 71000 DUKE OF GLOUCESTER entered revenue-earning service with BR (ex Crewe Works) in May 1954. Interestingly the loco designer's retirement from BR took place shortly before his 8P prototype emerged from the works.

The Standard Locomotive Group having submitted outline plans for their 8P Pacific design were granted special financing for the project, with the BR bosses expecting a modified Duchess-type 4-6-2 with four cylinders, a double blastpipe and chimney and built using bar frames.

The resultant replacement locomotive for No 46202 followed anything but those design criteria. The new Pacific emerged from the works as a three-cylinder locomotive which was itself a departure from BR Standard practice that hitherto had employed only two-cylinder designs on the smaller Class 6 (Clan) and Class 7 (Britannia) Pacific engines. Perhaps the most striking difference to the lineside observer was the addition of British Caprotti rotary cam poppet valve gear to the cylinders, driven by shafts attached to the centre driving wheels and easily discernable.

Generally when designing the 8P 4-6-2 the normal parameters of BR Standard design were followed and they included ensuring the upmost in steam producing capacity permitted by weight and clearance restrictions, simplicity, visibility and accessibility, the number of moving parts reduced to a minimum and the simplification of shed maintenance by increased use of mechanical lubricators and grease lubrication, and importantly a reduction in disposal time at sheds by the fitting of self-cleaning smokeboxes, rocking grates and self-emptying ash pans.

Over the years there has been a great deal written about the below expectation performances of this unique locomotive; however, with an early end to steam traction looming British Railways were reluctant at that time to address those problems, and in truth no great effort was made to rectify them.

The locomotive was to say the least not overly popular with footplate crews! In fact some drivers were said to have changed turns when faced with the prospect of being rostered to a 'heavy train' turn of duty with the reportedly sometimes shy steaming No 71000. However, and supposedly against all the odds, when in the hands of skilful footplate crews No 71000 did turn in some very good performances. 'The Duke' regularly worked West Coast Main Line (WCML) express services; in particular during the period 1956–8 the loco was often rostered to work the Crewe–Euston–Crewe section of the prestigious 'Mid-Day Scot' service.

'The Duke' was based at Crewe North shed (5A) for all of its operating life and was in its later years regularly employed on boat train and other express services on the undemanding North Wales Coast line between Crewe and Holyhead. However, the locomotive's reputation as a poor steamer followed it into what, with hindsight, many consider to have been a premature retirement in November 1962.

Caprotti valve gear

Caprotti valve gear is a distinctively different type of steam locomotive valve gear which was invented and first introduced by Italian engineer Arturo Caprotti. The system uses camshaft and associated poppet valves rather than the various types of piston valves more conventionally used by locomotive designers/builders. The Caprotti system was based on valves used in internal combustion engine design which Caprotti significantly changed to make the method suitable for use with steam engines.

The Caprotti system uses camshaft and associated poppet valves driven by a rotary shaft rather than the various types of piston valves more conventionally used by locomotive designers/builders. The valve gear can be clearly seen in this image of No 71000 taken at Crewe Works. *Keith Langston*

In the 1950s the system was further improved and the resulting equipment from that development became known as British Caprotti valve gear. Caprotti valve gear was fitted to the last two British railways built Black Fives Nos 44686–7, the last 30 BR Standard Class 5s, Nos 73125–54 and of course the Riddles prototype three-cylinder Class 8P Pacific 71000 DUKE OF GLOUCESTER.

Caprotti valve gear is said to facilitate a more efficient use of generated steam and benefits of the Caprotti system include the fact that much of the mechanism is enclosed, a factor which practically speaking means a reduction in damage caused by wear and tear in the harsh steam locomotive environment. The use of Caprotti poppet valve gear also allows independent control of the locomotive cylinders' admission and exhaust functions. An important downside to the system is the cost of manufacture which is often stated as being considerably higher than that for conventional piston valves gear.

For additional detailed information about the Riddles designed BR Standard Pacific locomotives please refer to the Pen & Sword Books publication ***British Steam-BR Standard Locomotives*** written by the same author. Please visit www.pen-and-sword.co.uk/British-Steam-BR-Standard-Locomotives.

Number	Name	Built	Date	Withdrawn
BR 71000	DUKE OF GLOUCESTER	BR Crewe	05/1954	11/1962 Preserved

BR 4-6-2 'Duke of Gloucester' class, BR number 71000

Introduced: 1954

Power Classification: 8P

Built: Crewe Works, 1 locomotive

Designer: Robert Riddles

Company: British Railways

Driving Wheel: 6ft 2ins

Boiler Pressure: 250psi superheated

Cylinders: 3 – 18ins diameter x 28ins stroke

Tractive Effort @ 85%: 32,160lbf

Valve Gear: Caprotti

Water Capacity: 4325 and 4725 gallons

Coal Capacity: 10 tons

BR 'Duke of Gloucester' class Pacific No 71000 DUKE OF GLOUCESTER was pictured at Crewe station on 31 May 1956 having just arrived with the 'Mid-Day Scot' working; note the young admirers. The BR Standard would be replaced by a Stanier Pacific for the continuation of the journey north. The 'Mid-Day Scot' ran in each direction between London Euston and Glasgow Central from 26 September 1927 until 13 June 1965, with an enforced break in service during the war years. *Peter Kerslake/The Duke of Gloucester Steam Locomotive Trust*

The A1 Steam Locomotive Trust inspired 'new build' Pacific steam locomotive No 60163 TORNADO made a splendid sight as it steamed along the demonstration line at Barrow Hill Roundhouse Railway Centre in May 2009. *David Gibson*

Chapter 31

2008

60163 Tornado – 50th Member of the legendary 'A1' Pacific Class

New Build A1

IN 1990 a group of people came together to share an extraordinary ambition – to construct a brand new Peppercorn 'A1' Pacific. They formed The 'A1' Steam Locomotive Trust and after nineteen years of incredible effort that locomotive, No 60163 TORNADO, moved under its own power for the first time in 2008.

At the start of 2009 perhaps the most impressive preservation milestone ever was passed when the newly built 'A1' Class 4-6-2 No 60136 TORNADO made its impressive first mainline run. The superbly engineered machine was the first standard gauge steam locomotive to be built in the UK since British Railways Standard 9F 2-10-0 No 92220 EVENING STAR rolled out of Swindon Locomotive Works on March 18th 1960. Accordingly it was also the first express passenger locomotive to be built in Britain since No 71000 DUKE OF GLOUCESTER left Crewe Loco Works in 1954.

Hopefully the 'A1' will be the first of many new UK-built mainline steam locomotives, as several other 'New Build' projects are currently underway. The project to build a 50th member of the long lamented Peppercorn 'A1' Pacific class locomotive, using 21st-century steam technology, reportedly cost in the region of £3 million.

A very important locomotive with a very important person in the driving seat! The 'new build' 'A1' Pacific is pictured at speed on the day of the naming ceremony. Joining the footplate crew was HRH Prince Charles, Prince of Wales; the location was Colton whilst en route to York. *Fred Kerr*

As the new loco entered its working life, and up to the present day, the 'A1 Trust' was still asking for continued monetary support. They make a very important point. 'The more regular donations we receive, the quicker TORNADO can pay off its debts and the more assured its working future will be.' TORNADO was named by Their Royal Highnesses the Prince of Wales and The Duchess of Cornwall in a ceremony held at York railway station at 10:00hrs on Thursday 19th February 2009.

Design

From the very beginning the Trust regarded TORNADO not as a replica or copy of any one of its forty-nine predecessors, but as the fiftieth A1. This simple decision gave the Trust licence to make small changes to the design to better suit modern manufacturing techniques and to fit in with the modern high-speed railway, while remaining demonstrably faithful to the greater part of the original design.

Manufacturing Economies

The original 'A1' class numbered forty-nine locomotives, which, because many components were shared with other classes, favoured manufacturing techniques suited to batch production. In particular, extensive use was made of steel castings. In most cases the cost of approval of other manufacturing techniques caused the Trust to choose steel castings as per the originals. However, for some items, such as the star stay which supports the brake cylinder, a fabrication was produced. Extensive use has been made of 'patterns' fashioned from expanded polystyrene which are ideal for one off items, and cost between one-third-and-a-half of a comparable wood pattern.

The principal change from the original design concerns the boiler. The locomotive's boiler was designed as a fully welded vessel with a steel firebox, as opposed to the original A1 design, which was of a riveted construction and was coupled with a copper firebox. The reasoning behind the decision was that, with the exception of a small cottage industry which supports the existing preservation movement, there was at the time judged to be no capacity to produce a large riveted boiler within the modern pressure vessel industry.

It was reasoned that this method of construction did not significantly increase the technical risk, as extensive use was made of welded boilers and steel fireboxes in the USA, and other overseas countries. Note also that in the UK the successful Bulleid-designed 'Merchant Navy' and 'West Country' classes had fully welded inner and outer steel fireboxes.

Requirements for modern operating conditions

Brakes – the 'A1' class was equipped with a steam brake for the locomotive and vacuum brake for the train. As it is expected that the locomotive will spend most of its operating time on the main line, the Trust decided to make air brakes the primary braking system for the 'new build' locomotive. To enable No 60163 to haul vacuum-braked stock on heritage railways, a vacuum ejector is fitted with the vacuum train pipe being controlled through an air/vacuum proportional valve. In addition to the automatic fail-safe air brake system, the locomotive is also equipped with a straight air brake to assist with shunting and coupling.

AWS/TPWS – the original locomotives were fitted with the BR vacuum brake AWS (Automatic Warning System). In modern mainline service TORNADO will require the new TPWS (Train Protection and Warning System). This is designed to be a direct replacement for the AWS as fitted to air-braked diesel and electric stock. Modern operating conditions require a data recorder to be fitted on all motive power running on Network Rail. Cab to lineside radio equipment was also to be fitted.

In addition to successfully hauling a great many mainline charter trains TORNADO has proved to be a very popular visitor to preserved railways throughout the UK and on those occasions draws huge admiring crowds of both families and railway enthusiasts. The engine is pictured during a May 2009 visit to the North York Moors Railway. *David Gibson*

Electrical system – arising from the above plus the intended fitment of video cameras to relay locomotive action to the train, there will be a significantly increased requirement for electrical power on the locomotive. As built, the 'A1s' had a 350-watt 24v AC turbo alternator fitted which powered light bulbs for marker lights, cab gauge lighting and certain lights for maintenance purposes. When the AWS was fitted, a separate 24v battery set was provided.

TORNADO therefore has a dual battery system: a vital service battery to power the AWS/TPWS and cab radio, and a general services battery for the other demands. The alternators continuously charge these, backed up if necessary by an auxiliary generator in the support coach or a mains shore supply when stabled. The charging circuitry has been designed to ensure preferential charging of the vital services battery.

Range and capacity

The 'A1' class locomotive tender has been redesigned internally eliminating the water scoop but increasing the water capacity from 5000 gallons (22,700 litres) to around 6200 gallons (28,150 litres) and correspondingly reducing coal capacity from 9 tons to 7.5 tons.

The range of a steam locomotive is governed by water capacity, lubricant consumption and fuel capacity. Water is the most significant limitation with most locomotives hauling

Royal Train duty. The 50th 'A1' Pacific No 60163 TORNADO is pictured on Royal Train duty in February 2009. Note the three-lamp 'Royal Train' code, only a train carrying the reigning monarch is authorised to carry the full four-lamp code. *Jeff Colledge*

loaded trains at express speeds being limited to about 100 miles (160km) between fillings of the tender. For the 'A1' class an average of 40–45 gallons (113–137 litres) per mile is to be expected. Thus the standard 5000-gallon (22,700-litre) capacity of the tender allowed an average of about 100 miles (160km) allowing 500 gallons (2,270 litres) in reserve.

With the capacity of the TORNADO tender augmented to 6200 gallons (27,240 litres) plus a possible 8000 gallons (36,320 litres) in a future second coupled vehicle, a range of around 300 miles (480km) non-stop would be practicable. This would allow operation from Euston to Carlisle or Kings Cross to Newcastle.

Full oil pots and lubricators would ensure a comfortable 300-mile (480km) range – the 'Elizabethan' non-stop runs totalled about 400 miles (640km), a total which included the shed movements at either end. The original locomotives had a coal capacity of 9 tons of coal which gave about 350 miles (560km) of range. TORNADO's reduced coal capacity of 7.5 tons will give a range of about 290 miles (470km).

The 'A1' class was designed to cope with the heaviest regular East Coast trains of the post-war period. These were regularly loaded to fifteen coaches or 550 tons. The locomotives were capable of maintaining 60–70 miles per hour (95–110km/hr) on level track. However, the greatest asset of TORNADO will be the ability to haul lighter (ten–eleven coach trains) at higher speeds, to fit in with modern traffic patterns.

On Saturday 6 October 2012, TORNADO made her last mainline run carrying a later style of British Railways dark green livery. The loco was then taken out of traffic in order to receive a change of livery during November 2012, when the former British Railways-style 'Express Passenger' dark blue livery (with the early BR emblem on the tender) was applied.

During the working life of the locomotive various livery changes are planned to take place. The Peppercorn engines were originally fitted with plain-topped (un-lipped) double chimney castings which were eventually changed for lipped chimneys, a move that many thought greatly improved the look of the class. Reportedly a chimney style change for TORNADO will also take place at some point in the future.

Chapter 32

PRESERVED PACIFICS

As the UK steam era came towards its end, and for the decade or so which followed, the steam locomotive preservation movement came into being. As a result of which there are fortunately a good number of working steam locos based at the 115 or so railway orientated heritage centers and museums around the country. The majority of the locos are either privately, trust or society owned and additionally there are a number in the care of the National Railway Museum, and they are often referred to as 'The National Collection'.

A good proportion of the engines have been restored to working condition with a selection of those prepared to a higher specification in order to a fulfill the criteria of the national network operators; those engines can therefore haul charter trains over approved sections of the mainline.

But the real good news is that in modern-day Britain steam is alive and well; most parts of the country have an active steam centre close by.

Regularly open to visitors, and in the main run by hard working groups of volunteers, the newly born railways attract volunteers and visitors in healthy numbers. And yes some modern-day boys and girls do still dream of becoming engine drivers!

It is fascinating that young people who were actually born after the steam era have now joined with those others who remember, and jointly enthusiastically restore and operate, not just locomotives but also railway stations, signal boxes etc. whilst tackling all manner of challenging engineering problems in order to keep preserved railway infrastructures intact. The lasting fascination can fairly be described as 'The Magic of Steam'.

Bulleid Pacifics seen at Eastleigh Works. Locos No 35028 CLAN LINE (MN), No 34070 MANSTON (BB) and No 34028 EDDYSTONE (WC) were all pictured there during a special event weekend in May 2009. *Fred Kerr*

Ex-London & North Eastern Railway preserved and new-build Pacific steam power pictured as lined up at the 'Barrow Hill Roundhouse Railway Centre', near Chesterfield on 3 April 2009, all the locomotives displaying named train headboards. From left to right: The 2008 completed newly built 'A1' No 60163 TORNADO displaying 'Yorkshire Pullman', 'A2' Pacific No 60532 BLUE PETER displaying 'The North Eastern', 'A4' Pacific No 60007 SIR NIGEL GRESLEY displaying 'The Elizabethan' and 'A4' Pacific No 60009 displaying 'The Heart of Midlothian'. *David Gibson*

The total of preserved engines includes forty-seven preserved Pacific types, all of which are 4-6-2 tender locos, as unfortunately none of the 'Pacific Tanks' made it into preservation. This chapter lists all of those locomotives and indicates where they are normally based; the details therein were correct as at mid-summer 2012, but be mindful that preserved locomotives are often the subject of loan arrangements between the various railways.

Ex-SR/BR 'West Country' Pacific No 34007 WADEBRIDGE is pictured double heading in September 2009 with re-built 'West Country' Pacific No 34028 EDDYSTONE on the Bluebell Railway. *Paul Pettitt*

Ex-SR/BR 'West Country and Battle of Britain' class

BR Number	Name	Date	Ex-BR	Location	Status 2012
34007	WADEBRIDGE	1945	1965	Mid Hants Railway	Operational
34010 R	SIDMOUTH	1945	1965	Herston Works Swanage	Restoration project
34016 R	BODMIN	1947	1964	Mid Hants Railway	Awaiting overhaul
34023	BLACKMORE VALE	1946	1967	Bluebell Railway	Awaiting overhaul
34027 R	TAW VALLEY	1946	1964	Severn Valley Railway	Under overhaul
34028 R	EDDYSTONE	1946	1964	Swanage Railway	Operational
34039 R	BOSCASTLE	1946	1965	Great Central Railway	Under overhaul
34046 R	BRAUNTON	1946	1965	West Somerset Railway	Operational
34051	WINSTON CHURCHILL	1946	1965	NRM York	Static display
34053 R	SIR KEITH PARK	1947	1965	Severn Valley Railway	Operational
34058 R	SIR FREDERICK PILE	1947	1964	Mid Hants Railway	Under restoration
34059 R	SIR ARCHIBALD SINCLAIR	1947	1966	Bluebell Railway	Under overhaul
34067	TANGMERE	1947	1963	Southall Railway Centre	Operational mainline passed
34070	MANSTON	1947	1964	Swanage Railway	Under repair
34072	257 SQUADRON	1948	1964	Herston Works Swanage	Restoration project
34073	249 SQUADRON	1948	1964	Riley & Sons Bury	Awaiting restoration
34081	92 SQUADRON	1948	1964	Nene Valley Railway	Under overhaul
34092	CITY OF WELLS	1949	1964	Keighley & Worth Valley Railway	Under overhaul
34101 R	HARTLAND	1950	1966	North Yorkshire Moors Railway	Under overhaul
34105	SWANAGE	1950	1964	Mid Hants Railway	Under overhaul

R denotes rebuilt locomotive

Ex-SR/BR 'West Country' Pacific No 21C123 (BR 34023) BLACKMORE VALE, in Southern Railway livery, was pictured at the Bluebell Railway in June 2009. *Paul Pettitt*

Ex-SR/BR 'Battle of Britain' Pacific No 34067 TANGMERE was pictured crossing the river Adur near Ford in West Sussex whilst on mainline charter duty. *Paul Pettitt*

Corfe Castle on the Swanage Railway is the backdrop for this stunning image of 'Battle of Britain' class Bulleid light Pacific No 34070 MANSTON taken on 27 February 2009. *Paul Pettitt*

Bulleid 'Battle of Britain' light Pacific No 34081 92 SQUADRON makes a fine sight heading away from Llangollen with an afternoon service for Carrog; No 34081 visited the Llangollen Railway during April 2007. *Fred Kerr*

Re-built ex-Southern Railway 'West Country' Pacific No 34028 EDDYSTONE was pictured whilst masquerading as a not preserved member of the class, No 34100 APPLEDORE, at Freshfield Curve, which is a popular location on the Bluebell Railway, 21 October 2007. *Paul Pettitt*

Ex-SR/BR 'Merchant Navy' class

BR Number	Name	Date	Ex-BR	Location	Status 2012
35005	CANADIAN PACIFIC	1942	1965	Mid-Hants Railway	Stored at Eastleigh Works out of use
35006	PENINSULAR & ORIENTAL S.N.CO.	1942	1965	Gloucester & Warwickshire Railway	Under restoration
35009	SHAW SAVILLE	1942	1964	East Lancashire Railway	Restoration project
35010	BLUE STAR	1942	1966	Colne Valley Railway	Restoration project
35011	GENERAL STEAM NAVIGATION	1944	1966	Sellindge Kent	Restoration project
35018	BRITISH INDIA LINE	1945	1964	East Lancashire Railway	Restoration project
35022	HOLLAND AMERICA LINE	1938	1963	East Lancashire Railway	Restoration project
35025	BROCKLEBANK LINE	1948	1964	Sellindge Kent	Restoration project
35027	PORT LINE	1948	1966	East Lancashire Railway	Under overhaul to mainline standard
35028	CLAN LINE	1948	1967	Stewarts Lane Depot	Operational mainline passed
35029	ELLERMAN LINES	1949	1966	NRM York	Static display (sectioned)

Ex-SR/BR 'Merchant Navy' class Pacific No 35005 CANADIAN PACIFIC was pictured at work leaving Consall Forge station with a train for Cheddleton during a 2008 visit to the Churnet Valley Railway. *David Gibson*

Ex-LMS 'Princess Royal' class

BR Number	Name	Date	Ex-BR	Location	Status 2012
46201	PRINCESS ELIZABETH	1933	1962	Tyseley	Operational Mainline passed
46203	PRINCESS MARGARET ROSE	1935	1962	Midland Railway Centre	Static display

Ex-LMS 'Princess Royal' class No 6201 PRINCESS ELIZABETH was pictured at Liverpool Lime Street station during a recreation of 'The Merseyside Express' service. In the later part of the steam era 'Princess Royal' class locomotives were regular performers on express services between Liverpool and London. *Keith Langston*

Another visitor during the September 2005 'The Great Gathering' held at Crewe Works was ex-LMS 'Princess Royal' class No 46203 PRINCESS MARGARET ROSE which was photographed at the world famous locomotive works. *Keith Langston*

Ex-LMS 'Princess Coronation/Duchess' class

BR Number	Name	Date	Ex-BR	Location	Status 2012
46229	DUCHESS OF HAMILTON	1938	1964	NRM York	Streamlined Static Display
46233	DUCHESS OF SUTHERLAND	1938	1964	Midland Railway Centre	Operational Mainline passed
46235	CITY OF BIRMINGHAM	1939	1964	Birmingham Museum	Static display

Ex-LMS 'Princess Coronation/Duchess' class No 46229 DUCHESS OF HAMILTON was pictured whilst working a down 'Ynys Mon Express' near to Beeston shortly before being withdrawn from service so that a streamlined casing could be added to the National Collection locomotive. *Keith Langston*

Ex-LMS 'Princess Coronation/Duchess' class pictured as No 6229 DUCHESS OF HAMILTON in streamlined form at the National Railway Museum York where the currently non-mainline ticketed engine is usually on static display. *Keith Langston*

In September 2005 'The Great Gathering' was held at Crewe Works; that wonderful event staged by, and for the benefit of, the 'Webb Crewe Works Charity Fund' looks increasingly likely to be the last steam celebration of any size to be held at the location. But who knows what the future may bring! Ex-LMS 'Princess Coronation/Duchess' class No 6233 DUCHESS OF SUTHERLAND (with support coach having just worked in from Derby) was pictured on that occasion. *Keith Langston*

The Chester–Holyhead route has been a happy hunting ground for restored mainline locomotives and Llandudno Junction station is used regularly as a watering point. Ex-LMS 'Princess Coronation/Duchess' class No 6233 DUCHESS OF SUTHERLAND was pictured there during such a visit. *Brian Jones*

Ex-LNER 'A4' class

BR Number	Name	Date	Ex-BR	Location	Status 2012
60007	SIR NIGEL GRESLEY	1937	1966	North Yorkshire Moors Railway	Operational
60008	DWIGHT D EISENHOWER	1937	1963	NRM of USA Wisconsin	Static display
60009	UNION OF SOUTH AFRICA	1937	1966	Markinch	Operational Mainline passed
60010	DOMINION OF CANADA	1937	1965	Canadian Railway Museum Delson	Static display
60019	BITTERN	1937	1966	Southall Railway Centre	Operational Mainline passed
60022	MALLARD	1938	1963	NRM York	Static Display

Ex-LNER 'A4' class Pacific No 4498 SIR NIGEL GRESLEY pictured during 1977 on the Shrewsbury–Chester leg of the 'Western Jubilee' charter train. *Keith Langston*

Ex-LNER 'A4' class Pacific No 60007 SIR NIGEL GRESLEY was pictured leaving Goathland on the North Yorkshire Moors Railway on 12 March 2008. *Fred Kerr*

Ex-LNER 'A4' class Pacific No 60009 UNION OF SOUTH AFRICA was pictured whilst hard at work near to Greenholme with a 'Cumbrian Mountain Express' working, from Manchester Victoria to Carlisle, on 28 July 2007. *Fred Kerr*

In July 2008 the NRM celebrated the 70th anniversary of Gresley Class 'A4' Pacific No 4468 MALLARD achieving the World Record speed of 126mph in 1938, by bringing together three mainline certified locomotives to join No 4468 for a weekend display in the NRM yard. The three mainline locomotives also worked stages of a two-day London–Edinburgh charter hauled by 'A4' class Pacifics including No 60019 BITTERN, which was pictured passing Colton Junction on 6 July with the York/London stage of the tour. *Fred Kerr*

In April 2008 the North Yorkshire Moors Railway held an 'LNER Weekend', the main attraction being three 'A4' class Pacifics in steam. On April 6 No 60009 UNION OF SOUTH AFRICA passed the loco shed at Grosmont with a Grosmont–Pickering service as sister loco No 60007 SIR NIGEL GRESLEY was being prepared for its next duty. Ex-LNER 'V2' class No 4771 GREEN ARROW is seen outside the shed. *Fred Kerr*

Ex-LNER 'A3' class

BR Number	Name	Date	Ex-BR	Location	Status 2012
60103	FLYING SCOTSMAN	1923	1963	NRM York	Under overhaul to mainline standard

Ex-LNER 'A3' Pacific No 60103 FLYING SCOTSMAN (with German-style smoke deflectors and double chimney) was pictured during a 1995 visit to the Llangollen Railway. *Keith Langston*

Ex-LNER 'A3' Pacific No 4472 FLYING SCOTSMAN, without smoke deflectors and with a single chimney, was pictured at the Severn Valley Railway during a September 1990 visit. *Keith Langston*

Ex-LNER/BR 'A2' class

BR Number	Name	Date	Ex-BR	Location	Status 2012
60532	BLUE PETER	1948	1966	NRM York	Under overhaul to mainline standard

Ex-LNER/BR 'A2' class Pacific No 60532 BLUE PETER pictured at Appleby on the Settle & Carlisle route whilst on mainline charter train duty. *David Gibson*

Ex-British Railways 'Britannia' class

BR Number	Name	Date	Ex-BR	Location	Status 2012
70000	BRITANNIA	1951	1966	Southall Railway Centre	Operational, mainline passed
70013	OLIVER CROMWELL	1951	1968	NRM/Tours	Operational, mainline passed

Ex-BR Standard 'Britannia' class engine No 70000 BRITANNIA was re-built for a second time and certified for mainline running in 2011. The loco was pictured at the Crewe works of London & North Western Railway Heritage Ltd resplendent in a newly applied BR Brunswick green livery. *Keith Langston*

Ex-BR Standard 'Britannia' class engine No 70013 OLIVER CROMWELL is part of the National Collection and in addition to visiting preserved railways the loco can often be seen hauling steam charters on the national network. *David Gibson*

Ex-British Railways 'Duke of Gloucester' class

BR Number	Name	Date	Ex-BR	Location	Status 2009
71000	DUKE OF GLOUCESTER	1954	1966	East Lancashire Railway	Operational, mainline passed

British Railways '8P' Riddles Standard Pacific No 71000 DUKE OF GLOUCESTER is seen at speed in July 2010 whilst heading the 'Cumbrian Coast Explorer' charter through Meathop. *Fred Kerr*

Ex-BR Standard Pacific No 71000 DUKE OF GLOUCESTER was pictured on the 'Cumbrian Coast Route' near to Parton on 3 July 2010 with 'The Cambrian Coast Explorer' charter train. The plume of steam at the rear of the tender indicates that the coal pusher is in use. *Fred Kerr*